Practical Serverless Applications with AWS

Harnessing the Power of Serverless Cloud Applications

Apoorva Prakash
Shaik Inthiyaz Basha

Apress®

Practical Serverless Applications with AWS: Harnessing the Power of Serverless Cloud Applications

Apoorva Prakash
Bangalore, Karnataka, India

Shaik Inthiyaz Basha
Nellore, Andhra Pradesh, India

ISBN-13 (pbk): 979-8-8688-1254-5
https://doi.org/10.1007/979-8-8688-1255-2

ISBN-13 (electronic): 979-8-8688-1255-2

Copyright © 2025 by Apoorva Prakash and Shaik Inthiyaz Basha

This work is subject to copyright. All rights are reserved by the Publisher, whether the whole or part of the material is concerned, specifically the rights of translation, reprinting, reuse of illustrations, recitation, broadcasting, reproduction on microfilms or in any other physical way, and transmission or information storage and retrieval, electronic adaptation, computer software, or by similar or dissimilar methodology now known or hereafter developed.

Trademarked names, logos, and images may appear in this book. Rather than use a trademark symbol with every occurrence of a trademarked name, logo, or image we use the names, logos, and images only in an editorial fashion and to the benefit of the trademark owner, with no intention of infringement of the trademark.

The use in this publication of trade names, trademarks, service marks, and similar terms, even if they are not identified as such, is not to be taken as an expression of opinion as to whether or not they are subject to proprietary rights.

While the advice and information in this book are believed to be true and accurate at the date of publication, neither the authors nor the editors nor the publisher can accept any legal responsibility for any errors or omissions that may be made. The publisher makes no warranty, express or implied, with respect to the material contained herein.

   Managing Director, Apress Media LLC: Welmoed Spahr
   Acquisitions Editors: James Robinson-Prior, Divya Modi
   Editorial Assistant: Gryffin Winkler

Cover designed by eStudioCalamar

Cover image designed by Kohji Asakawa from Pixabay

Distributed to the book trade worldwide by Springer Science+Business Media New York, 1 New York Plaza, Suite 4600, New York, NY 10004-1562, USA. Phone 1-800-SPRINGER, fax (201) 348-4505, e-mail orders-ny@springer-sbm.com, or visit www.springeronline.com. Apress Media, LLC is a California LLC and the sole member (owner) is Springer Science + Business Media Finance Inc (SSBM Finance Inc). SSBM Finance Inc is a **Delaware** corporation.

For information on translations, please e-mail booktranslations@springernature.com; for reprint, paperback, or audio rights, please e-mail bookpermissions@springernature.com.

Apress titles may be purchased in bulk for academic, corporate, or promotional use. eBook versions and licenses are also available for most titles. For more information, reference our Print and eBook Bulk Sales web page at http://www.apress.com/bulk-sales.

Any source code or other supplementary material referenced by the author in this book is available to readers on GitHub. For more detailed information, please visit https://www.apress.com/gp/services/source-code.

If disposing of this product, please recycle the paper

To my father, **Dr. Om Prakash Srivastava,** *to whom I owe everything and who inspired me but is not here to read this. Yes, life is like that sometimes!*

—*Apoorva Prakash*

To my parents **Shaik Alla Basha** *and* **Shaik Sabira Begum**. *They sacrificed their dreams to fulfill ours. Parents are the architects of our future, laying the foundation of our dreams. My father retired from the APSRTC on June 1, 2024, after a 35-year career.*

—*Shaik Inthiyaz Basha*

Table of Contents

About the Authors xv

About the Technical Reviewer xvii

Acknowledgments xix

Introduction xxi

Chapter 1: Introduction to AWS 1
   Cloud Computing Refresher 2
      Growth of Cloud Computing 2
      Types of Cloud Computing 4
      Cloud Computing Model Types 5
      Upsides and Downsides of Cloud Computing 6
   AWS Architecture and Services 8
      Importance of AWS 9
      AWS Architecture 9
      AWS Services 11
   Regions and Availability Zones 14
      Regions 15
      Availability Zones 16
   Identity and Access Management (IAM) 17
      Capabilities of IAM 18
      IAM User Credentials 19
      IAM Group 20
      IAM Policies 21

TABLE OF CONTENTS

CloudFormation and Cloud Development Kit 26
- CloudFormation 26
- Cloud Development Kit 28

CloudWatch 30
- Understanding CloudWatch Logs 31

Networking Basics 32
- Virtual Private Cloud (VPC) 33
- Subnets 34
- Security Group 35
- Internet Gateways 36
- Route Table 37
- NAT Gateways 38

Conclusion 40

Chapter 2: Frontend Development and Integration 43

Introduction 43

AWS Amplify 44
- Key Features of Amplify 44
- Key Benefits of Amplify 47
- How Amplify Works 48
- Working with AWS Amplify 49

API Gateway 51
- Key Features and Benefits of AWS API Gateway 52
- Use Cases for AWS API Gateway 53
- How AWS API Gateway Works 54
- Setting Up AWS API Gateway 58
- Security Features in AWS API Gateway 61
- Integrating AWS API Gateway with Frontend Development 63
- Optimizing Performance 65

TABLE OF CONTENTS

S3 (Simple Storage Service) 68
    Key Features and Benefits of AWS S3 69
    Use Cases for AWS S3 70
    How AWS S3 Works 71
    Setting Up AWS S3.. 76
    Security Features in AWS S3 81
    Integrating AWS S3 with Frontend Development........................... 84
    Optimizing Performance and Costs Using S3 88
AWS CloudFront 91
    Key Features and Benefits of AWS CloudFront 92
    How AWS CloudFront Works 93
    Setting Up AWS CloudFront 96
    Security Features in AWS CloudFront.. 100
    Integrating AWS CloudFront with Frontend Development 102
    Optimizing Performance with AWS CloudFront 105
Conclusion 108

Chapter 3: Data Engineering.. 111
    Introduction 111
    AWS Glue.. 112
        Use Cases of AWS Glue.. 113
        AWS Glue Key Components 113
        Features of AWS Glue 116
        Advantages of AWS Glue.. 117
        Disadvantages of AWS Glue.. 118
        Practical Guide to AWS Glue 119
    AWS Batch 127
        Use Cases for Batch Processing 128
        AWS Batch Key Components 128

vii

TABLE OF CONTENTS

    Features of AWS Batch 129
    Advantages of AWS Batch 131
    Disadvantages of AWS Batch 132
    Practical Guide to AWS Batch 133
AWS RedShift 134
    Use Cases of AWS Redshift 135
    Key Components of AWS Redshift 136
    Features of AWS Redshift 136
    Advantages of AWS Redshift 138
    Disadvantages of AWS Redshift 139
    Practical Guide to AWS Redshift 140
AWS Athena 141
    Use Cases of AWS Athena and Ad Hoc Querying 142
    Key Components of AWS Athena 143
    Features of AWS Athena 144
    Advantages of AWS Athena 145
    Disadvantages of AWS Athena 146
    Practical Guide to AWS Athena 147
Basics of Data Lake 149
    Use Cases of Data Lakes 150
    Key Components of Data Lakes 151
    Features of Data Lakes 152
    Advantages of Data Lakes 153
    Disadvantages of Data Lakes 155
    Designing a Data Lake Architecture 156
    Best Practices for Data Ingestion and Organization 158
Conclusion 159

TABLE OF CONTENTS

Chapter 4: Backend Development 161

Introduction 161

AWS Lambda Functions 162

    Use Cases for AWS Lambda Functions 163

    Key Components of AWS Lambda Functions 163

    Features of AWS Lambda Functions 165

    Advantages of AWS Lambda Functions 166

    Disadvantages of AWS Lambda Functions 167

    Practical Guide to AWS Lambda Functions 168

AWS Step Functions 172

    Use Cases for AWS Step Functions 172

    Key Components of AWS Step Functions 173

    Features of AWS Step Functions 174

    Advantages of AWS Step Functions 175

    Disadvantages of AWS Step Functions 176

    Practical Guide to AWS Step Functions 177

AWS Elastic Load Balancer 183

    Types of AWS Elastic Load Balancers 184

    Use Cases for AWS Elastic Load Balancers 185

    Key Components of AWS Elastic Load Balancers 186

    Features of AWS Elastic Load Balancers 187

    Advantages of AWS Elastic Load Balancers 188

    Disadvantages of AWS Elastic Load Balancers 189

    Practice Guide to AWS Elastic Load Balancers 189

AWS Certificate Manager 191

    Use Cases for AWS Certificate Manager 192

    Key Components of AWS Certificate Manager 192

    Features of AWS Certificate Manager 193

ix

TABLE OF CONTENTS

    Advantages of AWS Certificate Manager 195
    Disadvantages of AWS Certificate Manager 195
    Practical Guide to AWS Certificate Manager 196
  AWS Secrets Manager 197
    Use Cases of AWS Secrets Manager 198
    Key Components of AWS Secrets Manager 198
    Features of AWS Secrets Manager 199
    Advantages of AWS Secrets Manager 201
    Disadvantages of AWS Secrets Manager 202
    Practice Guide to AWS Secrets Manager 202
  AWS Simple Notification Service 207
    Use Cases for AWS Simple Notification Service 208
    Key Components of Simple Notification Service 208
    Features of Simple Notification Service 209
    Advantages of Simple Notification Service 211
    Disadvantages of Simple Notification Service 212
    Practical Guide to AWS Simple Notification Service 212
  AWS Simple Queue Service 213
    Use Cases for AWS Simple Queue Service 214
    Key Components of AWS Simple Queue Service 214
    Features of AWS Simple Queue Service 215
    Advantages of AWS Simple Queue Service 216
    Disadvantages of AWS Simple Queue Service 217
    Practical Guide to AWS Simple Queue Service 217
  Introduction to Databases 219
    SQL 220
    NoSQL 223

TABLE OF CONTENTS

AWS ElastiCache 227
    Use Cases for AWS ElastiCache 227
    Key Components of AWS ElastiCache 228
    Features of AWS ElastiCache 229
    Advantages of AWS ElastiCache 230
    Disadvantages of AWS ElastiCache 231
    Practical Guide to ElastiCache 231
Introduction to ECS and EKS in AWS 235
    Amazon Elastic Container Service (ECS) 235
    Amazon Elastic Kubernetes Service (EKS) 236
Conclusion 237

Chapter 5: Cloud DevOps 239
Introduction 239
AWS CodeCommit 240
AWS CodeBuild 240
    Use Cases of AWS CodeBuild 242
    Key Components of AWS CodeBuild 242
    Features of AWS CodeBuild 243
    Advantages of AWS CodeBuild 244
    Disadvantages of AWS CodeBuild 244
    Practical Guide to AWS CodeBuild 245
AWS CodePipeline 247
    Use Cases of AWS CodePipeline 248
    Key Components of AWS CodePipeline 248
    Features of AWS CodePipeline 249
    Advantages of AWS CodePipeline 249
    Disadvantages of AWS CodePipeline 250
    Practical Guide to AWS CodePipeline 250

xi

TABLE OF CONTENTS

AWS CloudWatch Monitoring 252
    Use Cases of AWS CloudWatch Monitoring 253
    Key Components of AWS CloudWatch Monitoring 253
    Features of AWS CloudWatch Monitoring 254
    Advantages of AWS CloudWatch Monitoring 255
    Disadvantages of AWS CloudWatch Monitoring 255
    Practical Guide to AWS CloudWatch Monitoring 255

AWS CloudWatch Alarms 258
    Use Cases of CloudWatch Alarms 259
    Key Components of CloudWatch Alarms 259
    Features of CloudWatch Alarms 260
    Advantages of CloudWatch Alarms 260
    Disadvantages of CloudWatch Alarms 261
    Practical Guide to CloudWatch Alarms 261

AWS CloudWatch Dashboards 263
    Use Cases of CloudWatch Dashboards 264
    Key Components of CloudWatch Dashboards 264
    Features of CloudWatch Dashboards 265
    Advantages of CloudWatch Dashboards 266
    Disadvantages of CloudWatch Dashboards 266
    Practical Guide and Examples of CloudWatch Dashboards 267

Conclusion 270

Chapter 6: Getting Hands-On: Creating First Serverless Application 273

Introduction 273
Understanding the Problem Statement 274
Designing the Solution 275
Planning the Implementation 278

TABLE OF CONTENTS

API Gateway Creation 279
Authorizer Lambda Creation 285
Configuring the Authorizer for GET Method Invocation 288
Creating S3 Bucket and DynamoDB 290
Process S3 CSV with Lambda, Stored in DynamoDB 292
RDS Database Creation 295
Creating Account in OpenWeatherAPI 301
Lambda to Fetch OpenWeatherAPI 302
Automating the Lambda Function 305
Reading Weather Information from MySQL DB 306

CloudWatch Monitoring 310
CloudWatch Dashboards 311
Conclusion 313

Index **315**

xiii

About the Authors

Apoorva Prakash is a distinguished IT professional and technical writer with a stellar 14-year track record of success across diverse roles. Currently serving as an Engineering Manager at Schneider Electric Pvt Ltd., India, Apoorva leads a dynamic team involved in multifaceted projects encompassing various cutting-edge technologies, notably specializing in AWS-based serverless cloud applications developed in Node.js and Python.

Apoorva's expertise extends to the meticulous architecture and implementation design of numerous portals, including expansive employee portals and ecommerce platforms, APIs showcasing his mastery in Liferay, Kubernetes, and data engineering and processing. As a Liferay-certified professional with over a decade of immersion in the platform, he coauthored the acclaimed book *Hands-On Liferay DXP* (Apress, 2022), solidifying his authority in the field.

Apoorva holds a master's in Computer Applications from the Apeejay Institute of Technology, School of Computer Science.

ABOUT THE AUTHORS

Shaik Inthiyaz Basha currently serves as a Platform Architect and Technical Expert at Schneider Electric Pvt Ltd., India. In this role, he is responsible for leading a team dedicated to developing serverless applications. Inthiyaz is recognized for his expertise in content management systems (CMS), Amazon Web Services (AWS), and other cloud platforms. He is a coauthor of the *Hands-On Liferay DXP* book and has demonstrated his proficiency through successful implementations of various Liferay components. In addition, he holds certifications such as Liferay Backend Developer (DXP).

Inthiyaz has been actively contributing to the field since 2011, leveraging his skills in Java, Liferay, AWS, and DevOps to develop CMS and serverless applications for major banking, employee, HR, and financial systems. His commitment to continuous learning is evident as he remains open to adopting new technologies and solutions.

Inthiyaz earned his master's degree in Computer Networks from Quba College of Engineering and Technology, affiliated with JNTUA University, Nellore, Andhra Pradesh, India.

About the Technical Reviewer

Ahmad Zaib is a seasoned IT professional with a distinguished 14-year career in backend web development, currently serving as a Senior Consultant at Deloitte. With a master's in Computer Applications from Apeejay Institute of Technology, he has established himself as an expert in Microsoft technologies and AWS serverless solutions.

Zaib plays a pivotal role in Deloitte's Human Capital division, where he leverages his expertise in C#, ASP.NET MVC, Python, and SQL Server to deliver innovative and impactful solutions. His extensive experience with AWS serverless architectures has enabled him to design and implement scalable, cloud-based applications that meet modern business needs. A strong advocate of Agile and Scrum methodologies, he consistently drives efficiency and productivity in fast-paced environments.

With a diverse portfolio spanning real-time systems and healthcare projects, Zaib is known for his problem-solving acumen and ability to think outside the box. His dedication to creating efficient, forward-thinking solutions underscores his reputation as a leader in the technology domain.

Acknowledgments

We extend our heartfelt gratitude to the remarkable individuals who have been instrumental in the creation of this book. Their unwavering support, encouragement, and invaluable contributions have been the bedrock of our journey. We are profoundly thankful for those rare souls whose words and presence have inspired us to push beyond our limits and achieve the extraordinary. Their humble support has been a constant source of strength, propelling us forward during the challenging process of writing.

To all those who have played a pivotal role in bringing this work to fruition, we offer our deepest appreciation. Your belief in us and this project has been transformative, and we are truly honored to acknowledge your significant impact on our endeavor.

- Mr. Ashutosh Naik, Director, Digital Strategy & Governance, Schneider Electric Pvt. Ltd.

    Thank you for your boundless kindness. I'm truly grateful for your generous spirit and unwavering support.

- Our families

    For allowing us to burn the midnight oil and spend weekends on this book.

- Finally, we extend our heartfelt gratitude to all those people of Schneider Electric who have contributed, directly or indirectly, to the creation of this book.

Introduction

Welcome to *Practical Serverless Applications with AWS: Harnessing the Power of Serverless Cloud Applications.*

In today's rapidly evolving technological landscape, cloud computing has become an indispensable part of modern software development. Among the various cloud providers, Amazon Web Services (AWS) stands out as a leader, offering a comprehensive suite of tools and services that empower developers to build scalable, efficient, and cost-effective applications. This book is your gateway to mastering serverless application development using AWS, providing you with the knowledge and hands-on experience needed to excel in this exciting field.

Why Serverless?

Serverless computing represents a paradigm shift in how we approach application development and deployment. By abstracting away the complexities of server management, serverless architectures allow developers to focus solely on writing code that delivers business value. AWS's serverless offerings provide automatic scaling, reduced operational overhead, and a pay-per-use model that can significantly optimize costs.

INTRODUCTION
What You'll Learn

This book is structured to take you on a comprehensive journey through the AWS ecosystem, focusing on serverless technologies and best practices. Here's what you can expect:

1. We'll start by laying a solid foundation with an introduction to AWS, covering its core concepts, architecture, and essential services.

2. You'll then dive into frontend development and integration, learning how to leverage AWS services to create responsive and scalable user interfaces.

3. Our exploration of data engineering will equip you with the tools and knowledge to build robust data pipelines and processing systems.

4. The backend development section will delve deep into serverless computing, showcasing how to create powerful, event-driven applications using AWS Lambda and related services.

5. We'll cover cloud DevOps practices, ensuring you can implement continuous integration and deployment pipelines for your serverless applications.

6. Finally, you'll put theory into practice by building your first end-to-end serverless application, consolidating all the knowledge gained throughout the book.

Whom This Book Is For

This book is designed for developers, architects, and technology enthusiasts who want to harness the power of AWS for serverless application development. Whether you're new to cloud computing or looking to expand your existing AWS skills, you'll find valuable insights and practical examples to guide your learning journey.

By the end of this book, you'll have the confidence and expertise to design, develop, and deploy serverless applications on AWS, opening up new possibilities for your projects and career.

Let's embark on this exciting journey into the world of serverless computing with AWS!

CHAPTER 1

Introduction to AWS

As you begin on your expedition into the world of serverless computing on Amazon Web Services (AWS), it is crucial to have a solid understanding of the fundamental concepts that underpin this powerful platform. In this chapter, you will delve into the fundamentals of cloud computing, explore the AWS architecture and services, and unravel the intricacies of regions, availability zones, and identity management. You will then dive into the world of infrastructure as code (IaC) by examining CloudFormation and the Cloud Development Kit (CDK), which enable us to create, manage, and provision your resources efficiently. To ensure the health and performance of your applications, we will introduce CloudWatch, AWS's comprehensive monitoring and observability service. Finally, you will explore the essential networking concepts within AWS, including Virtual Private Cloud (VPC), Internet Gateways, subnets, and NAT Gateways, which provide the foundation for secure and scalable networking in the cloud. At the conclusion of this chapter, you will have a deep knowledge of the core components and services that form the backbone of serverless computing on AWS, empowering you to build robust and scalable applications that harness the power of the cloud.

CHAPTER 1   INTRODUCTION TO AWS

Cloud Computing Refresher

The on-demand availability of computer system resources is called cloud computing. It is the delivery of services including storage, servers (physical and virtual), databases, software, development tools, and networking capabilities over the Internet without direct active management by the user.

Growth of Cloud Computing

The term cloud computing was initially introduced in the 1950s to detail Internet-related services and their growth, as shown in Figure 1-1, from distributed systems to the advanced technology known as *cloud computing*.

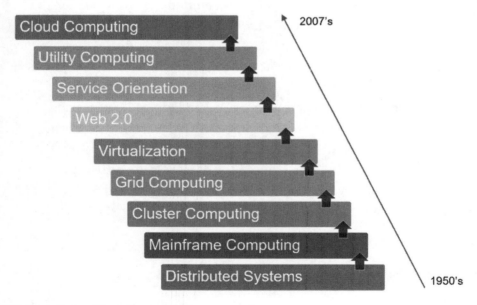

Figure 1-1. Cloud computing growth

1. **Distributed Systems:** A distributed system spreads tasks across independent computers but presents a single point of access for users.

2. **Mainframe Computing:** It was introduced in 1951. It refers to incredibly powerful and reliable computers, handling massive amounts of data and complex input/output tasks. But these were awfully expensive.

3. **Cluster Computing:** It emerged as a counterpoint to mainframe computing to reduce the cost up to some extent associated with mainframe computing in the 1980s. In cluster computing, the connection between each machine is by a network with high bandwidth.

4. **Grid Computing:** The groundwork for grid computing was laid in the 1990s. In grid computing, systems were dispersed across various locations, and the connections between these systems are via the Internet.

5. **Virtualization:** Virtualization creates a software layer on top of physical hardware, allowing users to run multiple independent systems (like operating systems) at the same time. It is a key technology powering cloud computing.

6. **Web 2.0:** Web 2.0 is an interface that transforms static web pages into dynamic and interactive experiences. It is the reason you can interact with and contribute to websites, not just passively view them. Web 2.0, which boomed around 2004, revolutionized how you connect and engage online. This shift toward user-generated content and collaboration fostered the rise of social media platforms like Google Maps, Facebook, and Twitter.

CHAPTER 1   INTRODUCTION TO AWS

7. **Service Orientations:** Service orientation is the architectural foundation for cloud computing. It allows for building applications that are flexible, scalable, and cost-effective. With this approach, two key concepts were introduced: QoS (Quality of Service) and SaaS (Software as a Service).

8. **Cloud Computing:** Cloud computing shifts data and software from local storage to remote servers, accessible through an Internet connection. Cloud computing is a technology where resources are provided as a service through the Internet. The data stored in the cloud can include files, images, documents, and other storable content. This is also sometimes referred to as utility computing.

Types of Cloud Computing

Major types of cloud computing services are listed below:

1. **IaaS (Infrastructure as a Service):** It provides scalable and customizable computing resources as needed such as virtual machines, storage, and networking, allowing organizations to outsource their IT infrastructure.

2. **PaaS (Platform as a Service):** It provides a comprehensive platform for entire application lifecycle, for developing, testing, deploying, and managing applications, providing the necessary infrastructure and tools, allowing developers to concentrate on building applications without any distraction about the underpinning hardware and software.

3. **SaaS (Software as a Service):** It provides access to software applications over the Internet, eliminating the need for organizations to install and maintain the software on their own devices, making it a convenient and scalable solution.

Cloud Computing Model Types

Major types of cloud computing models are listed below:

1. **Public Cloud:** Public cloud services are delivered by independent providers and are available to the public over the Internet, offering a cost-effective and scalable solution for organizations.

2. **Private Cloud:** Private cloud resources are isolated for a specific organization, providing more control, security, and customization options, but typically requiring a higher upfront investment.

3. **Hybrid Cloud:** Hybrid cloud integrates public and private cloud services, enabling organizations to balance the benefits of both models, including scalability, cost-effectiveness, and data security.

Figure 1-2 illustrates various components and services interconnected through cloud computing. It highlights how cloud computing integrates with private clouds, public clouds, hybrid computing, databases, storage, servers, applications, and mobile devices. It emphasizes the versatility and connectivity of cloud-based solutions.

CHAPTER 1 INTRODUCTION TO AWS

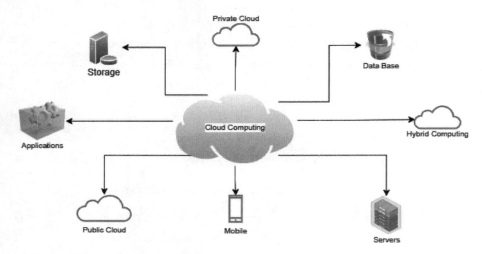

Figure 1-2. *Cloud computing*

Upsides and Downsides of Cloud Computing

In recent years, cloud computing has experienced substantial growth, delivering a multitude of benefits with some potential drawbacks. Let us explore the pros and cons of this technology.

Pros of Cloud Computing

1. **Cost Saving:** Cloud computing discards the necessity for businesses to invest in costly hardware and software, as well as the associated maintenance and IT support costs. Instead, businesses can reach computing resources on demand, paying only for what they utilized.

2. **Data Redundancy:** Cloud providers typically maintain multiple copies of data across distinct locations, ensuring that your information is protected against hardware failures or natural disasters.

3. **Data Replication:** Cloud services automatically replicate and back up your data, reducing the risk of data loss and providing an additional layer of protection.

4. **Malware Protection:** Cloud providers often have powerful security measures in place, including advanced malware protection, to safeguard your data from cyber threats.

5. **Flexibility:** Cloud computing allows you to extend your computing resources up or down as needed, adapting to changing business requirements.

6. **Reliability:** Cloud providers typically have robust infrastructure and redundancy measures in place, confirming high availability and uptime for your applications and data.

7. **High Accessibility:** Cloud-based services can be accessed remotely through an Internet connection, facilitating distributed work and teamwork.

8. **Scalable:** Cloud computing allows you to easily scale your computing resources to meet increasing demands, without the need for costly hardware upgrades.

Cons of Cloud Computing

1. **Internet Dependency:** Cloud computing requires a reliable and stable Internet connection to access your data and applications. Disruptions in Internet service can impact your ability to work.

2. **Limitations of Control:** When using cloud services, you have reduced control over your data and infrastructure compared to in-house solutions. This can be a concern for businesses with specific compliance or regulatory requirements.

3. **Issues in Privacy and Security:** While cloud providers maintain rigorous security protocols, there are still concerns about the potential for certificate thefts or unauthorized access to sensitive information.

4. **Data Breaches:** Cloud services can be vulnerable to data breaches, which can have grave consequences for businesses and their customers.

AWS Architecture and Services

AWS (Amazon Web Services) is a comprehensive, evolving cloud computing platform provided by Amazon. It is like a one-stop shop for businesses and individuals to access a variety of services online. These services fall into three main categories: Infrastructure as a Service (IaaS), Platform as a Service (PaaS), and Software as a Service (SaaS). AWS provides compute power, storage, and content delivery tools. It started with internal infrastructure for Amazon's retail operations in 2002. In 2006, AWS introduced its defining IaaS services. AWS pioneered the pay-as-you-go cloud model, offering scalable resources on demand.

AWS offers a variety of tools and products for enterprises and software developers in around 245 countries and territories. AWS services are widely used by government agencies, education institutions, and private organizations across the globe.

Importance of AWS

AWS (Amazon Web Services) boasts over 200 services, making it a one-stop shop for building virtually any application imaginable. This vast range of services caters to individuals, public sector agencies, and private companies alike.

1. **Cost-Effective Cloud Solutions:** AWS offers a broad spectrum of services, all delivered through the cloud, which translates to potentially lower costs compared to traditional IT infrastructure.

2. **Language and Network Agnostic:** No matter your preferred programming language or network setup, AWS integrates seamlessly, making it adaptable to various development environments.

3. **Open Collaboration:** AWS plays well with others! It allows you to connect and integrate with services from competing cloud providers, fostering a flexible and open ecosystem.

4. **Global Reach and Proven Track Record:** As the forerunner in cloud services, AWS benefits from a vast global network of data centers and a well-established customer base, making it a reliable choice for organizations worldwide.

AWS Architecture

AWS architecture refers to the way you design and configure various AWS services to build and run your applications on the AWS cloud platform. There is no single architecture that fits all, but there are some core principles and components to consider:

1. **Architectural Styles:** There are different architectural styles you can employ within AWS, like a simple three-tier web application structure or a more complex microservices architecture.

2. **Scalability:** AWS allows you to easily scale your resources up or down as your needs change. This means you can handle spikes in traffic or data storage without having to worry about infrastructure limitations.

3. **Flexibility:** AWS offers an extensive variety of services that can be used to build and run a variety of applications. This flexibility allows businesses to choose the tools that are ideally suited to their requirements.

4. **Security:** AWS is a secure platform that offers a variety of features to help businesses protect their data. These features include encryption, access controls, and monitoring.

5. **Reliability:** AWS is an exceptionally reliable platform that offers an elevated level of uptime and performance. This means that businesses can be confident that their applications will be available to users when they need them.

6. **Best Practices:** AWS provides a framework called AWS Well-Architected to help you build secure, high-performing, resilient, and cost-effective architectures. It includes best practices for designing and deploying systems on AWS.

7. **Cost Optimization:** When designing your AWS architecture, consider cost optimization strategies. There are various pricing models and tools to help you manage your AWS costs effectively.

Overall, a well-designed AWS architecture can bring significant benefits to your organization, offering security, scalability, flexibility, and cost efficiency.

AWS Services

Amazon Web Services (AWS) provides an extensive suite of cloud computing services that enable businesses and individuals to build, deploy, and manage applications on a robust and scalable infrastructure. These services span various domains, from compute power and storage solutions to advanced analytics and machine learning capabilities. In this overview, you will explore the main categories of AWS services, highlighting their key features and use cases:

1. **Compute:** The compute services offered by AWS include EC2 machines for virtual servers, AWS Lambdas for serverless computing, and Amazon ECS for container management. These options provide flexible and scalable computing power to run applications and services.

2. **Storage:** AWS Storage services provide secure and durable storage solutions for data of varied sizes and types. Examples include Amazon S3 for object storage, Amazon EBS for block storage, and Amazon Glacier for long-term archiving.

3. **Database:** AWS Database services offer a wide range of database options to suit diverse needs, from relational databases like Amazon RDS to NoSQL databases like Amazon DynamoDB and Amazon DocumentDB. These services provide scalability, high availability, and easy management.

4. **Networking and Content Delivery:** It enables secure and efficient communication between applications, users, and services. This includes Amazon VPC for virtual private networks, Amazon Route 53 for domain name system (DNS) management, and Amazon CloudFront for content delivery.

5. **Analytics:** AWS Analytics services provide powerful tools for data processing, analysis, and visualization. Examples include Amazon Athena for interactive SQL queries, Amazon EMR for big data processing, and Amazon QuickSight for business intelligence.

6. **Machine Learning:** It offers advanced artificial intelligence capabilities, from pretrained models for specific use cases to custom model development and deployment. Examples include Amazon SageMaker for training, building, and deploying machine learning models and Amazon Comprehend for natural language processing.

7. **Security:** AWS Security services help protect applications, data, and infrastructure from threats and maintain conformity with industry standards and regulations. This includes services like AWS IAM for identity and access management, AWS WAF for web application firewall, and AWS Shield for DDoS protection.

8. **Identity and Compliance:** AWS Identity and Compliance services provide tools for managing user identities, permissions, and compliance with various regulations. Examples include AWS IAM for identity and access management, AWS Organizations for managing multiple AWS accounts, and AWS Artifact for compliance documentation.

9. **IoT:** AWS IoT services enable the development, deployment, and management of Internet of Things (IoT) applications. This includes services like AWS IoT Core for device connectivity, AWS IoT Analytics for data analysis, and AWS IoT SiteWise for industrial asset management.

10. **Management and Governance:** AWS Management and Governance services help organizations effectively manage and monitor their AWS resources. Examples include AWS CloudFormation for infrastructure as code, AWS CloudTrail for logging and monitoring, and AWS Config for resource configuration management.

11. **Business Applications:** AWS Business Applications services provide cloud-based solutions for common business needs, such as email and collaboration (Amazon WorkMail), contact center management (Amazon Connect), and document storage and sharing (Amazon WorkDocs).

CHAPTER 1   INTRODUCTION TO AWS

Regions and Availability Zones

The infrastructure, which includes data centers and networking connectivity, remains essential for the functioning of every cloud application. In the context of AWS, this physical infrastructure is manifested as the AWS Global Infrastructure, which is composed of Availability Zones and Regions. Availability Zones are unique locations within a Region, each designed to operate autonomously in case of failures in other Availability Zones, while Regions are separate geographic areas designed to host isolated infrastructure. This setup ensures redundancy, fault tolerance, and low latency for applications deployed across the AWS cloud.

Let us understand them in detail with the help of Figure 1-3.

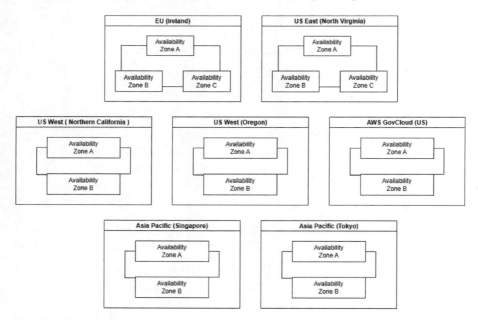

Figure 1-3. *AWS Regions and Availability Zones*

Regions

AWS Regions are specific geographic areas globally where AWS operates its data centers. Each Region is named after the location it serves. For instance, in Asia Pacific, there are Regions such as Singapore, Mumbai, and Hyderabad. Similarly, AWS has established Regions in North America, South America, Europe, Middle East, Asia Pacific, Australia, and New Zealand and is continuously expanding to cater to customer requirements. Each AWS Region is denoted by a geographical name and a unique Region code.

For example, "eu-west-1" represents the initial Region established in the western Europe, with the geographical name being Ireland.

It is important to note that AWS Regions function independently of each other. This signifies that your data is not automatically duplicated or transferred from one Region to another unless you explicitly provide consent and authorization for such actions.

When selecting an AWS Region for hosting applications and workloads, consider four key factors: latency, price, service availability, and compliance.

1. **Latency:** Opt for a Region close to your user base if your application is sensitive to latency. This minimizes wait times for customers.

2. **Price:** Prices may vary between regions due to local economies and operational aspects of data centers.

3. **Service Availability:** Not all AWS services are available in every Region. Refer to AWS documentation for a table listing the available services in each Region.

4. **Data Compliance:** GDPR policies for Countries and Regions vary drastically. They may have compliance requirements dictating that customer data must be stored in specific geographic territories. If applicable, choose a Region that aligns with your compliance needs.

Considering these aspects will help in making an informed decision about the most suitable AWS Region for your applications and workloads.

Availability Zones

It represents a virtual data center within an AWS region, open for use by any AWS client. Within each region, every zone possesses redundant and independent power, networking, and connectivity to minimize the risk of simultaneous failures in multiple zones. It is important to note that a common misunderstanding is the belief that a single zone equates to a solitary data center. Each zone is supported by one or more physical data centers, with the most extensive zones being supported by up to five. While a solitary availability zone can encompass multiple data centers, no two zones share the same data center.

To ensure equitable distribution of resources across the various zones within a specific region, Amazon uniquely assigns identifiers to zones for each account. As a result, one zone for one account may not rely on the same data centers for another account. Within each zone, the participating data centers are interconnected via redundant, low-latency private network links. Similarly, all zones within a region communicate with one another through redundant private network links. These intra- and inter-zone links play a crucial role in data replication for numerous AWS services, including storage and managed databases.

CHAPTER 1   INTRODUCTION TO AWS

Identity and Access Management (IAM)

AWS Identity and Access Management (IAM) serves as a robust and essential tool within the AWS ecosystem, providing a comprehensive suite of features for effective access management. IAM offers a centralized and holistic view of the entities authorized within your AWS account, encompassing the critical functions of authentication and authorization. Authentication involves verifying the identity of users, systems, and services attempting to access the AWS account, while authorization dictates the specific actions and resources these entities are permitted to use within the AWS infrastructure.

IAM not only governs access to the AWS account but also regulates interactions with the diverse array of AWS resources. This dual functionality ensures that only authorized entities can access the account and that they possess the necessary privileges to engage with the resources in a controlled manner. One of the key advantages of IAM is its ability to facilitate access allocation without the necessity of sharing sensitive access keys or passwords. Moreover, IAM enables granular permission assignment, allowing administrators to tailor access rights to individuals and services based on their specific responsibilities and requirements. This fine-grained control empowers administrators to define precise access levels, such as granting read-only permissions for particular AWS services, by meticulously selecting the actions and resources within those services that users can utilize. Ultimately, IAM empowers organizations to enforce robust access control measures, ensuring the security and integrity of their AWS environments while facilitating efficient and tailored access for authorized entities.

CHAPTER 1   INTRODUCTION TO AWS

Capabilities of IAM

IAM, or Identity and Access Management, offers a wide range of capabilities that are crucial for ensuring security and effectively managing access within your AWS account. Here is a detailed breakdown of its features:

1. **Global Operation:** IAM functions on a global scale, allowing users to access and manage configurations from any AWS Region using the AWS Management Console. This global accessibility provides a unified and centralized approach to managing access and security settings across different regions.

2. **Seamless Integration:** IAM seamlessly integrates with various AWS services by default. This integration ensures that access management and security measures extend across the entire spectrum of AWS services, enabling a consistent and comprehensive security posture.

3. **Password Policy Management:** With IAM, administrators can establish and enforce password policies, specifying complexity requirements and mandatory rotation intervals for users. This feature ensures that passwords adhere to specified security standards and are regularly updated to mitigate potential vulnerabilities.

4. **Multifactor Authentication (MFA):** IAM supports multifactor authentication (MFA), adding an extra sheet of security by demanding users to provide multiple forms of verification before accessing AWS resources, and mitigates the risks of unauthorized access attempts.

5. **Identity Federation:** IAM supports identity federation, allowing users who possess passwords from external sources such as corporate networks or Internet identity providers to gain temporary access to the AWS account. This feature streamlines access for users with existing credentials, enhancing flexibility and user experience while maintaining security.

6. **Accessibility and Cost:** IAM is available to all AWS customers at no extra cost, making it an inclusive and cost-effective solution for managing access and security within AWS accounts. This accessibility ensures that organizations of all sizes can leverage IAM's capabilities without incurring extra expenses.

IAM's extensive feature set, global operability, seamless integrations, and robust security measures make it a fundamental component for maintaining a secure and well-managed AWS environment.

IAM User Credentials

An IAM user is composed of a name and a specific set of credentials. When setting up a user, there is the option to grant the user using the following:

1. **Access to the AWS Management Console:** For AWS Management Console access, users are provided with a username and password.

2. **Programmatic Access:** Programmatic access to the AWS Command Line Interface (AWS CLI) and AWS Application Programming Interface (AWS API) is provided by creating a set of access keys that are compatible with the AWS CLI and AWS API.

IAM user credentials are considered permanent and remain with the user until there is a compelled rotation by administrators.

Upon creating an IAM user, there is the flexibility to assign permissions directly at the user level. While this may appear practical for a small user base, as the number of users contributing to your AWS solutions grows, managing permissions becomes more intricate. For instance, "n" number of users in your AWS account, overseeing access becomes challenging, and gaining an overarching understanding of who can execute specific actions on particular resources becomes unfeasible.

Considering this, the capability to group IAM users and allocate permissions at the group level offers a more organized approach, particularly in scenarios involving a large user base.

IAM Group

An IAM group functions as an amalgamation of users, with all users within the group inheriting the permissions assigned to that group. This approach simplifies the process of granting permissions to multiple users simultaneously, offering a more convenient and scalable method of managing user permissions within your AWS account. This practice of utilizing IAM groups is widely regarded as a best practice in AWS.

Suppose you are developing an application with multiple users operating within a single account. In that case, you may opt to categorize these users based on their teams. For instance, you might establish IAM groups for the development team, security team, DevOps team, and

CHAPTER 1   INTRODUCTION TO AWS

support team and subsequently assign each IAM user to the corresponding group based on their team. This strategy facilitates a clearer segregation of permissions within your organization and provides a seamless approach to accommodating new members, departures, and role changes within the organization.

Consider the following scenarios: When a new developer joins your AWS account to contribute to the application, you can effortlessly create a new user and assign them to the developer team without the need to individually determine their permissions. On the other hand, if there is permission needed to be added for a team, you do not have to modify it for everyone individually but to just update the IAM group accordingly, and it will reflect for everyone who are a part of that IAM group.

It is important to note the following characteristics of groups:

1. Groups can encompass multiple users.
2. Users can be part of multiple groups.
3. Groups cannot be nested within other groups.

By default, the root user possesses the capability to execute all actions on all resources within an AWS account. Conversely, when creating new IAM users, groups, or roles, these new IAM identities possess no default permissions within the AWS account and require explicit permission grants.

In IAM, permissions are granted through the utilization of IAM policies.

IAM Policies

An IAM policy serves as a JSON document outlining permissions within AWS. These policies offer reusability across various AWS services and can be assigned to multiple individuals and teams. AWS classifies policies into two primary categories:

1. **AWS Managed Policies:** These default policies are preconfigured within AWS, encompassing commonly utilized services and their associated read and write permissions.

2. **Customer-Managed Policies:** Users have the flexibility to create custom policies tailored to their specific requirements and use cases when default AWS managed policies do not align with their needs. This allows for a more personalized approach to policy creation.

Several types of policies are available for use in AWS; details for each policy type can be found below:

1. **Identity-Based Policies:** These policies encompass the assignment of managed and inline policies to IAM identities such as users, groups, or roles. They are crucial for providing permissions to a particular identity within the AWS environment.

2. **Resource-Based Policies:** Resource-based access controls involve embedding direct policy statements into specific assets. Notable instances of this approach include the security configurations for Amazon S3 storage and the trust frameworks associated with IAM roles. These integrated directives allocate privileges to designated entities, which may reside within the same organizational boundary or span across multiple accounts.

3. **Permissions Boundaries:** Apply a managed policy as the permissions boundary for an IAM entity to establish the upper limit of permissions that identity-based policies can provide. This approach does not directly assign permissions. Note that these boundaries do not restrict the maximum permissions that a resource-based policy can allocate to an entity.

4. **Organizations SCPs (Service Control Policies):** AWS Organizations service control policies (SCPs) serve as governance tools to establish the highest level of permissible permissions for users within an organization or organizational unit (OU). These policies restrict the permissions granted by identity-based or resource-based policies to entities within the account, without directly providing any permissions.

5. **Access Control Lists (ACLs):** Access Control Lists (ACLs) function as gatekeepers, managing how entities from external accounts interact with the resource they are linked to. Unlike standard policies, ACLs eschew the JSON policy structure, instead employing a unique structure. They function as cross-account permission systems, enabling specific services to access resources while excluding in-house entities from their purview.

6. **Session Policies:** Session policies in AWS serve as sophisticated control mechanisms when utilizing roles or federated identities via the CLI or API. These policies function as constraints, narrowing down the authorizations provided by the role or user's identity-based policies for the duration of the session. Rather than directly conferring permissions, session policies function as restrictive filters, fine-tuning access rights for the temporary session period.

AWS policies can be created in JSON or YAML documents and comprise several elements, explained below:

1. **Version:** Version indicates the desired version of the policy language.

2. **Statement:** This serves as the primary policy component, acting as a container for the remaining elements elaborated in the subsequent points. A policy may contain one or more statement blocks.

3. **Sid (Optional):** Sid stands for Statement ID. It indicates an elective statement ID to distinguish between statements.

4. **Effect:** It specifies whether a resource is accessible or restricted based on the policy's permissions.

5. **Action:** This function specifies which actions can be executed by which service.

6. **Resource:** It consists of the resource (or list of resources) for which the IAM policy is made.

```json
{
    "Version": "2012-10-17",
    "Statement": [
        {
            "Sid": "AllowListBucket",
            "Effect": "Allow",
            "Action": "s3:ListBucket",
            "Resource": "arn:aws:s3:::practical-aws",
            "Condition": {
                "StringLike": {"s3:prefix": [""]}
            }
        },
        {
            "Sid": "AllowGetObject",
            "Effect": "Allow",
            "Action": "s3:GetObject",
            "Resource": "arn:aws:s3::: practical-aws/*"
        },
        {
            "Sid": "DenyPutObject",
            "Effect": "Deny",
            "Action": "s3:PutObject",
            "Resource": "arn:aws:s3::: practical-aws/*"
        }
    ]
}
```

Figure 1-4. *IAM policy*

Here is an example in Figure 1-4 of a simple IAM policy. The highlight of the policy is to understand the following actions:

1. AllowListBucket: Allows listing the contents of the bucket

2. AllowGetObject: Allows retrieving objects from the bucket

3. DenyPutObject: Denies uploading objects to the bucket

This IAM policy grants specific permissions for an S3 bucket named "practical-aws." It allows users to list the contents of the bucket using the "s3:ListBucket" action, which is limited to the root directory (empty prefix). The policy also permits retrieving objects from the bucket using the "s3:GetObject" action, granting access to all objects within the bucket. However, the policy includes a "DenyPutObject" statement that explicitly denies users the ability to upload new objects using the "s3:PutObject" action. This combination of allowing list and get operations while denying put operations ensures that users can view the contents of the bucket and download existing objects, but are prevented from modifying the bucket by adding new objects. The policy demonstrates how IAM policies can be used to fine-tune access control for specific actions on an S3 bucket, enabling administrators to grant the necessary permissions while restricting potentially harmful actions.

CloudFormation and Cloud Development Kit
CloudFormation

AWS CloudFormation simplifies AWS resource management by allowing users to define and deploy templates, reducing manual provisioning efforts. These templates consist of the needed AWS resources, such as Lambda, Amazon EC2, or Amazon RDS DB instances, etc., which enable CloudFormation to automate the resource provisioning and configuration seamlessly. This eliminates the need for individual resource setup and dependency management, streamlining the process and allowing users to focus more on their applications within AWS. CloudFormation's efficiency becomes evident in various scenarios, showcasing its ability to streamline resource management tasks.

In diverse use cases, CloudFormation proves its value by enabling swift and consistent resource deployment. Whether it is setting up complex multitier applications or replicating infrastructure across different environments, CloudFormation's templates ensure resource consistency and reliability. By abstracting the underlying infrastructure details, CloudFormation empowers users to automate resource provisioning, promoting agility and minimizing the time and effort drained on manual configuration. These scenarios underscore CloudFormation's role in simplifying resource management and fostering efficient application development within AWS.

AWS CloudFormation helps in automation of AWS resource provision.

AWS CloudFormation facilitates auto scaling by allowing users to define scaling policies and resources in templates, ensuring that additional instances are provisioned automatically based on defined conditions. This streamlines the implementation of auto scaling, promoting efficient resource utilization within AWS environments.

AWS CloudFormation seamlessly integrates with assorted services such as CodePipeline and Jenkins CI/CD pipelines, enabling automated deployment and streamlining the integration of resources across different platforms. This facilitates efficient and automated deployment processes, enhancing overall operational agility within AWS environments.

Let us simplify this. CloudFormation operates by taking a JSON or YAML template and then orchestrating the provisioning of resources accordingly. Once the template is submitted, CloudFormation generates a stack directly linked to the created resources. Consequently, if the stack is deleted, the associated services are also removed. Figure 1-5 highlights the flow how the CloudFormation template works.

CHAPTER 1　INTRODUCTION TO AWS

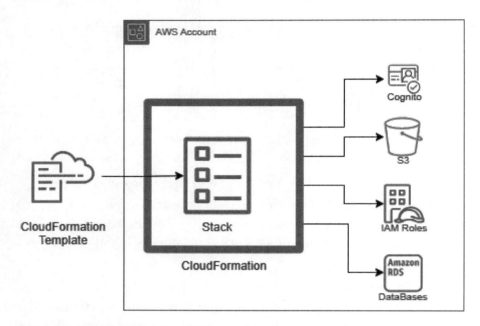

Figure 1-5. *CloudFormation template*

While CloudFormation is effective for resource definition in AWS, it comes with significant drawbacks. Templates require explicit definition of all app resources, leading to lengthy templates and creating huge YAML and JSON files which are difficult to manage. To address and simplify these issues, AWS introduced another service named CDK, which we will see in the next section.

Cloud Development Kit

The AWS Cloud Development Kit (CDK) serves as a robust framework empowering the utilization of reusable components for the construction of cloud environments. These reusable components are referred to as constructs. Within Integrated Development Environments, developers can leverage libraries and components to fashion and generate cloud services seamlessly. AWS CDK streamlines the process of infrastructure

CHAPTER 1   INTRODUCTION TO AWS

development by offering a straightforward and accessible approach facilitated by programming languages. This innovative framework revolutionizes the traditional methods of cloud environment creation, enabling developers to craft intricate and scalable infrastructures efficiently. With AWS CDK, developers gain a powerful tool that not only simplifies the process of building cloud environments but also enhances the overall agility and flexibility of cloud development operations.

The AWS CDK speeds up cloud development by enabling the use of familiar programming languages for application modeling.

Internally, CDK leverages CloudFormation to transform your code into a CloudFormation template. A CDK application comprises multiple stacks, which eventually translate into CloudFormation stacks. However, it is better to perceive them as coded versions of your CloudFormation stacks. This approach simplifies the process. The crucial point to note is that despite the internal utilization of CloudFormation, there is no direct interaction with YAML or JSON templates anymore. The process is depicted in Figure 1-6.

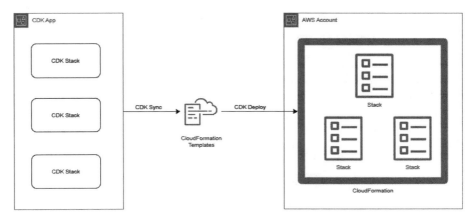

Figure 1-6. *CDK: Cloud Development Kit*

29

CHAPTER 1   INTRODUCTION TO AWS

CloudWatch

Amazon CloudWatch offers real-time surveillance of AWS resources and applications running on it. This service allows you to collect and monitor quantifiable indicators that reflect the performance of your resources and software. On the CloudWatch home page, you can automatically view metrics for all AWS services in use, and you can create custom dashboards to show metrics for your specific applications and selected metric collections. Moreover, you can set up alarms to monitor metrics, receive notifications, or automate resource adjustments when thresholds are exceeded. For instance, you can monitor CPU usage and disk activity of your Amazon EC2 instances to make decisions about scaling up or down based on the data. CloudWatch offers comprehensive visibility into resource usage, application performance, and operational status across your system.

One of the remarkable aspects of CloudWatch is that you only require an AWS account to begin using it. As a managed service, it lets you focus on monitoring tasks without the need to manage the underlying infrastructure.

Various AWS services automatically transmit metrics to CloudWatch at no cost, providing one data point per metric per five-minute interval. This automatic data collection offers visibility into your systems without any additional effort or cost, which is known as basic monitoring. While basic monitoring suffices for many applications, for those running on EC2 instances, you can achieve greater granularity by posting metrics every minute which is referred to as detailed monitoring, albeit incurring an additional fee.

Access to CloudWatch is available through various methods, including the Amazon CloudWatch Console, the AWS CLI, the CloudWatch API, and the AWS SDKs. These options provide flexibility in how users can interact with CloudWatch through numerous ways, catering to different preferences and needs.

Understanding CloudWatch Logs

Considering that log data can originate from various sources makes it crucial to organize and maintain logs carefully. Understanding this framework will enable you to effectively manage and analyze the log data, ensuring that you can derive meaningful insights and take necessary actions based on the information gathered.

1. **Log Event:** A log event represents an entry of an activity captured from the monitored application or resource. Each log event includes a timestamp indicating when the activity occurred and an associated event message providing specific details about the recorded activity. Understanding these log events is fundamental for effectively tracking and analyzing the behavior of the monitored application or resource.

2. **Log Stream:** Following the recording of log events, they are organized into log streams, forming continuous sequences of related log events associated with the same monitored resource. For instance, log streams consolidate all the log events generated by an EC2 or Lambda, allowing users to conveniently filter or query these streams to gain valuable insights. Understanding this grouping of log events into streams is pivotal for efficiently managing and extracting meaningful information from the log data.

3. **Log Groups:** After log events are grouped into log streams, these streams are further organized into what are known as log groups. A log group consists of multiple log streams that are configured with the same retention and permissions settings. For instance, when application log data from multiple EC2 instances is sent to CloudWatch Logs, a log group can be fired by grouping these individual log streams. This practice of grouping log streams into log groups is beneficial as it helps in maintaining a well-organized structure for the logs.

Networking Basics

Communication between devices (and services in AWS context) is facilitated through networks. AWS Networking empowers the establishment of rapid, dependable, and secure networks. AWS presents an assortment of cloud services characterized by their on-demand nature, high availability, and remarkable scalability. The amalgamation of various AWS services such as Amazon VPC, Amazon Gateway, Load Balancers, Amazon Route 53, and others culminates in the formation of a comprehensive AWS network. Each of these services plays a pivotal role in shaping an intricate Amazon Network. A comprehensive understanding of the array of Amazon services contributing to network creation is essential for a profound insight into AWS Networking; however, you will understand about VPN, NAT (Network Address Translation) Gateways, subnets, and ENI (Elastic Network Interface), which are basic building blocks of AWS Network.

When accessing a website or using an application, the data and requests travel from your device to a server hosting the website or application and back. This is referred to as the request-response model. This journey involves multiple hops, such as Wi-Fi, ISP networks, undersea fiber cables, etc. However, with cloud technology, global deployment becomes swift and efficient. For instance, AWS facilitates rapid deployment of applications across various physical locations, reducing latency and enhancing user experience. AWS infrastructure revolves around Regions and Availability Zones, enabling universally available, fault-tolerant, and scalable operation of applications and databases.

Virtual Private Cloud (VPC)

An AWS VPC (Virtual Private Cloud) serves as an independent network within the AWS cloud, resembling a conventional data center network as shown in Figure 1-7. In other words, you can say that it is a private cloud inside the cloud. Amazon VPC empowers the creation of a secluded virtual network for Amazon resources, ensuring privacy and enabling restricted operations. Hosting an Amazon VPC is open to any user with an AWS account, and it can be managed with the help of various tools and services. These tools include the following:

1. Amazon Web Service Management Console
2. Amazon CLI (Command Line Interface)
3. Amazon SDK
4. Query API

Amazon VPC offers a private network that is isolated from the external world, allowing users to conduct operations that are not meant for public access.

CHAPTER 1   INTRODUCTION TO AWS

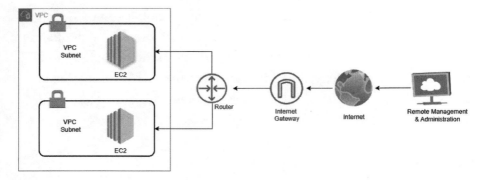

Figure 1-7. *AWS Networking*

A well-configured VPC encompasses various essential services, including gateways, Load Balancers, and subnets, all combined to form an independent virtual environment. Additionally, multiple levels of security measures are implemented alongside these services. The VPC is initially segmented into subnets, interlinked via route tables, and equipped with a load balancer.

Subnets

In the context of AWS subnets, a subnet functions as a smaller, distinct segment of the network encompassing specific machines within a designated area as shown in Figure 1-7. Within a single availability zone, the flexibility exists to incorporate numerous subnets. It is essential to note that each subnet is confined within a single availability zone. When it comes to connectivity, public subnets are linked to an Internet Gateway, facilitating Internet accessibility, while private subnets are intentionally isolated from Internet connectivity. Additionally, every subnet within the Virtual Private Cloud (VPC) necessitates association with a routing table.

The subdivision of large networks into smaller interconnected ones serves to alleviate network congestion. With the potential to accommodate up to 200 user-defined subnets within a range, this approach enables efficient network management and optimized data flow.

Security Group

AWS Security Groups function as virtual firewalls, controlling network traffic to and from your AWS resources. They enforce rules for inbound and outbound connections, enhancing security by permitting only authorized traffic.

Key Points

1. **Inbound Rules:** Control which traffic is permitted to enter your resources. You define these rules by specifying the allowed protocol (e.g., TCP, UDP), port range (e.g., 80 for HTTP), and the source of the traffic (e.g., specific IP addresses, other security groups).

2. **Outbound Rules:** Determine which traffic is allowed to leave your resources. Similar to inbound rules, you define these by specifying the protocol, port range, and the destination of the traffic.

3. **Stateful Behavior:** When a resource receives traffic that is allowed by an inbound rule, the response traffic is automatically permitted to leave the resource, even if it doesn't explicitly match an outbound rule. This simplifies many common network scenarios.

4. **Flexibility with Multiple Groups:** You can associate multiple security groups with a single resource. This provides granular control and allows for more complex traffic flow configurations.

5. **Default Security Group:** Every Virtual Private Cloud (VPC) has a default security group. By default, this group allows all outbound traffic but blocks all inbound traffic, acting as a crucial first line of defense.

6. Only allow the minimum necessary traffic for your applications to function.

7. Name your security groups and rules clearly to understand their purpose at a glance.

8. Regularly review your security groups and rules to ensure they are up to date and necessary.

Internet Gateways

Enabling communication between a VPC and the Internet, an Internet Gateway (or IGV) serves as a horizontally scalable, redundant, and universally available component within the Virtual Private Cloud infrastructure as shown in Figure 1-7. Sometimes referred to as a virtual router, it plays a pivotal role in facilitating bidirectional traffic flow between instances in the VPC and the Internet. By establishing the crucial link between the VPC and the Internet, an Internet Gateway mandates the presence of a public subnet within the VPC, requiring instances within that subnet to possess public IP addresses for Internet communication. Functioning as a conduit between the VPC and the Internet, it undertakes the essential task of translating private IP addresses within the VPC to public IP addresses, making it an indispensable component for Internet accessibility within the VPC. For instance, when hosting a web server within a VPC, an Internet Gateway becomes instrumental in making it reachable from the Internet.

The components hosted within a VPC, such as EC2 instances or Lambdas, gain the capability to connect with and access the Internet using Internet Gateway.

CHAPTER 1   INTRODUCTION TO AWS

It is crucial to understand that each VPC can only have one Internet Gateway (IGW). Additionally, once resources are active within a particular VPC, the associated IGW cannot be removed.

Route Table

Within Amazon Web Services (AWS), a VPC route table serves as a collection of rules dictating the path of network traffic originating from your subnet or gateway as shown in Figure 1-7. One VPC can accommodate multiple route tables as necessary to cater to its operational demands. Every subnet, representing a specific range of IP addresses within a VPC, is linked to a route table governing the flow of traffic between these subnets. At the core of these route tables lies the destination address, determining the trajectory of the network. These tables play a pivotal role in managing CIDR blocks of IPv4/IPv6, private and public subnets, VPC endpoints, network gateways, and more, forming an indispensable component of network architecture within AWS.

Effectively leveraging route tables is essential for orchestrating secure and efficient network traffic within your AWS environment. By defining the paths for traffic targeting on exact criteria, like destination addresses, these tables make sure that data gets transported seamlessly with security standards between various service instances of your VPC. As a fundamental building block for network management, understanding and configuring route tables optimally is key for upholding robust and reliable network infrastructure within AWS.

There are two types of route table:

1. **Default Route Table:** The default route table in AWS VPCs is automatically generated upon VPC creation, orchestrating traffic flow across linked subnets. It comes equipped with a built-in local route for intra-VPC traffic.

37

Subnets are automatically linked to this table unless explicitly assigned elsewhere. While it is recommended to assign subnets explicitly to avoid issues, the choice ultimately rests with the user. The default route table facilitates Internet interaction within the VPC, making it suitable for general networking needs.

2. **Custom Route Table:** The custom route table, as the name implies, is user created and offers greater flexibility compared to default tables. It remains empty until the user adds routes, allowing for tailored configuration. Users can create multiple custom route tables, with the responsibility to manually bind subnets and revise routing paths on demand. Custom route tables are explicitly associated and are ideal for complex networking scenarios, providing the necessary control for intricate routing requirements within the VPC.

NAT Gateways

The AWS NAT Gateway, an abbreviation for Network Address Translation, represents a managed service within Amazon Web Services that scales according to your usage. This service facilitates Internet access for instances configured within a private subnet. However, without appropriate routing, external access to these instances remains unattainable.

Essentially, a NAT Gateway provides Internet connectivity to instances in a private subnet, ensuring they are not exposed to external traffic. This is key to maintaining a secure environment and control over sensitive data and applications. By managing the traffic flow and enabling secure connectivity, the NAT Gateway plays a pivotal role in ensuring the integrity and confidentiality of your network. Its scalability and managed nature make it an asset for any organization leveraging AWS services.

> **AWS NAT Gateway acts as a vital intermediary, effectively shielding your private instances from external threats while allowing them to harness the power of the Internet.**

Two types of AWS NAT Gateways exist, the public and the private, explained below:

1. **Public NAT Gateways:** Operate within a public subnet, enabling Internet access from instances in private subnets while barricading external access without appropriate routing. This setup ensures that the instances in private subnets remain shielded from unsanctioned external connections, bolstering network security.

2. **Private NAT Gateways:** Predominantly facilitate communication between VPCs or VPCs and Transit Gateway. Notably, they do not support access to Elastic IP. These private gateways hold significant importance in maintaining secure and controlled interconnectivity between VPCs, ensuring the protection of sensitive data and applications from unauthorized access. Understanding these distinctions is pivotal for effectively architecting and securing network infrastructures within AWS.

CHAPTER 1   INTRODUCTION TO AWS

Conclusion

In this chapter, you have gained a holistic look at the world of cloud computing, its growth, and the key pros and cons of adopting this technology. We have also delved into the importance of AWS, its architecture, and the diverse services it offers, including regions, availability zones, Identity and Access Management (IAM), CloudFormation, Cloud Development Kit, and CloudWatch.

1. **Cloud Computing – Refresher, Growth Pros and Cons:** The adoption of cloud technologies has surged dramatically in the past decade, driven by its cost-effectiveness, scalability, and flexibility. The advantages of cloud computing include reduced infrastructure costs, increased collaboration, and automatic software updates. As a cornerstone of modern IT strategy, cloud computing is being embraced by companies looking to optimize their digital resources and drive productivity gains. However, there are also challenges, such as the need for good Internet connectivity and potential security risks.

2. **AWS Architecture and Services:** Amazon Web Services (AWS) stands as a premier cloud service provider, delivering an extensive array of solutions tailored to meet diverse business requirements. The architecture of AWS is crafted to ensure scalability, security, and dependability for applications hosted in the cloud. Gaining insight into AWS offerings like Elastic Compute Cloud (EC2), Simple Storage Service (S3), and Relational Database Service (RDS) is essential for maximizing the advantages of cloud computing.

3. **Regions and Availability Zones:** AWS regions and availability zones are critical components of its architecture. Regions are geographic locations where AWS resources are available, and availability zones are data centers within these regions. This setup ensures high availability and fault tolerance for applications, allowing businesses to maintain uptime and performance upon a data center outage.

4. **Identity and Access Management (IAM):** IAM is fundamental to maintaining robust security in cloud environments, empowering companies to regulate user access and permissions for AWS cloud resources. IAM provides a robust framework for controlling who can access what, ensuring that specific actions are limited to users with the appropriate permissions. A strong IAM strategy is fundamental to maintaining the security and integrity of systems in the cloud.

5. **CloudFormation and Cloud Development Kit:** CloudFormation and Cloud Development Kit (CDK) are tools that streamline the provisioning, deployment, and oversight of cloud-based assets. CloudFormation enables users to specify and control their infrastructure using code, while CDK provides a programming model for defining cloud resources programmatically. These tools streamline the cloud deployment process, reducing errors and improving efficiency.

CHAPTER 1   INTRODUCTION TO AWS

6. **CloudWatch:** CloudWatch is a monitoring and logging service that helps businesses track and analyze their cloud resources. It provides real-time data on resource utilization, performance, and availability, enabling proactive issue detection and resolution. CloudWatch acts as a critical guardian, overseeing the vitality and efficiency of software running in cloud environments.

7. **Networking Basics:** The role of networking within the cloud is fundamental to cloud architecture. The VPC service from AWS furnishes a protected, stand-alone environment for managing cloud resources. Subnets, security groups, Internet Gateways, route tables, and NAT Gateways are key components of VPC that help manage network traffic and ensure secure communication between resources. Understanding these networking basics is vital for designing and deploying robust cloud infrastructure.

In conclusion, cloud computing has established itself as a critical aspect of the modern IT landscape, offering numerous benefits and challenges. Understanding AWS architecture, regions, availability zones, IAM, CloudFormation, CloudWatch, and networking basics is essential for leveraging the full spectrum of cloud computing possibilities. By mastering these concepts, businesses can build scalable, secure, and efficient cloud-based solutions that drive growth and productivity.

By mastering the concepts and services discussed in this chapter, you will be well prepared to navigate the cloud computing ecosystem and utilize AWS to develop and deploy scalable, secure, and efficient applications.

CHAPTER 2

Frontend Development and Integration

Introduction

Amidst the swiftly advancing domain of web development, frontend technologies play a crucial role in delivering seamless user experiences. This chapter delves into the integration of frontend development with Amazon Web Services (AWS), exploring powerful tools and services that streamline the way of designing, implementing, and scaling up web applications. You'll examine AWS Amplify, a comprehensive platform for frontend and backend development, AWS CloudFront for content delivery, API Gateway for managing APIs, and S3 (Simple Storage Service) for efficient storage solutions. By understanding these services and their integration, developers can create robust, scalable, and high-performance web applications that leverage the full potential of AWS infrastructure.

CHAPTER 2 FRONTEND DEVELOPMENT AND INTEGRATION

AWS Amplify

Offered by Amazon Web Services (AWS), AWS Amplify serves as a robust development platform that simplifies the process of building, deploying, and managing scalable web and mobile applications. Launched in 2017, AWS Amplify is designed to cater to both frontend and backend development needs, making it a perfect option for developers aiming to effortlessly build full-stack applications. By leveraging AWS's robust infrastructure, Amplify provides a unified interface that integrates seamlessly with various AWS services, permitting developers to dedicate more attention to application logic rather than the complexities of infrastructure management. This platform is particularly beneficial for developers who want to accelerate application development without delving into the complexities of backend configuration and deployment. Amplify's ability to support popular frontend frameworks and its extensive set of tools and services make it a powerful ally in the modern development landscape.

Key Features of Amplify

With AWS Amplify, developers can access a suite of features designed to streamline the creation of both web and mobile applications. Some notable features are

1. **Authentication:** Amplify provides built-in authentication capabilities powered by Amazon Cognito as shown in Figure 2-1, allowing developers to easily implement secure user sign-up, sign-in, and access control. It supports various authentication methods, including social logins via platforms like Google and Facebook, and offers multifactor authentication and password encryption for enhanced security.

CHAPTER 2　FRONTEND DEVELOPMENT AND INTEGRATION

2. **API Integration:** With AWS Amplify, developers can effortlessly create and manage REST and GraphQL APIs. The platform integrates with AWS services like AWS AppSync as shown in Figure 2-1, enabling real-time data synchronization and offline capabilities. This feature simplifies the process of connecting applications to backend data sources, ensuring seamless communication between the client and server.

3. **Storage:** Amplify offers secure cloud storage solutions through Amazon S3 as shown in Figure 2-1, allowing applications for the storage and retrieval of user-generated items such as images, videos, and documents. The storage module supports categorization of data into public, private, and protected access levels, ensuring data security and scalability.

CHAPTER 2   FRONTEND DEVELOPMENT AND INTEGRATION

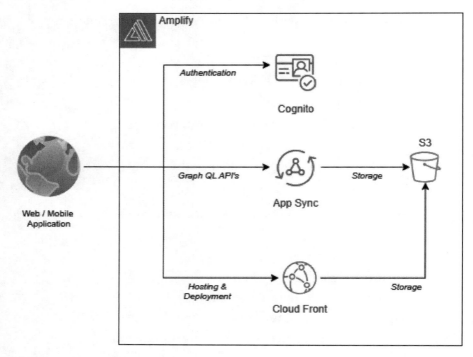

Figure 2-1.   *AWS Amplify features*

4. **Hosting and Deployment:** AWS Amplify provides a fully managed hostig service that supports continuous deployment of web applications. Developers can deploy static and dynamic websites with ease using Git-based workflows, and the platform automatically handles scaling and content delivery through the Amazon CloudFront global edge network as shown in Figure 2-1.

Key Benefits of Amplify

AWS Amplify provides numerous benefits that enhance the development experience:

1. **Rapid Development:** Amplify accelerates the development process by offering prebuilt components and a streamlined workflow. Developers can quickly configure backends, integrate APIs, and deploy applications with minimal code, reducing time to market for new features and updates.

2. **Scalability and Performance:** Built on AWS's robust infrastructure, Amplify ensures applications can scale effortlessly to handle varying levels of traffic. The platform's integration with AWS services like Amazon CloudFront guarantees low-latency content delivery, enhancing application performance.

3. **Cost-Effectiveness:** With Amplify's pay-as-you-go pricing model, developers can effectively manage expenses. This approach allows businesses to optimize their budget by only paying for the services they use, all while benefiting from AWS's powerful resources.

4. **Seamless Integration:** Amplify's seamless integration with other AWS services simplifies the process of adding functionalities like authentication, storage, and analytics to applications. This integration reduces the complexity of managing multiple services and enhances application capabilities.

CHAPTER 2   FRONTEND DEVELOPMENT AND INTEGRATION

5. **User Experience:** The unified interface of Amplify, along with its support for popular frontend frameworks, ensures a seamless user experience across multiple platforms and devices. This aspect is especially valuable for developers aiming to develop cross-platform applications with a harmonious design and functionality.

How Amplify Works

AWS Amplify acts as a development platform that eases the process of developing full-stack web and mobile applications through the integration of various AWS services. It operates through a combination of tools and services that facilitate both frontend and backend development. The process begins with Amplify Studio or the Amplify CLI, which allows developers to visually or programmatically configure the app's backend. This setup includes defining data models, authentication rules, and other backend resources.

Once the backend is configured, Amplify provides libraries and UI components to connect the frontend of the application to these backend resources. This connection is crucial for enabling features like authentication, data storage, and real-time data synchronization. Amplify's DataStore, for instance, allows for seamless data synchronization between the app and the cloud, powered by AWS AppSync.

For deployment, Amplify offers a fully managed CI/CD pipeline that automates the build and deployment process. Developers can link their Git repositories to Amplify, allowing for continuous deployment whenever changes are pushed. This integration ensures the application is always updated and capable of automatically scaling to manage increased traffic.

Overall, AWS Amplify simplifies the development workflow by providing a unified interface for managing both frontend and backend resources, thereby accelerating the development and deployment of scalable applications.

CHAPTER 2   FRONTEND DEVELOPMENT AND INTEGRATION

Working with AWS Amplify

1. Log in to the AWS Console if you haven't already.

2. Search for AWS Amplify in the AWS Console.

3. Select AWS Amplify to open the Amplify Console as shown in Figure 2-2.

Figure 2-2. *AWS Amplify Console*

4. Amplify requires read-only access to your repository and branch.

5. If you're using a GitHub repo for the first time, you need to authenticate on GitHub using your GitHub username and password.

49

CHAPTER 2   FRONTEND DEVELOPMENT AND INTEGRATION

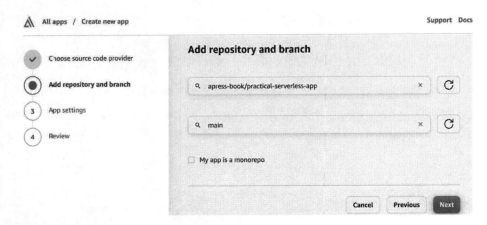

Figure 2-3. *Adding repository to Amplify*

6. As shown in Figure 2-3, you can add a GitHub repo to Amplify after successful authentication.

7. After adding a repository branch, we need to configure build settings as shown in Figure 2-4.

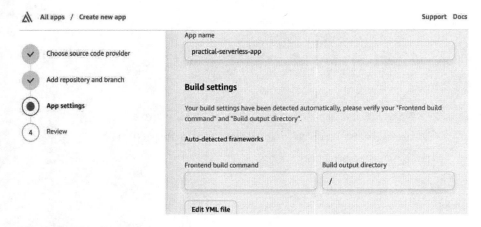

Figure 2-4. *Configure build settings in Amplify*

CHAPTER 2   FRONTEND DEVELOPMENT AND INTEGRATION

8. And then review the repository details and app settings to deploy and save.

Figure 2-5. *Review of app settings in Amplify Console*

9. The app will be deployed to the domain.

10. Go to All apps on the left panel as shown in Figure 2-5, select your app, click the branch as per the given branch name, then click deploy.

API Gateway

AWS offers Amazon API Gateway as a fully managed service that allows developers to efficiently create, publish, maintain, monitor, and secure APIs regardless of scale. As the entry point for API requests, it facilitates applications in accessing data, business logic, or functionalities provided by backend services. API Gateway supports the creation of RESTful, HTTP, and WebSocket APIs, making it versatile for various application needs. By handling tasks such as traffic management, authorization, and monitoring using API Gateway, developers can dedicate their attention to building

51

CHAPTER 2   FRONTEND DEVELOPMENT AND INTEGRATION

applications without dealing with infrastructure management. The pay-as-you-go pricing model, along with integration with other AWS services, makes it an appealing choice for managing scalable APIs.

Amazon API Gateway streamlines API development and management by offering a robust platform that integrates with AWS services. It supports various API types, including RESTful, HTTP, and WebSocket APIs, catering to different application needs. API Gateway manages API calls, traffic, authentication, and access control. It features a monitoring dashboard and integrates with Amazon CloudWatch for metrics and logging. Ideal for serverless applications, it works with AWS Lambda to execute backend logic without server management, providing scalability and a comprehensive feature set.

Key Features and Benefits of AWS API Gateway

Let's explore the key features of AWS API Gateway:

1. **Scalability and Elasticity:** API Gateway can handle thousands of concurrent API calls, automatically scaling to accommodate traffic spikes without manual intervention. This elasticity ensures that applications remain responsive under varying loads.

2. **Integration with AWS Services:** API Gateway's seamless integration with AWS Lambda, IAM, and additional AWS services enables developers to easily construct serverless applications. This integration supports secure and efficient communication between APIs and backend systems.

3. **Cost-Effectiveness:** By using a pay-as-you-go pricing system, API Gateway charges only for the API calls and data transferred, providing a cost-

effective solution for businesses of any scale. The tiered pricing model helps to further cut costs as usage expands.

4. **Security:** Offering robust security features such as AWS IAM policies, Lambda authorizers, and Amazon Cognito user pools, API Gateway provides flexible and powerful methods for authenticating and authorizing API access.

5. **Comprehensive Monitoring and Logging:** Integrated with Amazon CloudWatch, API Gateway provides detailed metrics and logging capabilities. Developers can monitor API performance, set up alarms, and troubleshoot issues using CloudWatch logs.

Use Cases for AWS API Gateway

Let's explore the key use cases of AWS API Gateway:

1. **Microservices Architecture:** API Gateway is ideal for managing microservices, acting as a central hub for routing requests to various backend services. It simplifies the process of exposing microservices to external clients while handling cross-cutting concerns like security and monitoring.

2. **Serverless Applications:** API Gateway, when integrated with AWS Lambda, allows for the creation of serverless applications where backend logic runs in response to API calls. This setup reduces infrastructure management overhead and allows for rapid development and deployment.

3. **Real-Time Communication:** WebSocket APIs provided by API Gateway facilitate real-time communication applications, such as chat applications and live dashboards. This capability allows for bidirectional data flow between clients and servers, supporting dynamic and interactive user experiences.

4. **Legacy System Integration:** API Gateway can act as a proxy for legacy systems, enabling modern applications to interact with older infrastructure. By providing a unified API interface, it simplifies the integration process and extends the life of legacy systems.

5. **Mobile and Web Applications:** As a backend for mobile and web applications, API Gateway offers a scalable and secure interface for accessing application data and functionality. Its feature of generating SDKs for diverse platforms expedites development and deployment.

How AWS API Gateway Works

AWS API Gateway is a robust service that streamlines API creation and management, allowing developers to effortlessly connect applications to backend services. It serves as a conduit for API requests, offering features such as traffic management, authorization, and monitoring. Supporting both RESTful and WebSocket APIs, it meets diverse application needs. By integrating with AWS Lambda and other services, it aids in developing serverless applications, enabling developers to concentrate on business logic instead of infrastructure. Understanding its components and integration capabilities is crucial for maximizing its potential in building scalable applications.

CHAPTER 2 FRONTEND DEVELOPMENT AND INTEGRATION

API Gateway Components

The API Gateway's architecture is built around three core components: resources, methods, and stages as shown in Figure 2-6. These elements work together to define how APIs are structured, accessed, and managed across different environments. Let's understand them.

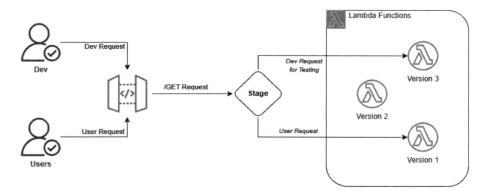

Figure 2-6. *API Gateway components*

1. **Resources:** In AWS API Gateway, a resource is a logical entity that represents an API endpoint. Resources are organized in a hierarchical structure, similar to a file system, and can represent different parts of an API, such as users, products, or orders. Each resource can have one or more methods associated with it, defining how the resource can be accessed. Resources provide a way to structure an API, making it intuitive and easy to navigate. They can be configured with specific settings, such as authorization and caching, to optimize performance and security.

CHAPTER 2   FRONTEND DEVELOPMENT AND INTEGRATION

2. **Methods:** Methods in API Gateway define the type of HTTP request that can be made to a resource, such as GET, POST, PUT, DELETE, etc. Each method can be configured with specific integrations, request and response models, and authorization settings. Methods determine how requests are processed and responses are generated, allowing for fine-tuned control over API behavior. By supporting various HTTP methods, API Gateway enables developers to build comprehensive APIs that handle different types of interactions with backend services.

3. **Stages:** Stages in API Gateway represent different versions or environments of an API, such as development, testing, and production. Each stage can have its own settings, including logging, throttling, and deployment history. Stages allow developers to manage and test APIs in isolated environments before deploying them to production. They provide a mechanism for versioning APIs, ensuring that changes can be made and tested without affecting live applications. By using stages, developers can maintain a clear separation between different API environments, enhancing the development and deployment process.

RESTful APIs vs. WebSocket APIs

AWS API Gateway supports both RESTful and WebSocket APIs, each catering to distinct communication needs. See details below to understand their differences and ideal use cases:

CHAPTER 2   FRONTEND DEVELOPMENT AND INTEGRATION

1. **RESTful APIs:** RESTful APIs in API Gateway are designed for traditional web applications, where clients communicate with servers using HTTP methods. They are stateless and follow the principles of Representational State Transfer (REST), making them suitable for CRUD operations and resource-based interactions. RESTful APIs are easy to cache, scale, and secure, making them a popular choice for many applications. They are ideal for scenarios where the client and server can operate independently, and the communication is request-response based. RESTful APIs in API Gateway can be integrated with various AWS services, providing a flexible and powerful solution for building modern web applications.

2. **WebSocket APIs:** WebSocket APIs in API Gateway facilitate real-time, two-way communication between clients and servers by maintaining a persistent connection. This allows continuous data exchange, making them perfect for applications needing real-time updates, like chat apps, live dashboards, and gaming platforms. With low-latency communication and the ability to handle many concurrent connections, WebSocket APIs enhance interactive and dynamic user experiences, broadening API Gateway's capabilities.

Integration with AWS Lambda and Other AWS Services

Integrating AWS API Gateway with AWS Lambda and other services is crucial for building serverless applications. API Gateway serves as a bridge, allowing HTTP requests to trigger Lambda functions, enabling scalable

CHAPTER 2 FRONTEND DEVELOPMENT AND INTEGRATION

APIs without infrastructure management. It facilitates authentication, authorization, and throttling for secure access. Integration with services like DynamoDB, S3 (Simple Storage Service), and SNS (Simple Notification Service) allows developers to create versatile, comprehensive serverless solutions within the AWS ecosystem.

Setting Up AWS API Gateway

1. Log in to the AWS Console if you haven't already.
2. Navigate to CloudFormation Service and upload a template for API Gateway.
3. Figure 2-7 is a sample template for API Gateway.

CHAPTER 2 FRONTEND DEVELOPMENT AND INTEGRATION

```
AWSTemplateFormatVersion: '2010-09-09'
Description: Practical Serverless App API Gateway
Resources:

  ApiGatewayRestApi:
    Type: AWS::ApiGateway::RestApi
    Properties:
      ApiKeySourceType: HEADER
      Description: Practical Serverless App API Gateway
      Name: serverless-api

  ApiGatewayResource:
    Type: AWS::ApiGateway::Resource
    Properties:
      ParentId: !GetAtt ApiGatewayRestApi.RootResourceId
      PathPart: 'practical-aws'
      RestApiId: !Ref ApiGatewayRestApi

  ApiGatewayMethod:
    Type: AWS::ApiGateway::Method
    Properties:
      ApiKeyRequired: false
      AuthorizationType: NONE
      HttpMethod: GET
      Integration:
        ConnectionType: Mock
      ResourceId: !Ref ApiGatewayResource
      RestApiId: !Ref ApiGatewayRestApi

  ApiGatewayModel:
    Type: AWS::ApiGateway::Model
    Properties:
      ContentType: 'application/json'
      RestApiId: !Ref ApiGatewayRestApi
      Schema: {}
```

Figure 2-7. *API Gateway sample template*

CHAPTER 2   FRONTEND DEVELOPMENT AND INTEGRATION

4. "AWSTemplateFormatVersion" and "Description" provide the version and description of the CloudFormation template, respectively.

5. The "Resources" section defines the resources to be created. In this case, it creates an API Gateway named "`serverless-api`" and a resource named "`practical-aws.`"

6. "Type: AWS::ApiGateway::RestApi" specifies the resource type for API Gateway.

7. The "Properties" section contains the configuration for the API Gateway. In this example, you set the name of the REST API to "sample-api."

8. "Type: AWS::ApiGateway::Resource" specifies the resource type for the API Gateway resource.

9. The "Properties" section contains the configuration for the API Gateway resource.

10. "Type: AWS::ApiGateway::Method" specifies the method type for the API Gateway.

11. "Type: AWS::ApiGateway::Model" specifies the API Gateway model.

12. You can also add other types like "Type: 'AWS::ApiGatewayV2::Stage,'Type: 'AWS::ApiGatewayV2::DomainName,'Type: AWS::Logs::LogGroup,Type: 'AWS::ApiGatewayV2::ApiMapping,'Type: AWS::Route53::RecordSet" based on your requirement.

Security Features in AWS API Gateway

AWS API Gateway offers strong security features to safeguard APIs from unauthorized access and ensure secure data transmission, crucial for serverless applications. It provides authentication, authorization, traffic management, and API monitoring, maintaining data integrity and confidentiality. Using AWS IAM, Amazon Cognito, and Lambda Authorizers, it enables precise access control. Throttling and rate limiting prevent abuse, while Amazon CloudWatch integration ensures comprehensive logging and monitoring, empowering developers to build secure APIs.

Authentication and Authorization with IAM, Cognito, and Lambda Authorizers

To secure APIs effectively, AWS API Gateway offers multiple authentication and authorization options, including IAM, Cognito, and Lambda Authorizers. Read the following to understand how each method provides unique security benefits and use cases:

1. **IAM Authentication:** AWS IAM offers a secure method for controlling access to API Gateway resources. Developers can use IAM policies to specify who can access APIs and what actions they can perform. IAM authentication is well suited for internal APIs or when integrating with other AWS services, utilizing AWS's strong security framework to manage permissions and access control.

2. **Amazon Cognito:** Amazon Cognito simplifies user authentication by providing a scalable user directory and identity federation capabilities. Using Cognito, developers can authenticate users via social identity providers, such as Google or Facebook, or even through a custom user pool. This approach is well suited for public-facing APIs, as it allows for seamless integration with external identity providers while maintaining strong security controls.

3. **Lambda Authorizers:** Lambda Authorizers offer a versatile and customizable method for implementing authentication and authorization logic. By leveraging a Lambda function, developers can create custom authorization strategies, such as token validation or IP whitelisting. This method provides the flexibility to implement complex authentication scenarios tailored to specific application requirements, making it a powerful tool for securing APIs.

Throttling and Rate Limiting

Throttling and rate limiting are vital features in AWS API Gateway for controlling API traffic and preventing abuse. By setting request limits within a specific time frame, developers can ensure fair usage and protect backend services from overload. API Gateway allows configuration of both account-level and API-specific throttling, offering precise traffic management. These settings can be tailored to accommodate bursts of traffic while maintaining stability. Rate limiting prevents denial-of-service attacks by restricting requests from individual clients, ensuring resource availability for all users. Implementing these features helps maintain API performance and reliability under heavy load.

CHAPTER 2   FRONTEND DEVELOPMENT AND INTEGRATION

Logging and Monitoring with CloudWatch

AWS API Gateway's integration with Amazon CloudWatch provides comprehensive logging and monitoring capabilities, enabling developers to gain insights into API performance and usage patterns. CloudWatch collects detailed metrics, such as request count, latency, and error rates, allowing developers to monitor API health and identify potential issues. By setting up CloudWatch alarms, developers can receive notifications when certain thresholds are breached, enabling proactive response to performance degradation or security incidents. Additionally, API Gateway can be configured to log request and response data, providing valuable information for troubleshooting and auditing purposes. These logs can be analyzed to identify trends, optimize API performance, and ensure compliance with security policies. By leveraging CloudWatch's powerful monitoring and logging features, developers can maintain high levels of security and reliability for their APIs, ensuring a seamless user experience.

Integrating AWS API Gateway with Frontend Development

Handling CORS (Cross-Origin Resource Sharing)

Browsers implement Cross-Origin Resource Sharing (CORS) as a key security measure to restrict web applications from requesting resources from a domain other than the one that served the page. In the context of AWS API Gateway, CORS must be configured to allow web applications hosted on different domains to access APIs securely. Proper CORS configuration is essential to prevent unauthorized access while enabling legitimate cross-origin requests. AWS API Gateway provides mechanisms to handle CORS for both REST and HTTP APIs, guaranteeing that your API resources can only be accessed by approved domains.

CHAPTER 2   FRONTEND DEVELOPMENT AND INTEGRATION

To enable CORS in AWS API Gateway, you need to configure the appropriate HTTP headers, such as "Access-Control-Allow-Origin," "Access-Control-Allow-Methods," and "Access-Control-Allow-Headers" as shown in Figure 2-8. These headers define three things – which origins are authorized for access of the API, which HTTP methods are permitted, and headers that can be part of the requests. CORS settings are done via the AWS Management Console, AWS CLI, or by using Swagger extensions for more complex setups.

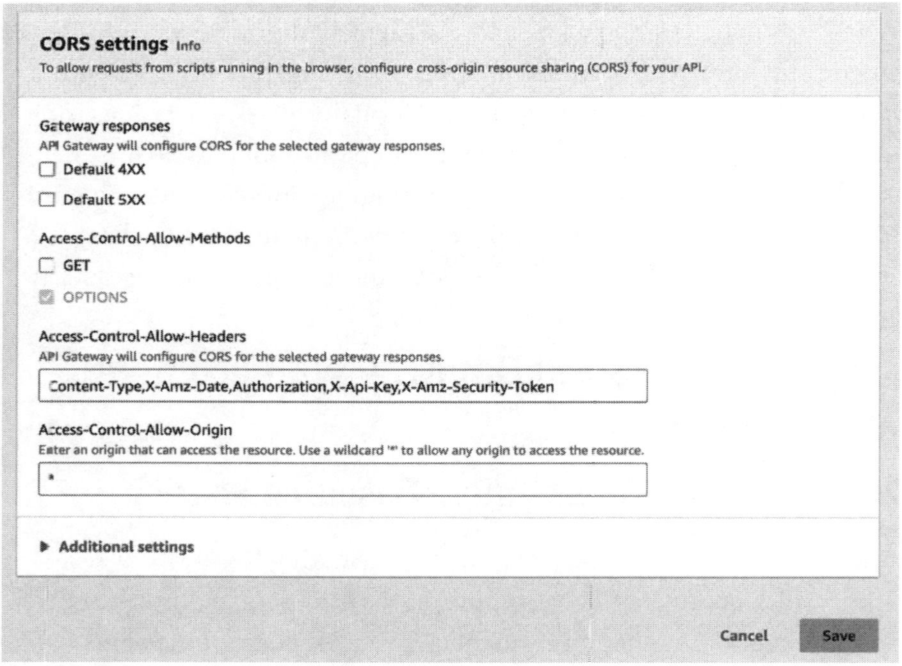

Figure 2-8.   Enabling CORS using AWS Console

For REST APIs, enabling CORS involves creating an OPTIONS method for each resource that requires cross-origin access. This method is used to handle preflight requests, which browsers send to determine if the actual request is safe to execute. The OPTIONS method should be

CHAPTER 2 FRONTEND DEVELOPMENT AND INTEGRATION

configured with a mock integration to return the necessary CORS headers. Additionally, the actual methods (e.g., GET, POST) must be configured to include the Access-Control-Allow-Origin header in their responses.

For HTTP APIs, CORS configuration is slightly different. API Gateway automatically handles preflight requests and appends the specified CORS headers to the responses. You can specify allowed origins, methods, and headers directly in the CORS configuration settings. This approach simplifies the process, as the API Gateway manages the CORS headers without requiring manual configuration of the OPTIONS method.

One common challenge with CORS in AWS API Gateway is ensuring that all responses, including error responses, contain the necessary CORS headers. This can be particularly tricky with proxy integrations, where the backend service must return the appropriate headers. To address this, developers should ensure that their backend services are configured to include CORS headers in all responses or use API Gateway's integration response mapping to add them.

Optimizing Performance

Optimizing performance in AWS API Gateway is crucial for delivering fast and reliable API responses, especially in serverless applications where efficiency and scalability are paramount. Performance optimization involves implementing strategies that reduce latency, manage traffic effectively, and ensure that APIs can handle varying loads without degradation. By leveraging caching, fine-tuning configurations, and following best practices, developers can enhance the performance of their APIs, providing users with a seamless experience. API Gateway offers several features and tools that aid in optimizing performance. These strategies include caching, throttling, and connecting other performance optimization services. Understanding how to utilize these features effectively is key to maximizing the potential of your serverless applications.

CHAPTER 2   FRONTEND DEVELOPMENT AND INTEGRATION

Caching Strategies with API Gateway

Caching is a powerful technique for improving API performance by storing responses and serving them from a cache rather than making repeated calls to the backend as shown in Figure 2-9. In AWS API Gateway, caching can be enabled at the stage level, allowing developers to cache responses for specific API methods. By configuring cache settings as shown in Figure 2-10, such as time to live (TTL), cache data encryption, and cache capacity, developers can control how long responses are stored and how much data the cache can hold. Caching reduces the load on backend services, decreases latency, and speeds up response times for data that is often requested.

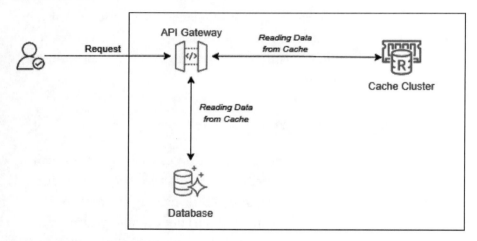

Figure 2-9. *API Gateway caching*

API Gateway provides flexible caching options, allowing developers to cache responses based on request parameters, headers, or query strings. This granularity ensures that only the necessary data is cached, optimizing cache utilization. Additionally, cache invalidation can be managed through cache key policies, ensuring that stale data is not served to clients. By implementing effective caching strategies, developers can significantly enhance API performance, reduce costs associated with backend processing, and provide a better user experience. Figure 2-10 is a sample template for API caching.

```
StageName : Test
MethodSettings:
    - ResourcePath: "/*"
      HttpMethod: "*"
      CachingEnabled: true
      CahcheTtlInSeconds: 300
      CacheDataEncrupted: false
      ThrottlingBurstLimit: 2000
      ThrottlingRateLimit: 1000
      CacheClusterEnabled: true
      CacheClusterSize: "0.5"
```

Figure 2-10. Sample template code for API caching

Best Practices for AWS API Gateway Performance Optimization

To optimize performance in AWS API Gateway, developers should follow a set of best practices that address various aspects of API design and configuration. One key practice is to minimize payload sizes by compressing responses and using efficient data formats like JSON or Protocol Buffers. Smaller payloads result in faster transmission and reduced latency.

Another important practice is to implement throttling and rate limiting to manage traffic and prevent overloading backend services. By setting appropriate limits, developers can ensure that APIs remain responsive under heavy load and that resources are allocated fairly among users.

CHAPTER 2   FRONTEND DEVELOPMENT AND INTEGRATION

Additionally, developers should optimize integration settings by choosing the most efficient integration type for their use case, such as direct integrations with AWS services or using Lambda functions for complex logic. Tools like Amazon CloudWatch, when used to monitor and analyze API performance, can uncover discoveries into bottlenecks and areas for improvement.

Implementing these best practices helps developers improve API performance and reliability, ensuring they cater to the needs of current serverless applications.

S3 (Simple Storage Service)

Amazon Simple Storage Service (S3) is a powerful object storage solution offered by AWS, designed to store and retrieve vast amounts of data from anywhere on the Internet. Its high durability, availability, and security make it a vital tool for businesses and developers seeking cloud storage solutions. S3's object storage architecture manages data as objects, which include the data itself, metadata, and a unique identifier. This structure is ideal for handling large volumes of unstructured data, such as media files and logs. S3 offers a scalable, secure environment that supports diverse use cases, including data lakes, content distribution, and big data analytics, with features like versioning, lifecycle policies, and flexible access controls.

Amazon S3's architecture revolves around buckets and objects, where buckets serve as containers for storing objects. Each object comprises a file and its metadata, identified uniquely within a bucket by a key. This setup allows for flexible data management and seamless integration with other AWS services, making S3 a versatile storage solution. S3 provides a simple web interface for storing and retrieving data at any scale, boasting 99.999999999% durability and 99.99% availability. It automatically replicates objects across multiple systems to enhance data durability. The service is highly scalable, with a cost-effective pricing model that charges users based on actual storage and data transfer usage. S3 supports various storage classes optimized for different access patterns and costs and integrates with AWS services like Lambda, CloudFront, and IAM, extending its capabilities and making it central to AWS's cloud infrastructure.

Key Features and Benefits of AWS S3

There are various key features and benefits of AWS S3, and the main ones are elaborated below:

1. **Versioning:** AWS S3's versioning feature is essential for data recovery, allowing users to preserve, retrieve, and restore every version of an object. It acts as a safeguard against accidental deletions and overwrites, enabling easy reversion to previous states. This is particularly useful for applications needing audit trails and historical data analysis.

2. **Lifecycle Policies:** S3's lifecycle policies automate data transitions between storage classes, optimizing cost and performance. By moving data to cost-effective storage as it ages, such as transitioning from S3 Standard to S3 Glacier, these policies simplify data management and free organizations to focus on strategic tasks.

3. **Security Features:** AWS S3 prioritizes security with robust features like server-side encryption, ACLs, and bucket policies. These tools protect data from unauthorized access, allowing users to set precise permissions via AWS IAM. This security framework helps meet compliance requirements and safeguard sensitive information.

4. **Global Infrastructure:** AWS S3's global infrastructure ensures low latency and high availability by allowing data storage in multiple regions. Integrated with AWS CloudFront, it accelerates content delivery worldwide, minimizing downtime and enhancing user experience. This setup is ideal for businesses with a global reach, supporting seamless data access.

5. **Ease of Use:** S3 offers a user-friendly interface accessible to both technical and nontechnical users. Managed through the AWS Management Console, CLI, or SDKs, it provides flexibility in data interaction. Its simple web service interface facilitates easy data transfers and operations, empowering organizations to manage data efficiently without extensive technical expertise.

Use Cases for AWS S3

There are various use cases for AWS S3, and the main ones are explained below:

1. **Data Storage, Backup, and Recovery:** AWS S3 is a reliable choice for data storage, backup, and recovery, thanks to its high durability and availability. Organizations can store critical data and backups, ensuring swift recovery from data loss or system failures. Its versioning feature adds an extra layer of protection, making S3 scalable and cost-effective for safeguarding data assets.

2. **Content Distribution and Hosting:** S3 is ideal for hosting static websites, distributing media files, and delivering content globally. Its integration with AWS CloudFront ensures efficient content delivery, reducing latency and enhancing user experience. S3's global infrastructure makes it a popular choice for companies aiming to improve their online presence and reach.

3. **Big Data Analytics and Data Lakes:** S3's capacity to store large volumes of structured and unstructured data makes it perfect for building data lakes. It supports analytics and machine learning workloads, offering valuable insights. Compatibility with AWS services like Amazon Athena and AWS Glue enhances its utility, enabling data-driven decisions and competitive advantages.

4. **Disaster Recovery:** S3's disaster recovery features are vital for protecting data in case of disasters or outages. Cross-region replication allows automatic data duplication across multiple AWS regions, ensuring business continuity and minimizing downtime. S3's reliability and global reach make it a trusted solution for disaster recovery planning.

How AWS S3 Works

Understanding how AWS S3 works is crucial for leveraging its capabilities effectively. This section delves into the core components and functionalities of S3, including buckets and objects as shown in Figure 2-11, the data consistency model, and storage classes and lifecycle policies. By exploring these topics, you will gain a comprehensive understanding of how to utilize S3 for various storage needs and optimize their serverless applications.

CHAPTER 2   FRONTEND DEVELOPMENT AND INTEGRATION

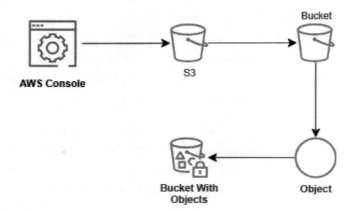

Figure 2-11.   Overview of AWS S3

Buckets and Objects

In AWS S3, data is stored in a structure composed of buckets and objects. A bucket is a container for objects, which is the data entities in S3. Each bucket is created within a specific AWS region and has a globally unique name. Buckets serve as the top-level namespace for storing data and can hold an unlimited number of objects.

An object in S3 stores metadata, a unique identifier, and data. This unique identifier is referred to as key. Any data type, such as text, images, videos, or backups, can be stored in S3. Metadata contains information of the object, such as its content type, its size, and create/modify date. The unique identifier is used for the retrieval of the object from a bucket.

When uploading objects to a bucket, users can specify access permissions to control who can read or write the data. Access control mechanisms are supported by S3, which include bucket policies, ACLs, and IAM roles. These features make sure the security of stored objects and its accessibility to authorized users.

CHAPTER 2   FRONTEND DEVELOPMENT AND INTEGRATION

Buckets can also be configured with additional settings, such as versioning, which allows users to maintain multiple versions of an object. This is particularly useful for data recovery and auditing purposes. Another feature is bucket logging, which enables users to track access requests and monitor usage patterns.

Data Consistency Model

AWS S3 utilizes a comprehensive data consistency framework to uphold data integrity and accessibility. For new objects, it offers strong read-after-write consistency, enabling immediate access to the most current version of data once it is stored. This feature ensures users can swiftly access newly uploaded content, which is essential for applications requiring instant data retrieval, such as content delivery networks (CDNs) and real-time analytics. For overwriting PUTS and DELETES, S3 employs eventual consistency, meaning changes might take time to propagate. During this interval, users may still access the previous version of the object, but S3 assures that updates will eventually be reflected across all copies.

The consistency framework is crafted to balance performance with reliability, providing strong consistency for new objects and eventual consistency for updates and deletions. This approach ensures data is always accessible and quickly retrievable, supporting applications that demand immediate data access. Additionally, S3 supports multipart uploads, allowing large objects to be uploaded in smaller segments, enhancing upload performance and enabling resumption in case of network disruptions. Once all segments are uploaded, S3 assembles them into a single object while maintaining consistency guarantees. Overall, S3's data consistency model is a crucial feature that ensures data reliability and availability, making it a trusted solution for storing essential data.

CHAPTER 2   FRONTEND DEVELOPMENT AND INTEGRATION

Storage Classes

There are various S3 storage classes, optimized for various access patterns and cost, which are elaborated below:

1. **S3 Standard:** This default category is crafted for frequently accessed data, providing low latency, high throughput, 99.999999999% durability, and 99.99% availability, making it perfect for content distribution and big data analytics.

2. **S3 Intelligent-Tiering:** Automatically transitions data between frequent and infrequent access tiers based on usage trends, optimizing storage expenses without impacting performance, with a nominal monthly monitoring fee per object.

3. **S3 Standard-IA (Infrequent Access):** Designed for data accessed less often but requiring swift access, offering reduced storage costs and higher retrieval charges, ideal for long-term storage, backups, and disaster recovery.

4. **S3 One Zone-IA:** Stores data in a single availability zone, providing lower costs but decreased availability and durability, suitable for infrequently accessed data that can be easily recreated.

5. **S3 Glacier:** Offers economical storage for seldom-accessed data, with retrieval times ranging from minutes to hours, suitable for archival data, compliance, and digital preservation.

6. **S3 Glacier Deep Archive:** The most cost-effective category for data rarely accessed, requiring retrieval times of 12 hours or more, ideal for long-term data retention like regulatory archives.

Lifecycle Policies

AWS S3 lifecycle policies allow users to program the management of their data, optimizing storage costs and performance. These policies enable users to define rules that transition objects between different storage classes. It can also delete the objects based on rules.

For example, a lifecycle policy can be set to move objects kept in Standard S3 storage class to S3 Standard-IA if it is not accessed for 60 days. Further, this object will be moved to S3 Glacier if it is not accessed for 180 days as shown in Figure 2-12. This automated process helps reduce costs, like Standard-IA and S3 Glacier low-cost storage classes, as it becomes less frequently accessed.

```
<LifecycleConfiguration>
    <Rule>
        <ID>object-id</ID>
        <Filter>
            <Prefix>logs/</Prefix>
        </Filter>
        <Status>Enabled</Status>
        <Transition>
            <Days>60</Days>
            <StorageClass>STANDARD_IA</StorageClass>
        </Transition>
        <Transition>
            <Days>180</Days>
            <StorageClass>GLACIER</StorageClass>
        </Transition>
        <Expiration>
            <Days>365</Days>
        </Expiration>
    </Rule>
</LifecycleConfiguration>
```

Figure 2-12. *AWS S3 lifecycle configuration*

Lifecycle policies also support the expiration of objects, allowing users to automatically delete objects that are no longer needed. This is particularly useful for managing data retention policies and making sure that abide with compliance mandates.

To create a lifecycle policy, users can specify a set of rules in the AWS Management Console, AWS CLI, or AWS SDKs. Each rule defines the actions to be taken on a specific set of objects, depending on their age or other factors. Once the policy is created, S3 automatically applies the rules to the specified objects, streamlining data management and reducing operational overhead.

Setting Up AWS S3

1. Log in to the AWS Console if you haven't already.
2. Search for S3.
3. Then click the Create Bucket button; it will redirect to the page as shown in Figure 2-13.

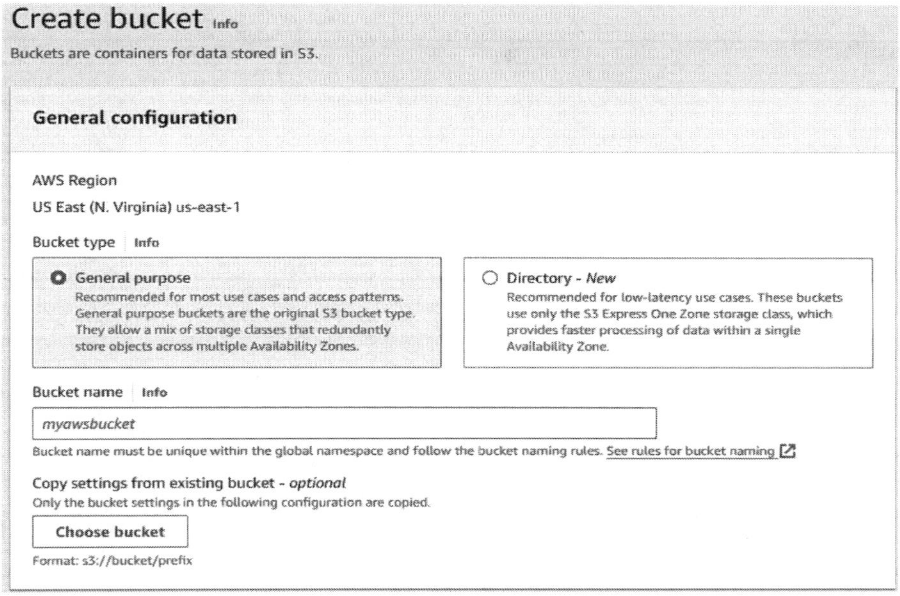

CHAPTER 2   FRONTEND DEVELOPMENT AND INTEGRATION

Figure 2-13.   *Screen for creating S3 in AWS Console*

4. Select Object Ownership based on requirement and block public access. Refer to Figure 2-14.

77

CHAPTER 2 FRONTEND DEVELOPMENT AND INTEGRATION

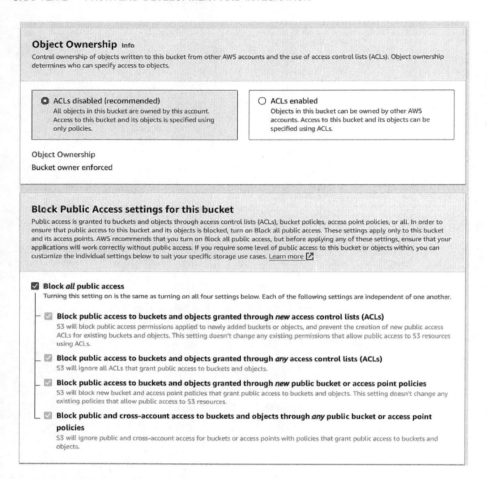

Figure 2-14. *Ownership and access of S3*

5. Then you need to select the versioning type of encryption as shown in Figure 2-15.

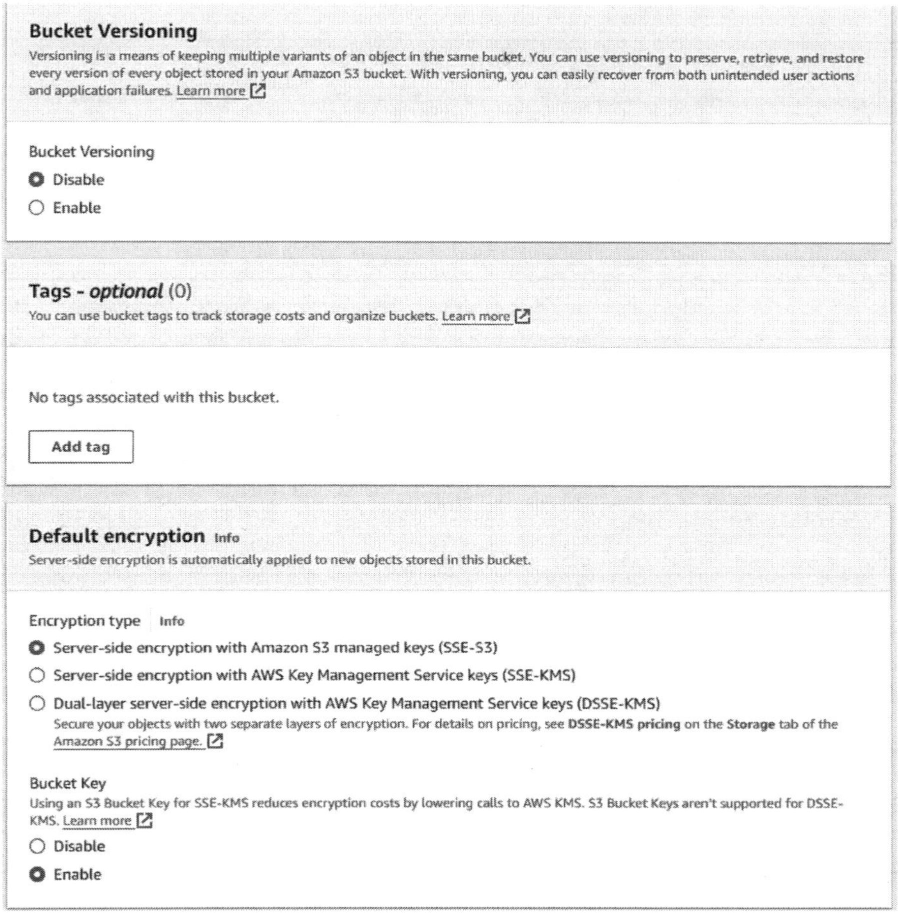

CHAPTER 2   FRONTEND DEVELOPMENT AND INTEGRATION

Bucket Versioning
Versioning is a means of keeping multiple variants of an object in the same bucket. You can use versioning to preserve, retrieve, and restore every version of every object stored in your Amazon S3 bucket. With versioning, you can easily recover from both unintended user actions and application failures. Learn more

Bucket Versioning
- ◉ Disable
- ○ Enable

Tags - *optional* (0)
You can use bucket tags to track storage costs and organize buckets. Learn more

No tags associated with this bucket.

[Add tag]

Default encryption Info
Server-side encryption is automatically applied to new objects stored in this bucket.

Encryption type   Info
- ◉ Server-side encryption with Amazon S3 managed keys (SSE-S3)
- ○ Server-side encryption with AWS Key Management Service keys (SSE-KMS)
- ○ Dual-layer server-side encryption with AWS Key Management Service keys (DSSE-KMS)
  Secure your objects with two separate layers of encryption. For details on pricing, see **DSSE-KMS pricing** on the **Storage** tab of the Amazon S3 pricing page.

Bucket Key
Using an S3 Bucket Key for SSE-KMS reduces encryption costs by lowering calls to AWS KMS. S3 Bucket Keys aren't supported for DSSE-KMS. Learn more
- ○ Disable
- ◉ Enable

Figure 2-15. *Versioning and encryption type in S3*

6. Next, click the Create button to set up the S3 bucket.

7. You can also create a bucket by using a CloudFormation template. Figure 2-16 shows a sample CloudFormation template for creating S3.

79

CHAPTER 2   FRONTEND DEVELOPMENT AND INTEGRATION

```
AWSTemplateFormatVersion: "2010-09-09"
Description: This is a cloud formation explaining S3 bucket creation
and configuration

Parameters:
  BucketName: { Type: String, Default: "object-storage-bucket" }

Resources:
  AccessLogBucket:
    Type: "AWS::S3::Bucket"
    Properties:
      AccessControl: LogDeliveryWrite

  MainBucket:
    Type: "AWS::S3::Bucket"
    Properties:
      BucketName: !Ref BucketName
      BucketEncryption:
        ServerSideEncryptionConfiguration:
          - ServerSideEncryptionByDefault:
              SSEAlgorithm: AES256
      LoggingConfiguration:
        DestinationBucketName: !Ref AccessLogBucket

Outputs:
  MainBucketName:
    Description: Name of the main bucket
    Value: !Ref MainBucket
  LogBucketName:
    Description: Name of the access log bucket
    Value: !Ref AccessLogBucket
```

Figure 2-16. Sample CloudFormation template for S3

Security Features in AWS S3

Ensuring security is crucial for any cloud storage service, and AWS S3 is no exception. AWS S3 offers a comprehensive suite of security controls designed to protect data from unauthorized access and ensure compliance with various regulatory standards. These features include encryption, access control mechanisms, and detailed logging and monitoring capabilities. By leveraging these tools, users can secure their data both at rest and in transit, manage access permissions with precision, and maintain a detailed audit trail of all interactions with their S3 resources. This chapter explores the key security features of AWS S3, providing insights into how they can be effectively utilized to protect data.

Encryption at Rest and in Transit

To safeguard data, AWS S3 employs robust encryption techniques for both storage (at rest) and transmission. Server-side encryption (SSE) is employed for encrypting data while it is in storage (at rest). This encrypts data when it is stored and decrypts it when a request is made for its retrieval. Users can choose from several encryption options, including SSE-S3, which uses Amazon's managed keys; SSE-KMS, which integrates with AWS KMS (Key Management Service) for additional control; and SSE-C, which lets developers work with encryption keys of their choice.

In addition to SSE, S3 also provides client-side encryption, where data is encrypted before it is uploaded to S3 and decrypted after it is downloaded. This contributes an additional security measure, ensuring that data remains protected even before it reaches the S3 service.

Access Control with IAM, Bucket Policies, and ACLs

AWS S3 provides a range of access control tools to manage permissions and secure data. AWS IAM is a key component, allowing developers

CHAPTER 2   FRONTEND DEVELOPMENT AND INTEGRATION

to define granular permissions for their S3 resources. IAM enables the creation of roles and policies, specifying who is permitted access-specific buckets and objects and which actions they are authorized to take.

Bucket policies are another powerful tool for controlling access. These JSON-based policies are attached directly to S3 buckets and define permissions for users and groups. Bucket policies are used for exposing buckets publicly, restricting access to certain IP addresses, or allowing cross-account access, providing flexibility in managing permissions.

Access Control Lists (ACLs) offer a more granular level of control, allowing users to specify permissions for individual objects within a bucket. ACLs can assign read or write permissions to particular users or groups, adding an extra security layer.

By combining IAM, bucket policies, and ACLs, AWS S3 offers a comprehensive access control framework that allows) users to manage permissions with precision and guarantee that only authorized individuals can access the data.

```
{
  "Version": "2012-10-17",
  "Statement":[{
    "Effect": "Allow",
    "Action": "s3:*",
    "Resource": ["arn:aws:s3:::practical-serverless-bucket/*"]
    }
  ]
}
```

Figure 2-17. *Sample AWS IAM policy*

In Figure 2-17, a sample IAM policy grants permission to perform all actions on objects within the "`practical-serverless-bucket`" S3 bucket.

CHAPTER 2   FRONTEND DEVELOPMENT AND INTEGRATION

```
{
  "Version": "2012-10-17",
  "Statement": [
    {
      "Effect": "Allow",
      "Principal": {
        "AWS": "arn:aws:iam::012345678910:role/my-bucket-access"
      },
      "Action": "s3:ListBucket",
      "Resource": "arn:aws:s3::: practical-serverless-bucket"
    }
  ]
}
```

Figure 2-18. *Sample AWS S3 bucket policy*

In Figure 2-18, the sample S3 bucket policy will enable the IAM role *my-bucket-access* under the account 012345678910 to use the AWS S3 GET Bucket (ListObjects) operation.

Logging and Monitoring with AWS CloudTrail and S3 Access Logs

AWS S3 provides detailed logging and monitoring capabilities to help users maintain visibility into their data and ensure compliance with security policies. AWS CloudTrail allows tracking API calls made to S3, providing a complete audit trail of all actions performed on S3 resources. CloudTrail logs include information such as the identity of the requester, the time of the request, and the actions taken, enabling users to monitor access and detect unauthorized activities as shown in Figure 2-19.

83

CHAPTER 2 FRONTEND DEVELOPMENT AND INTEGRATION

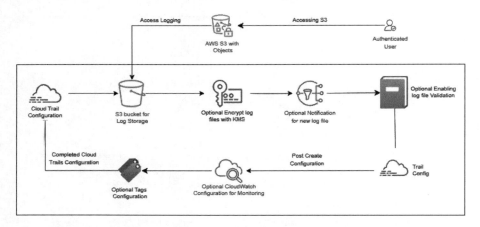

Figure 2-19. *Logging and monitoring with CloudTrail and S3*

In addition to CloudTrail, detailed records of requests to S3 buckets are available through S3 Access Logs. These logs capture information about the requester, the request type, and the response, allowing users to analyze access patterns and identify potential security issues. S3 Access Logs can be configured to capture both successful and failed requests, providing a comprehensive view of all interactions with S3 resources.

By leveraging CloudTrail and S3 Access Logs, users can gain valuable insights into their S3 environments, monitor for suspicious activities, and ensure compliance with security and regulatory requirements. These logging and monitoring tools are crucial for maintaining a secure and well-audited storage environment in AWS S3.

Integrating AWS S3 with Frontend Development

1. Log in to the AWS Console if you haven't already.

2. Create an S3 bucket by performing the steps as discussed in the section "Setting Up AWS S3."

CHAPTER 2   FRONTEND DEVELOPMENT AND INTEGRATION

3. New AWS buckets are private by default. You need to make your S3 bucket public to meet your specific needs for a static website hosting; for that, you need to uncheck "Block all public access" while creating a bucket as shown in Figure 2-20.

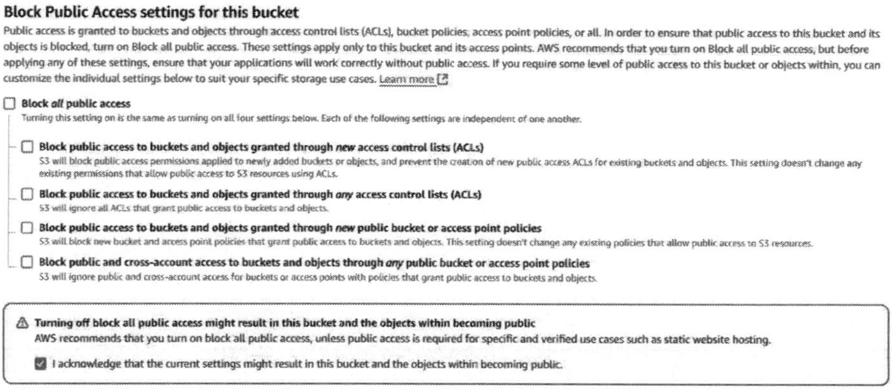

Figure 2-20. Unblock all public access

4. Once your bucket is created, select it from the list of buckets. Go to the "Properties" tab and enable "Static website hosting" as shown in Figure 2-21.

85

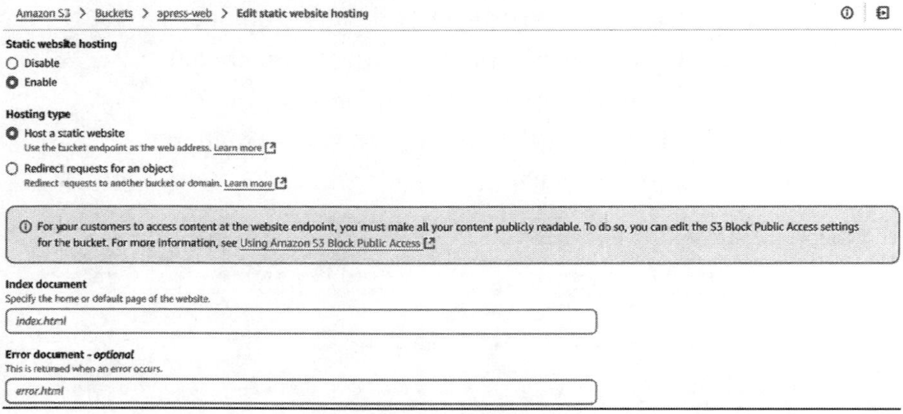

CHAPTER 2   FRONTEND DEVELOPMENT AND INTEGRATION

Figure 2-21. Enabling static website hosting

5. Enter the "Index document" (e.g., "index.html") and "Error document" (e.g., "error.html") if you have one as shown in Figures 2-22 and 2-23.

```
<!DOCTYPE html>
<html>
    <head>
        <title>Static Website loading</title>
    </head>
    <body style="background-color: green">
        <h1>Hello! This is simple static hosting using AWS S3!</h1>
    </body>
</html>
```

Figure 2-22. Index.html file

86

```
<!DOCTYPE html>
<html>
   <head>
       <title>Static Website Error loading</title>
   </head>
   <body style="background-color: red">
       <h1>Hello! This is the error page for static hosting!</h1>
   </body>
</html>
```

Figure 2-23. *error.html file*

6. Go to the "Overview" tab of your bucket. Click the "Upload" button to add your static website files (HTML, CSS, JavaScript, images, etc.).

7. You can either drag and drop files or use the upload interface.

8. Select the uploaded files in your bucket.

9. Go to the "Actions" drop-down and choose "Make public."

10. Confirm that you want to make the files public. This is necessary to allow public access to your website content.

11. After making the file public, your static website should be accessible at the endpoint provided in the "Static website hosting" section of your bucket's properties. It will look like this: `https://your-bucket-name.s3-website-region.amazonaws.com`.

12. And that's it! Your static website should now be hosted on AWS S3 and accessible to the public. Remember that S3 is designed for hosting static content. If your website requires server-side processing or dynamic content, you might need additional services like AWS Lambda, Amazon API Gateway, or a different hosting solution.

Optimizing Performance and Costs Using S3

A range of features in Amazon S3 helps boost performance and control costs, making it a powerful storage service. For businesses leveraging serverless applications, it is crucial to efficiently manage resources and guarantee that data is delivered quickly and with minimum cost. AWS S3 provides various strategies and tools to achieve these goals, including caching mechanisms, cost-effective storage classes, and performance optimization best practices. By implementing these strategies, organizations can enhance their application's performance, reduce latency, and manage storage expenses effectively. This section explores how to optimize performance and costs using AWS S3, focusing on caching strategies, cost management, and performance best practices.

Caching Strategies with CloudFront Integration

Integrating Amazon S3 with Amazon CloudFront, a content delivery network (CDN), is a highly effective strategy for improving performance. CloudFront utilizes edge locations around the world to cache content, lowering latency by delivering data from the nearest location to the user. This caching mechanism is particularly beneficial for static content, such as images, videos, and web assets, which can be served quickly to users regardless of their geographic location.

CloudFront's caching capabilities can be customized using cache behaviors, which allow users to define how different types of content are cached. For instance, users can set specific cache expiration times for certain file types or use query string parameters to differentiate cached content. By fine-tuning these settings, organizations can optimize cache efficiency and reduce the load on their S3 buckets.

Additionally, CloudFront provides features like dynamic content delivery and SSL/TLS encryption, ensuring secure and efficient content distribution. By leveraging CloudFront's caching strategies, businesses can significantly enhance the performance of their serverless applications, providing a seamless user experience while reducing data transfer costs.

Cost Management with Storage Classes and Lifecycle Policies

AWS S3 extends a variety of storage classes designed to manage costs based on how data is accessed. By selecting the appropriate storage class, businesses can manage expenses effectively. For frequently accessed data, the S3 Standard class provides high availability and low latency. For infrequently accessed data, S3 Standard-IA and S3 One Zone-IA offer lower storage costs with slightly higher retrieval fees. For archival data, S3 Glacier and S3 Glacier Deep Archive provide the least storage costs, suitable for extended-term storage.

Lifecycle policies further enhance cost management by automating data transitions between storage classes. Users can define rules to move data to more cost-effective classes as it gets older or becomes less frequently accessed.

By strategically utilizing storage classes and lifecycle policies, organizations can optimize their storage expenses, ensuring that they only pay for the resources they need while maintaining efficient data management.

CHAPTER 2   FRONTEND DEVELOPMENT AND INTEGRATION

Best Practices for AWS S3 Performance Optimization

Ensuring best practices in place, businesses can optimize the performance of their serverless applications using AWS S3, ensuring fast, reliable, and cost-effective data storage and retrieval. Let's have a look on the following to understand:

1. **Multipart Uploads:** For large files, using multipart uploads can significantly enhance performance. This method breaks files into smaller parts, allowing them to be uploaded concurrently. It improves upload speed and reliability, as failed parts can be retried without affecting the entire upload. Multipart uploads are especially beneficial for serverless applications that handle large datasets or media files.

2. **Data Compression:** Compressing data before uploading to S3 can reduce storage costs and improve transfer speeds. By minimizing file sizes, organizations can decrease the amount of data transferred and stored, leading to cost savings. Compression is particularly useful for text-based files and logs, where significant size reductions can be achieved.

3. **Efficient Data Retrieval:** Implementing efficient data retrieval strategies is crucial for performance optimization. This includes using range GET requests to download only the necessary parts of an object and leveraging S3 Select to fetch only specific parts from within an object. These techniques reduce data transfer and processing times, enhancing application performance.

4. **Monitoring and Analytics:** Regularly monitoring S3 usage and performance metrics can support the discovery of bottlenecks and the efficient allocation of resources. AWS provides tools like AWS CloudWatch and AWS Cost Explorer to track performance and costs. By analyzing these metrics, organizations can make informed decisions to improve efficiency and reduce expenses.

AWS CloudFront

AWS offers Amazon CloudFront, a CDN (content delivery network) aimed at enhancing the distribution speed of web content. It achieves this by routing user requests through a worldwide network of edge locations, ensuring content is delivered, offering minimal latency and fast transfer rates. CloudFront is particularly beneficial for applications requiring rapid content delivery, such as websites, APIs, and video streaming services. Caching content at edge locations allows CloudFront to minimize the load on origin servers and enhances the end-user experience by minimizing latency. This service seamlessly integrates with other AWS offerings, such as Amazon S3, EC2, and Lambda@Edge, making it a versatile choice for developers already utilizing the AWS ecosystem.

Content delivery networks (CDNs) are essential for improving the speed and reliability of web content delivery. This proximity reduces latency, ensuring faster load times for websites and applications. CDNs like CloudFront work by caching static and dynamic content, such as HTML pages, JavaScript files, images, and videos, at edge locations across the globe. Upon the access of a content, the CDN directs the request to the nearest edge server, significantly enhancing performance and reducing the load on the origin server. Additionally, CDNs provide security benefits by mitigating distributed denial-of-service (DDoS) attacks and other

CHAPTER 2   FRONTEND DEVELOPMENT AND INTEGRATION

malicious threats. By distributing content efficiently and securely, CDNs are a crucial need in modern web infrastructure, ensuring a seamless user experience across the globe.

Amazon CloudFront is a fast, secure, and globally distributed content delivery network (CDN) service that efficiently delivers web content to users worldwide with low latency and high transfer speeds.

Key Features and Benefits of AWS CloudFront

AWS CloudFront's combination of performance, integration, security, and cost-effectiveness makes it best suitable for businesses seeking optimization for their content delivery strategies. Let's understand the benefits of AWS CloudFront:

1. **Global Reach and Low Latency:** AWS CloudFront utilizes a vast network of edge locations worldwide, ensuring content is delivered with minimal delay. By routing user requests to the nearest edge server, CloudFront reduces latency and provides high-speed data transfer, enhancing the user experience significantly.

2. **Seamless Integration with AWS Services:** CloudFront integrates effortlessly with other AWS ecosystems such as Amazon S3, EC2, and Lambda@Edge. Developers can leverage existing AWS infrastructure for content delivery, simplifying setup and management while cutting costs linked to data transmission between AWS services.

CHAPTER 2   FRONTEND DEVELOPMENT AND INTEGRATION

3. **Enhanced Security Features:** CloudFront offers robust security measures, including SSL/TLS encryption, AWS Shield for DDoS protection, and AWS Web Application Firewall (WAF). These features ensure secure content delivery and protect against common web threats, providing peace of mind for businesses handling sensitive data.

4. **Cost-Effective Content Delivery:** By caching content at edge locations, it minimizes the need for repeated server requests, lowering bandwidth costs. Additionally, AWS offers flexible pricing models and no transfer fees for data fetched from AWS origins, making CloudFront an economical option for businesses of any size.

5. **Customizable and Programmable Edge Computing:** With CloudFront, developers can run serverless code at edge locations using Lambda@Edge. This capability allows for real-time content customization and processing closer to users, improving application responsiveness, and reducing latency.

How AWS CloudFront Works

The architecture of AWS CloudFront is built around a global network of points of presence (PoPs) and regional edge caches, designed to deliver content efficiently and reliably. PoPs, also known as edge locations, are strategically placed data centers that cache content close to users. This proximity reduces latency, ensuring faster delivery of web content. CloudFront also employs regional edge caches, which act as a mid-tier caching layer between the origin server and the edge locations. These caches help retain less frequently accessed content longer, reducing the need to fetch it from the origin server repeatedly.

CHAPTER 2 FRONTEND DEVELOPMENT AND INTEGRATION

The AWS global network, which underpins CloudFront, provides high bandwidth, resilience, and redundancy. This ensures consistent performance and shields users from Internet instabilities. The architecture is designed to minimize video delivery latency, reduce congestion, and provide high availability. CloudFront's architecture also supports edge computing capabilities through services like Lambda@Edge and CloudFront Functions. These services allow developers to run code at edge locations, enabling real-time content customization and processing closer to users.

CloudFront's architecture is highly scalable, capable of handling varying traffic patterns and peak loads efficiently. This scalability is crucial for applications like video streaming, where demand can fluctuate significantly. As shown in Figure 2-24, by working closely with customers, AWS continuously expands and scales its edge locations to meet current and future traffic demands.

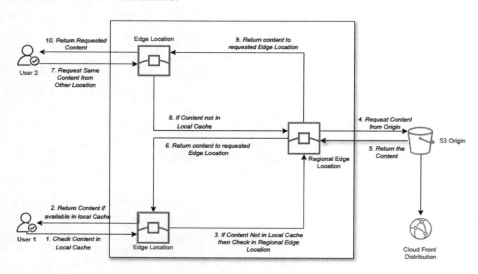

Figure 2-24. *CloudFront architecture*

Overall, the architecture of AWS CloudFront is designed to provide a robust, flexible, and efficient content delivery solution that meets the needs of diverse applications and industries.

Edge Locations and Regional Edge Caches

Edge locations and regional edge caches are critical components of AWS CloudFront's infrastructure. Edge locations, or PoPs, are data centers distributed globally to cache content close to users, reducing latency and improving load times. When a user requests content, CloudFront forwards the request to the nearest edge location, ensuring optimal performance. In case the requested content is unavailable at the edge location, CloudFront fetches it from the nearest regional edge cache or the origin server.

Regional edge caches serve as an intermediary caching layer between edge locations and origin servers. They store content that is not frequently accessed enough to remain in edge locations, reducing the need to fetch it from the origin server repeatedly. This setup helps improve performance for less popular content, ensuring it is still delivered efficiently. By maintaining a larger cache, regional edge caches help keep more content local to users, minimizing latency and enhancing the overall user experience.

Distribution Types: Web and RTMP

AWS CloudFront supports different types of distributions to cater to various content delivery needs. The primary distribution types are Web and RTMP (Real-Time Messaging Protocol):

1. **Web Distribution:** This type is used for delivering static and dynamic web content, including HTML, CSS, JavaScript, and images. Web distributions are best suited for websites and applications that need fast and reliable content delivery. They support both HTTP and HTTPS protocols, providing secure content delivery. Web distributions also offer features like geo-restriction, custom error pages, and logging, allowing businesses to tailor the content delivery experience to their needs.

2. **RTMP Distribution:** Although AWS has deprecated RTMP distributions, they were previously used for streaming media content using the Real-Time Messaging Protocol. RTMP distributions enabled live and on-demand video streaming, providing a smooth viewing experience. Despite the deprecation, AWS CloudFront continues to support media streaming through other protocols, ensuring high-quality content delivery for video applications.

AWS CloudFront's support for different distribution types allows businesses to choose the most suitable option for their content delivery requirements, ensuring optimal performance and user satisfaction.

Setting Up AWS CloudFront

1. Log in to the AWS Console if you haven't already.
2. Navigate to CloudFormation Service.
3. Figure 2-25 is a sample template to set up CloudFront with CloudFormation.

CHAPTER 2   FRONTEND DEVELOPMENT AND INTEGRATION

```
    publicDistribution:
   Type: AWS::CloudFront::Distribution
   Properties:
     DistributionConfig:
       Origins:
         - DomainName: private-bucket.s3.us-east-2.amazonaws.com
           Id: S3-private-bucket
           S3OriginConfig:
             OriginAccessIdentity: !Sub 'origin-access-identity/cloudfront/${CloudFrontOriginIdentity}'
       Enabled: 'true'
       Comment: "Practical Serverless Applications"
       DefaultCacheBehavior:
         AllowedMethods:
           - GET
           - HEAD
         TargetOriginId: S3-private-bucket
         ForwardedValues:
           QueryString: 'false'
           Cookies:
             Forward: none
         ViewerProtocolPolicy: redirect-to-https
       ViewerCertificate:
         CloudFrontDefaultCertificate: 'true'
```

Figure 2-25. *CloudFormation template for CloudFront*

4. Upload the CloudFormation template (refer to Figure 2-26).

97

CHAPTER 2   FRONTEND DEVELOPMENT AND INTEGRATION

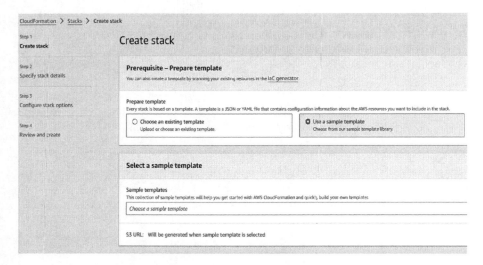

Figure 2-26.   Upload sample CloudFormation template using AWS Console

5. Create a simple S3 bucket by using AWS Console with the name "private-bucket."

6. As shown in Figure 2-25, you need to give an S3 bucket origin while creating CloudFront. In the example, "private-bucket" is your origin S3 bucket.

7. You need to update the S3 bucket policy for CloudFront access. Figure 2-27 is a sample template for updating the bucket policy.

CHAPTER 2 FRONTEND DEVELOPMENT AND INTEGRATION

```
BucketPolicy:
    Type: AWS::S3::BucketPolicy
    Properties:
      Bucket: private-bucket
      PolicyDocument:
        Version: '2012-10-17'
        Statement:
          - Effect: Allow
            Principal:
              AWS: !Sub 'arn:aws:iam::cloudfront:user/CloudFront Origin Access Identity ${CloudFrontOriginIdentity}'
            Action: 's3:GetObject'
            Resource: arn:aws:s3:::private-bucket/*
```

Figure 2-27. *Template to update S3 bucket policy for CloudFront*

8. As shown in Figure 2-25, you are defining a cache by using "DefaultCacheBehavior:".

9. You also need to define the type of access which you are using for S3 by CloudFront; in the example, you have defined it by using "OriginAccessIdentity."

10. Figure 2-28 is a sample template for "${CloudFrontOriginIdentity}".

CHAPTER 2　FRONTEND DEVELOPMENT AND INTEGRATION

```
CloudFrontOriginIdentity:
    Type: AWS::CloudFront::CloudFrontOriginAccessIdentity
    Properties:
        CloudFrontOriginAccessIdentityConfig:
            Comment: 'origin identity'
```

Figure 2-28. *Template to create origin access identity for CloudFront*

Security Features in AWS CloudFront

AWS CloudFront is not only a robust content delivery network but also a secure platform that ensures the protection of data as it is distributed globally. Security is a paramount concern for businesses handling sensitive information, and CloudFront addresses this with a suite of features designed to safeguard content and user data. Among these features are SSL/TLS encryption, which secures data during transport, and access control mechanisms like signed URLs and signed cookies, which control content access to authorized users. By implementing these security measures, CloudFront helps businesses maintain data integrity and confidentiality, ensuring that content is delivered securely and efficiently.

SSL/TLS Encryption

SSL/TLS encryption is a fundamental security feature in AWS CloudFront, providing secure data transmission between clients and servers. By encrypting data in transport, SSL/TLS guarantees that confidential information, such as user credentials and payment details, is protected from interception and tampering by malicious actors. CloudFront supports both HTTP and HTTPS protocols, with HTTPS providing the encrypted communication channel necessary for secure data exchange.

CloudFront allows businesses to use their own SSL/TLS certificates or leverage AWS Certificate Manager (ACM) to manage certificates seamlessly. This flexibility enables organizations to maintain control over their encryption standards while benefiting from the scalability and reliability of AWS infrastructure. Additionally, CloudFront supports HTTP/2 and IPv6, further enhancing security and performance. By implementing SSL/TLS encryption, CloudFront ensures that data integrity and confidentiality are maintained throughout the content delivery process, providing peace of mind for both businesses and end users.

Access Control with Signed URLs and Signed Cookies

Access control is a critical aspect of content security, and AWS CloudFront offers robust methods to control access to permitted users through signed URLs and signed cookies. These features enable businesses to control who can view their content, guaranteeing that just authenticated users have access to confidential or premium content.

1. **Signed URLs:** Signed URLs are helps in granting temporary access to certain content. They include an expiration timeline, following which the URL expires. This feature is particularly useful for delivering time-sensitive content, such as pay-per-view events or limited-time offers. By generating signed URLs, businesses can guarantee that only rightful users can access the content, preventing unauthorized sharing or access.

2. **Signed Cookies:** Signed cookies provide a way to control access to multiple files or resources without requiring individual signed URLs for each. They are ideal for applications where users need access to a range of content, such as subscription-based services. By setting signed cookies, businesses can manage user sessions and restrict access based on user authentication, guaranteeing that only rightful users can get the content.

By utilizing signed URLs and signed cookies, AWS CloudFront provides businesses with flexible and effective access control options, ensuring that content is delivered securely and only to intended recipients. These features help maintain data security and integrity, supporting businesses in protecting their valuable digital assets.

Integrating AWS CloudFront with Frontend Development

1. As a demo, you can will host a simple website – a website that has only an index.html file as shown in Figure 2-29.

```
<!DOCTYPE html>
<html>
   <head>
       <title>Simple SPA</title>
   </head>
   <body style="background-color: lightpink">
       <h1>Hello! This is the simple static hosting!</h1>
   </body>
</html>
```

Figure 2-29. *Index.html file*

CHAPTER 2   FRONTEND DEVELOPMENT AND INTEGRATION

2. Log in to the AWS Console if you haven't already.

3. Navigate to S3 which you have created with the name "private-bucket."

4. Upload the "Index.html" into the bucket name "private-bucket" which has CloudFront bucket policy (refer to Figure 2-30).

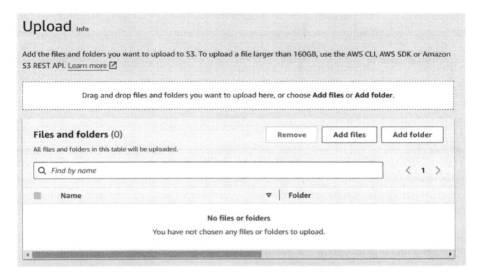

Figure 2-30. *AWS Console screen to upload file to S3 bucket*

5. For "index.html," set "cache-control = no-cache" so that CloudFront can detect its latest version and serve the same. Otherwise, you will start wondering about the reason why you're not finding the latest code rendered.

6. Now you will configure CloudFront for the index. html file by using a CloudFormation template. Figure 2-31 shows a sample template for CloudFront.

CHAPTER 2   FRONTEND DEVELOPMENT AND INTEGRATION

```
Outputs:
  CloudFrontDist:
    Value:
      Ref: CloudFrontDistribution

Resources:
  CloudFrontDistribution:
    Type: AWS::CloudFront::Distribution
    DependsOn:
      - S3Bucket
    Properties:
      DistributionConfig:
        Origins:
          - DomainName: private-bucket.s3.us-east-2.amazonaws.com
            Id: S3-private-bucket
            S3OriginConfig:
              OriginAccessIdentity: !Sub 'origin-access-identity/cloudfront/${CloudFrontOriginIdentity}'
        Enabled: "true"
        Comment: Practical Serverless Applications
        DefaultRootObject: index.html
        CustomErrorResponses:
          - ErrorCode: 404
            ResponseCode: 200
            ResponsePagePath: /index.html
          - ErrorCode: 403
            ResponseCode: 200
            ResponsePagePath: /index.html
        HttpVersion: http2
        Aliases:
          - web.example.com
        ViewerCertificate:
          AcmCertificateArn: "arn:aws:acm:us-east-1:Id-of-IAM-User:certificate/1xxxxxxx-xxxx-xxxx-xxxx-xxxxxxxxxxxx"
          MinimumProtocolVersion: TLSv1.2_2021
          SslSupportMethod: sni-only
        DefaultCacheBehavior:
          AllowedMethods:
            - DELETE
            - GET
            - HEAD
            - OPTIONS
            - PATCH
            - POST
            - PUT
          Compress: true
          TargetOriginId: S3-private-bucket
          ForwardedValues:
            QueryString: "false"
            Cookies:
              Forward: none
          ViewerProtocolPolicy: redirect-to-https
```

Figure 2-31.   *Configure CloudFront for frontend development*

CHAPTER 2   FRONTEND DEVELOPMENT AND INTEGRATION

7. *Aliases* is the alternate domain name you want to give, instead of the default CloudFront domain (d1xxxxxxxxxx.cloudfront.net).

8. AcmCertificateArn is the ARN of the certificate. Make sure you've imported the certificate for the given alias (domain). It's a requirement of AWS.

9. After getting the requested certificate in AWS Certificate Manager (ACM), note the given CNAME records and add it to your DNS provider Cloudflare or AWS Route 53, etc.

10. Now, add another CNAME record with the domain name (web.example.com in your case) with the value of CloudFront URL (d1xxxxxxxxxx.cloudfront.net). Make sure its proxy status must be DNS only.

Optimizing Performance with AWS CloudFront

AWS CloudFront is a dynamic content delivery network (CDN) that significantly enhances the performance of web applications by reducing latency and improving data transfer speeds. By leveraging a global network of edge locations, CloudFront caches content closer to end users, ensuring rapid delivery. However, to fully harness CloudFront's capabilities, it's essential to implement effective performance optimization strategies. These include utilizing caching strategies and cache invalidation, setting up appropriate cache policies and time to live (TTL) settings, and employing Lambda@Edge for content customization. By optimizing these elements, businesses can ensure that their applications deliver content swiftly and efficiently, providing an exceptional user experience.

105

CHAPTER 2   FRONTEND DEVELOPMENT AND INTEGRATION

Caching Strategies and Cache Invalidation

Caching is a core component of AWS CloudFront's performance optimization. By storing copies of content at edge locations, CloudFront reduces the need to fetch data from the origin server, minimizing latency and improving load times. Effective caching strategies involve determining which content should be cached and for how long. Static content, such as images and CSS files, can be cached for extended periods, while dynamic content may require more frequent updates.

Cache invalidation is crucial for ensuring that users receive the most up-to-date content. CloudFront allows for manual cache invalidation, enabling businesses to remove outdated content from edge locations. This process can be automated using the AWS Bash tool command, ensuring that content changes are reflected promptly across all edge locations. By implementing strategic caching and cache invalidation practices, businesses can optimize performance while maintaining content accuracy.

Setting Up Cache Policies and TTL (Time to Live)

Cache policies and TTL settings play a vital role in controlling how long content is cached at edge locations. TTL determines the duration for which cached content remains valid before CloudFront checks the origin server for updates. Setting appropriate TTL values is essential for balancing performance and content freshness. Longer TTLs reduce the frequency of origin server requests, enhancing performance, while shorter TTLs ensure that users receive the latest content.

CloudFront allows for the creation of custom cache policies, enabling businesses to define caching behavior based on specific requirements. These policies can be tailored to different content types, ensuring that each piece of content is cached optimally. By configuring cache policies and TTL settings effectively, businesses can maximize CloudFront's performance benefits while ensuring that users receive accurate and timely content.

CHAPTER 2   FRONTEND DEVELOPMENT AND INTEGRATION

Using Lambda@Edge for Customization

Lambda@Edge is a powerful feature of AWS CloudFront that enables developers to run serverless code at edge locations, allowing for real-time content customization and processing as shown in Figure 2-32. This capability is particularly useful for applications requiring dynamic content modification, such as personalized user experiences or A/B testing.

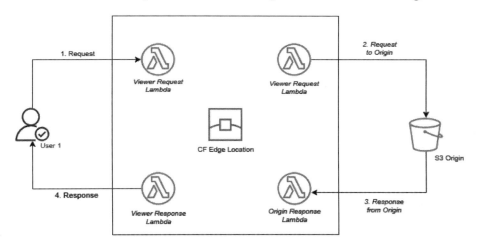

Figure 2-32. *Lambda@Edge*

With Lambda@Edge, developers can execute code in response to CloudFront events, such as viewer requests or origin responses. This allows for on-the-fly content transformation, such as image resizing, language localization, or security header insertion. By processing content closer to users, Lambda@Edge reduces latency and improves application responsiveness.

The flexibility of Lambda@Edge empowers businesses to implement sophisticated content customization strategies without the need for additional infrastructure. By leveraging this feature, organizations can enhance user experiences and optimize application performance, ensuring that content is delivered efficiently and effectively.

CHAPTER 2   FRONTEND DEVELOPMENT AND INTEGRATION

Conclusion

In this chapter, the key aspects of frontend development and integration using AWS services were summarized. Each point highlights the unique contributions of AWS Amplify, CloudFront, API Gateway, and S3 in creating efficient and scalable web applications:

1. **AWS Amplify:** AWS Amplify revolutionizes frontend development by providing a comprehensive set of tools and services. It simplifies the process of building and deploying web applications, offering features like authentication, API management, and serverless functions. Amplify's integration with other AWS services makes it an invaluable asset for developers seeking to create scalable and feature-rich applications quickly and efficiently.

2. **API Gateway:** API Gateway serves as a crucial component in building scalable and secure APIs for frontend applications. It provides features like request throttling, API versioning, and authentication, enabling developers to create robust and manageable APIs. API Gateway's seamless integration with AWS Lambda and other services allows for the creation of serverless architectures, reducing operational overhead and improving scalability.

3. **S3 (Simple Storage Service):** S3 offers a reliable and cost-effective solution for storing and retrieving data in frontend applications. Its high durability, availability, and scalability make it ideal for hosting static websites, storing user-generated content,

CHAPTER 2   FRONTEND DEVELOPMENT AND INTEGRATION

and managing application assets. S3's integration with other AWS services, such as CloudFront and Amplify, creates a powerful foundation for building efficient and scalable web applications.

4. **AWS CloudFront:** AWS CloudFront enhances website performance and user experience through its global content delivery network. By caching content at edge locations worldwide, CloudFront significantly reduces latency and improves load times for users across different geographical regions. Its integration with other AWS services, such as S3 and API Gateway, creates a powerful ecosystem for delivering dynamic and static content efficiently.

CHAPTER 3

Data Engineering

Introduction

In the rapidly evolving landscape of data management, this chapter delves into the critical realm of data engineering, focusing on the powerful tools and services offered by Amazon Web Services (AWS). This chapter serves as a comprehensive guide to understanding how AWS Glue, AWS Batch, AWS Redshift, AWS Athena, and the fundamentals of data lakes can transform raw data into actionable insights. AWS Glue simplifies the process of data preparation and integration, offering a serverless environment that automates the tedious tasks of data extraction, transformation, and loading (ETL). Meanwhile, AWS Batch provides an efficient way to run batch processing workloads, enabling you to execute thousands of jobs with ease. AWS Redshift, a fully managed data warehouse, allows for the rapid querying and analysis of vast datasets, while AWS Athena offers a serverless query service that lets you analyze data directly in Amazon S3 using standard SQL. The chapter also explores the concept of data lakes, which provide a centralized repository to store all structured and unstructured data at any scale. By the end of this chapter, you will gain a solid understanding of how these AWS services can be leveraged to build robust, scalable, and efficient data engineering pipelines, enabling your organization to fully leverage its data assets' potential.

CHAPTER 3   DATA ENGINEERING

> ETL stands for extract, transform, and load, a data processing framework used to gather data from various sources, transform it into a suitable format, and load it into a target system for analysis or reporting.

AWS Glue

AWS Glue is a fully managed extract, transform, and load (ETL) service from AWS that streamlines data preparation for analytics. It is designed to simplify the complexities of data integration by automating the processes of discovering, cataloging, cleaning, enriching, and transforming data. AWS Glue supports a variety of data sources, such as Amazon S3, Amazon RDS, and Amazon Redshift, making it an ideal choice for organizations aiming to optimize their data workflows. Its serverless architecture removes the need for infrastructure management, allowing users to concentrate on data processing tasks. This service is especially advantageous for data engineers and scientists who need to prepare data for machine learning, business intelligence, and application development.

> A fully managed AWS service is one where AWS handles the underlying infrastructure and operational tasks, allowing users to focus solely on using the service without worrying about maintenance or scaling.

AWS Glue offers a robust set of tools, including a data catalog, an ETL engine, and a scheduler, all integrated into a unified platform. The Glue Data Catalog serves as a centralized repository for metadata, making data easily searchable and accessible across AWS services. The ETL engine supports both Python and Scala, providing flexibility for writing custom scripts. AWS Glue Studio, the service's visual interface, allows users to create ETL jobs with minimal coding, enhancing efficiency. Additionally, the service includes job scheduling and monitoring features to ensure smooth and efficient data pipeline operations. Overall, AWS Glue empowers organizations to leverage their data effectively, fostering insights and innovation.

Use Cases of AWS Glue

AWS Glue is instrumental in building and managing data lakes, allowing organizations to efficiently store, catalog, and analyze large datasets. By automating the ETL process, it simplifies data preparation for analytics, enabling businesses to extract insights from both structured and unstructured data. Its seamless integration with AWS services like Amazon S3 and Redshift makes it ideal for creating scalable and cost-effective data lakes that support advanced analytics and machine learning.

Another significant use case for AWS Glue is real-time data processing and analytics. Organizations can leverage AWS Glue to automate the transformation and loading of streaming data from sources such as IoT devices or application logs into analytics platforms. This capability is essential for businesses that require timely insights from continuously generated data, such as monitoring system performance, detecting anomalies, or personalizing customer experiences in real time, thereby enhancing decision-making and operational efficiency.

AWS Glue Key Components

AWS Glue is a powerful ETL service, and components such as Data Catalog, ETL Jobs, Crawlers, and Triggers are integral to its functionality, each playing a crucial role in managing and processing data efficiently. These components work together to automate and streamline data

CHAPTER 3 DATA ENGINEERING

workflows, enabling organizations to derive insights and make data-driven decisions more effectively. Below, each component is explained in detail with the reference of the Glue architecture as shown in Figure 3-1.

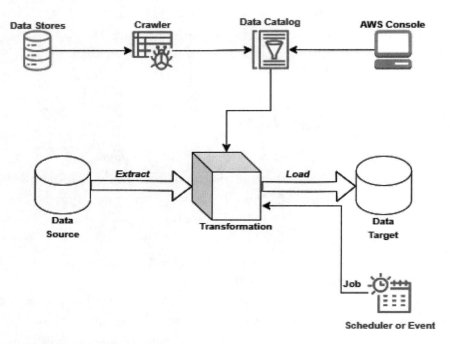

Figure 3-1. *Glue architecture*

1. **Data Catalog:** The AWS Glue Data Catalog is a centralized repository for metadata that stores details about data sources, schemas, and transformations. It acts as an index, making data easily searchable and accessible across AWS services. The Data Catalog supports schema versioning and automatic detection of schema changes, ensuring data integrity and facilitating data governance and compliance. This unified view of data assets helps organizations efficiently manage their data landscape.

2. **ETL Jobs:** ETL Jobs in AWS Glue are scripts that automate the extraction, transformation, and loading of data, written in Python or Scala and executed in a serverless environment. These jobs are crucial for converting raw data into analysis-ready formats, handling complex transformations like data cleaning and aggregation. AWS Glue Studio provides a visual interface for creating and managing ETL jobs with minimal coding, enhancing productivity and streamlining data pipeline development.

3. **Crawlers:** Crawlers in AWS Glue are automated tools that scan data sources to identify their schema and update the Data Catalog with metadata. They support various data sources, such as Amazon S3 and Amazon RDS, and ensure the Data Catalog remains current by detecting new data and schema changes. This automation reduces manual schema management efforts, allowing organizations to focus on extracting value from their data.

4. **Triggers:** Triggers in AWS Glue are mechanisms that start ETL jobs based on specific conditions or schedules, automating data workflows. They can initiate jobs at set intervals or in response to events, such as new data arrivals, enabling dynamic data pipelines. Triggers help maintain data freshness and availability, facilitating timely insights and decision-making while reducing the need for manual intervention.

CHAPTER 3   DATA ENGINEERING

Features of AWS Glue

AWS Glue boasts a plethora of features, each designed to elevate your data integration experience. Among these, the most prominent and transformative are elaborated upon below:

1. **Serverless Architecture:** AWS Glue is a fully managed, serverless data integration service that removes the need for infrastructure management, allowing users to focus on data processing tasks. Its serverless nature ensures automatic scaling of resources based on workload demands, optimizing performance and cost efficiency. This scalability is particularly advantageous for handling varying data volumes and complex ETL processes. AWS Glue also integrates seamlessly with other AWS services like Amazon S3, Redshift, and RDS, offering a cohesive environment for data management and analytics without the burden of server management.

2. **Automated Schema Discovery:** AWS Glue streamlines data extraction and transformation through automated schema discovery. Using Crawlers, it connects to various data sources, analyzes the data, and automatically infers the schema and data types, reducing the manual effort required for schema definition and maintenance. The discovered schema is stored in the AWS Glue Data Catalog, serving as a centralized metadata repository. This automation accelerates the ETL process, ensuring consistency and accuracy in data representation and facilitating seamless integration and querying across diverse data sources.

3. **Built-In Transformations:** AWS Glue provides a comprehensive set of built-in transformations for complex data processing tasks, such as filtering, mapping, joining, and aggregating data. These prebuilt transformations can be easily managed through AWS Glue's visual interface, allowing users to create and iterate on ETL workflows without extensive coding. This feature enhances productivity and reduces time to insight for data engineers and analysts. Additionally, AWS Glue supports custom transformations using Python or Scala, offering flexibility to implement specialized logic and meet unique business requirements, thereby extending the ETL process's capabilities.

Advantages of AWS Glue

AWS Glue offers a multitude of advantages that make it a powerful tool for data integration and ETL processes. Among these, the most significant benefits are detailed below, showcasing the transformative impact AWS Glue can have on your data engineering endeavors.

1. **Ease of Integration with AWS Services:** AWS Glue seamlessly integrates with AWS services like Amazon S3, Redshift, RDS, and Athena, creating a unified ecosystem for data management. This integration simplifies data movement and transformation across platforms without complex configurations, enhancing interoperability and governance. It streamlines workflows, reduces complexity, and accelerates data-driven initiatives.

2. **Cost-Effectiveness with Pay-As-You-Go Pricing:** AWS Glue offers a cost-effective pay-as-you-go pricing model, charging users based on resources consumed during ETL jobs. This eliminates upfront infrastructure costs and allows scaling according to demand. By paying only for usage, businesses optimize costs, benefiting from automatic resource scaling for efficient performance within budget constraints.

3. **Scalability and Flexibility:** AWS Glue's serverless architecture enables automatic scaling to handle data processing tasks of any size, ensuring optimal performance without manual intervention. It supports various data formats and sources, offering flexibility to adapt to changing data landscapes. This scalability empowers businesses to efficiently manage data and respond to market demands.

Disadvantages of AWS Glue

While AWS Glue is a powerful tool, it does have a few limitations. These are discussed below, highlighting areas where users might encounter challenges:

1. **Initial Learning Curve:** AWS Glue can present a steep learning curve for newcomers, especially those unfamiliar with AWS services or ETL processes. The complexity of setting up data catalogs, crawlers, and jobs can be daunting initially. Users may need to invest time in understanding the service's intricacies and best practices. However, once mastered, AWS Glue's robust features can significantly streamline data integration tasks, making the initial effort worthwhile.

CHAPTER 3   DATA ENGINEERING

2. **Potential Latency in Job Execution:** Another challenge with AWS Glue is the potential latency in job execution. Since it operates in a serverless environment, there can be delays in job startup times, particularly during peak usage periods. This latency might affect time-sensitive data processing tasks. While AWS Glue offers scalability and flexibility, users should be aware of these potential delays and plan their workflows accordingly to ensure timely data processing and delivery.

Practical Guide to AWS Glue

1. Log in to the AWS Console if you haven't already.
2. Search for AWS Glue in the search bar and then click AWS Glue, then you will redirect to the screen as shown in Figure 3-2.

Figure 3-2.   AWS Glue screen in AWS Console

119

CHAPTER 3 DATA ENGINEERING

3. As shown in Figure 3-2, first of all, you have to create the necessary policy and role for AWS Glue to be able to watch the logs and connect to S3.

4. You implement a new IAM policy specifically for Glue. A sample policy JSON is shown in Figure 3-3. You can select Glue as the service and use this JSON to define the policy's rules.

```
{
    "Version": "2012-10-17",
    "Statement": [
        {
            "Sid": "VisualEditor0",
            "Effect": "Allow",
            "Action": "iam:PassRole",
            "Resource": "arn:aws:iam::<account_id>:role/*"
        }
    ]
}
```

Figure 3-3. *Sample policy JSON*

5. Customize the policy by entering your account ID in the "*account_id*" field. Choose a suitable name for the policy. Then, create an IAM role linked to this policy. Don't forget to include these other policies as well:

   a. AwsGlueSessionUserRestrictedNotebookPolicy

   b. AmazonS3FullAccessV2

   c. CloudWatchFullAccessV2

   d. AWSGlueServiceRole

6. glue-iam-policy: Now either create a new bucket or use an existing bucket to get the initial data and upload the final data. This part is important since the bucket name should include "aws-glue."

CHAPTER 3   DATA ENGINEERING

7. Upload a sample CSV file into this bucket with some key. You are going to use this file as your main source of data.

8. Now you can create the database from AWS Glue ➤ Databases ➤ Add database.

9. Let's add a new table to this database to track the metadata of objects in your S3 bucket. You can either use a crawler to generate the table schema or customize it manually.

10. You'll manually modify the schema by choosing S3 as the data source as shown in Figure 3-4 and browsing to the location of your new object. Make sure to select the directory instead of an individual file.

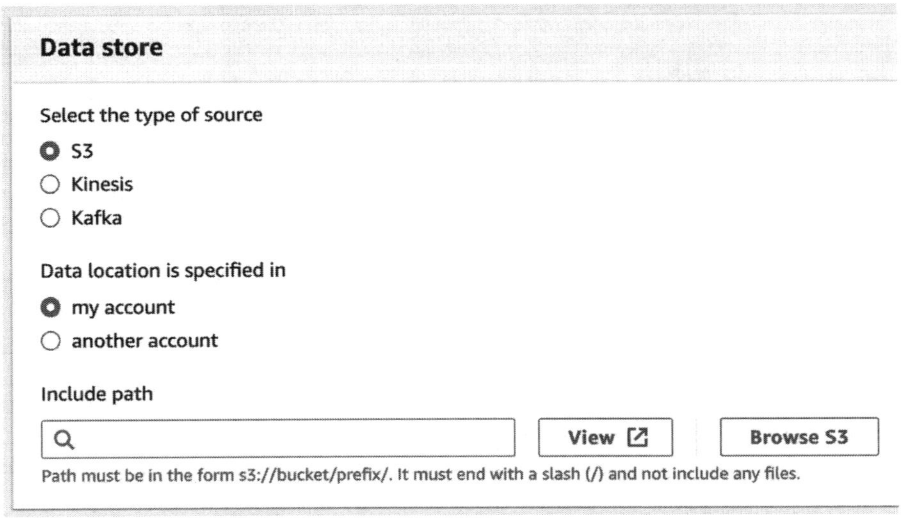

Data store

Select the type of source
- ● S3
- ○ Kinesis
- ○ Kafka

Data location is specified in
- ● my account
- ○ another account

Include path

[🔍   ]   [View ↗]   [Browse S3]

Path must be in the form s3://bucket/prefix/. It must end with a slash (/) and not include any files.

Figure 3-4. Choose a source data for Glue

121

CHAPTER 3   DATA ENGINEERING

11. The primary distinction between a crawler and a custom schema is that a crawler detects the schema automatically but incurs costs. Because of this, you chose a custom schema. A crawler would have handled everything else, except the schema, which it would have determined automatically. Additionally, we could have established a schema registry for frequently used data catalogs.

12. Once you've created the data catalog, including the database and table, we can proceed to create the Glue ETL job.

13. This Glue ETL job's primary function is to transform the source CSV file, using the Glue Data Catalog, and then save the modified data in Parquet format to S3. It will also create a corresponding target data catalog to store metadata about the resulting object.

14. You are going to create a job using the Spark script editor as shown in Figure 3-5. Before reviewing the script, you can configure it. First, we should name your script and select the recently created IAM role.

CHAPTER 3   DATA ENGINEERING

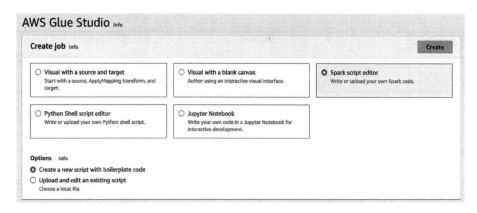

Figure 3-5. *Creating Glue job*

15. Since the data volume isn't large, you can use the minimum resource configuration for this job. We'll choose two workers of type G 1X.

16. Once your script is configured, you can create it. Glue will automatically generate the initial portion, creating a Glue dynamic frame. You'll add specific imports and then convert the Glue dynamic frame into a Spark data frame as shown in Figure 3-6.

123

CHAPTER 3　DATA ENGINEERING

```
import sys
from awsglue.transforms import *
from awsglue.utils import getResolvedOptions
from pyspark.context import SparkContext
from awsglue.context import GlueContext
from awsglue.job import Job
from awsglue.dynamicframe import DynamicFrame
from pyspark.sql import functions as F
from pyspark.sql.window import Window

## @params: [JOB_NAME]
args = getResolvedOptions(sys.argv, ['JOB_NAME'])

sc = SparkContext()
glueContext = GlueContext(sc)
spark = glueContext.spark_session
job = Job(glueContext)
job.init(args['JOB_NAME'], args)

glue_dynamic_frame_initial = 
glueContext.create_dynamic_frame.from_catalog(database='db_Name',
table_name='tb_Name')

df_spark = glue_dynamic_frame_initial.toDF()
```

Figure 3-6. Sample Glue job script

17. You are going to prepare your Spark data frame for further steps as shown in Figure 3-7.

```
    def prepare_dataframe(df):
    """Rename the columns, extract sample and drop unnecessary
columns. Remove NULL records"""
    df_renamed = df.withColumnRenamed("New Name1", "old_Name1") \
        .withColumnRenamed("New Name2", "old_Name2") \
    df_sample__added = df_renamed.withColumn("sample",
F.sample(sample))
    df_final =
df_year_added.filter((F.col("shape_reported").isNotNull()) &
(F.col("SampleColumnName").isNotNull()))
    return df_final
```

Figure 3-7. Sample Spark dataframe

18. Now you will convert your Spark data frame back into a Glue dynamic frame as shown in Figure 3-8. This will be used for writing the data to the S3 bucket and creating a corresponding table in the Data Catalog.

CHAPTER 3 DATA ENGINEERING

```
        df_final = create_final_dataframe(df_joined)

# From Spark dataframe to glue dynamic frame
glue_dynamic_frame_final = DynamicFrame.fromDF(df_final, glueContext,
"glue_etl")

# Write the data in the DynamicFrame to a location in Amazon S3 and a
table for it in the AWS Glue Data Catalog
s3output = glueContext.getSink(
 path="s3://bucketname/targetname",
 connection_type="s3",
 updateBehavior="UPDATE_IN_DATABASE",
 partitionKeys=[],
 compression="snappy",
 enableUpdateCatalog=True,
 transformation_ctx="s3output",
)

s3output.setCatalogInfo(
 catalogDatabase="dbbame", catalogTableName="tablename"
)
s3output.setFormat("glueparquet")
s3output.writeFrame(glue_dynamic_frame_final)

job.commit()
```

Figure 3-8. *Sample script writing data to S3*

19. After completing the script page as described, you can save the script and execute it. You can monitor the script's status in the Runs tab. We should wait for the run to finish successfully.

20. Alternatively, you can create the ETL job using a Jupyter Notebook. The steps are quite similar to the Spark script, so there's no need to examine the Jupyter Notebook code in detail. Here are the differences between the Spark script and Jupyter Notebook: "For the initial creation of the ETL job, Jupyter Notebook is a preferable choice over a Spark script. The notebook enables us to specify the resource allocation within the code itself."

21. You can add a schedule to your newly created Glue ETL job. To run the job on a recurring basis, you should use a Cron expression.

AWS Batch

AWS Batch is a powerful, fully managed service that enables developers to efficiently run batch computing workloads on the AWS cloud. It eliminates the need for complex infrastructure management, allowing users to focus on designing and implementing their batch jobs. AWS Batch dynamically provisions the optimal quantity and type of compute resources based on the volume and specific requirements of the submitted batch jobs. This service seamlessly integrates with other AWS offerings, making it an ideal choice for organizations looking to streamline their data processing pipelines and enhance overall operational efficiency.

At its core, AWS Batch automates the process of scheduling, scaling, and executing batch computing workloads across a fleet of Amazon EC2 instances. It leverages Docker containers to ensure consistency and portability across different computing environments. The service supports a wide range of job types, from simple scripts to complex multi-node parallel jobs, making it versatile enough to handle diverse computational needs. AWS Batch also provides detailed monitoring and logging capabilities, enabling users to track job progress, identify bottlenecks, and optimize resource utilization effectively.

Use Cases for Batch Processing

Batch processing is utilized in a wide range of industries and for numerous use cases. In financial services, it's commonly used for risk analysis, fraud detection, and end-of-day transaction processing. Scientific research benefits from batch processing for genomic sequencing, climate modeling, and drug discovery simulations. Media and entertainment companies utilize it for video transcoding and rendering complex visual effects. In the realm of IoT and big data, batch processing is crucial for analyzing large datasets from sensors and devices. Ecommerce platforms employ batch processing for inventory updates, recommendation engine training, and customer behavior analysis. These diverse applications showcase the versatility and importance of batch processing in modern data-driven organizations.

AWS Batch Key Components

The key components of AWS Batch are listed below, each playing a crucial role in the service's functionality and efficiency:

1. **Jobs and Job Definitions:** Jobs are the core work units in AWS Batch, typically consisting of scripts, executables, or Docker containers. Job Definitions serve as templates, specifying how these jobs should be run, including resource requirements like vCPUs and memory, as well as the container images to be used.

2. **Job Queues and Schedulers:** Job Queues hold submitted jobs until they can be executed. The Scheduler, an internal system, evaluates these queues to determine when, where, and how to run jobs based on their dependencies and resource requirements. This component ensures efficient resource allocation and job prioritization.

3. **Compute Environments:** These are the managed or unmanaged compute resources where batch jobs are executed. Compute Environments can be dynamically scaled and can utilize various EC2 instance types, including cost-effective Spot Instances, to meet the demands of submitted jobs.

4. **Advanced Job Features:** AWS Batch supports Array Jobs for running multiple similar jobs quickly, Multi-node Parallel Jobs for distributed computing tasks, and Job Dependencies for creating complex workflows. These features enhance the service's flexibility and ability to handle diverse computational needs.

Features of AWS Batch

AWS Batch offers a suite of robust features designed to simplify and enhance batch processing tasks. The main features of AWS Batch are elaborated below, showcasing its capabilities in transforming how batch workloads are managed and executed:

CHAPTER 3   DATA ENGINEERING

1. **Dynamic Resource Provisioning:** AWS Batch automatically provisions the optimal type and number of compute resources based on the specific requirements of submitted jobs. This dynamic scaling ensures that resources are efficiently utilized, reducing costs and eliminating the need for manual intervention. By leveraging Amazon EC2 and Spot Instances, AWS Batch provides flexibility and cost-effectiveness, enabling users to focus on their applications without worrying about underlying infrastructure complexities.

2. **Seamless Container Integration:** With support for Docker containers, AWS Batch ensures that applications are portable and consistent across different environments. This feature allows developers to package their code, dependencies, and configurations into a single container, simplifying deployment and execution. The use of containers also enhances security and reliability, as each job runs in its isolated environment, minimizing conflicts and ensuring smooth operation across diverse workloads.

3. **Comprehensive Job Management:** AWS Batch provides an intuitive interface for managing and monitoring batch jobs. Users can easily submit, schedule, and track jobs, with detailed logging and reporting features that offer insights into job performance and resource utilization. This comprehensive job management capability allows for efficient troubleshooting and optimization, helping organizations to streamline their workflows and achieve better operational efficiency.

4. **Scalability and Flexibility:** Designed to handle workloads of any scale, AWS Batch can efficiently manage both small- and large-scale batch processing tasks. Its flexible architecture supports a wide range of job types, from single-node tasks to complex multi-node parallel computations. This scalability ensures that AWS Batch can adapt to the evolving needs of businesses, providing a robust solution for diverse computational challenges across various industries.

Advantages of AWS Batch

AWS Batch provides numerous advantages that enhance the efficiency and effectiveness of batch processing. The main advantages of AWS Batch are detailed below, highlighting its transformative impact on managing computational workloads:

1. **Cost Optimization with Spot Instances:** AWS Batch allows users to take advantage of Amazon EC2 Spot Instances, which can significantly reduce computing costs. Spot Instances enable access to unused EC2 capacity at discounted rates, making it an economical choice for running batch jobs. By automatically selecting the most cost-effective resources, AWS Batch helps organizations optimize their spending while maintaining performance, ensuring that budget constraints do not hinder the execution of large-scale workloads.

2. **Scalability and Flexibility:** AWS Batch is designed to accommodate workloads of any size, offering unmatched scalability and flexibility. It can efficiently

manage both small, single-node tasks and large, complex multi-node computations. This adaptability ensures that AWS Batch can meet the diverse needs of businesses, allowing them to scale operations seamlessly as demands grow. Whether handling routine data processing or intensive computational tasks, AWS Batch provides a robust solution that evolves with organizational requirements.

3. **Simplified Job Management:** AWS Batch streamlines the process of managing batch jobs with its user-friendly interface and comprehensive monitoring tools. Users can easily submit, schedule, and track jobs, gaining valuable insights into performance and resource utilization through detailed logs and reports. This simplification reduces the administrative burden, allowing teams to focus on core tasks rather than infrastructure management. By enhancing visibility and control, AWS Batch empowers organizations to optimize workflows and improve overall productivity.

Disadvantages of AWS Batch

While AWS Batch offers many benefits, it also has some disadvantages that users should consider. Complexity in Configuring Compute Environments - Setting up compute environments in AWS Batch can be complex, especially for users unfamiliar with AWS infrastructure. Configuring the right mix of resources, security settings, and networking options requires a deep understanding of AWS services. This complexity can lead to potential misconfigurations, impacting performance and security. Organizations may need to invest time in training or seek expert assistance to ensure that their compute environments are optimized for their specific workload requirements:

CHAPTER 3   DATA ENGINEERING

1. **Potential Delays in Job Scheduling:** AWS Batch may experience delays in job scheduling, particularly during peak usage times or when relying heavily on Spot Instances. These delays can affect time-sensitive workloads, as jobs might wait in a queue longer than expected before execution. While AWS Batch aims to optimize resource allocation, external factors like spot market fluctuations can introduce unpredictability. Users need to account for these potential scheduling delays when planning their batch processing tasks to ensure timely completion.

Practical Guide to AWS Batch

1. Log in to the AWS Console if you haven't already.
2. Search for AWS Batch in the search bar and then click AWS Batch, then you will redirect to the page as shown in Figure 3-9.

Figure 3-9. *AWS Batch screen*

133

3. You will add a widget. This widget displays detailed information about a single job queue.

4. For a single job queue, choose Add widget.

5. Specify the job queue. Select the job statuses you want to display. (Optional) If you don't need to compute environment properties, hide them. Choose the desired compute environment properties. Click Add.

6. You will add another widget for "CloudWatch Container Insights."

7. This widget shows combined statistics for AWS Batch compute environments and jobs. To add container insights, select "Add widget." Choose the desired compute environment, then click Add.

8. To add job logs, select "Add widget." Enter the job ID of the job you want to see, then click Add. This widget gathers various logs from your jobs into a single place.

AWS RedShift

AWS Redshift is a fully managed, petabyte-scale data warehouse service in the cloud, designed to handle large-scale data analytics. It allows organizations to efficiently analyze massive datasets using SQL-based tools and business intelligence applications. Redshift's architecture is built on a massively parallel processing (MPP) model, which enables it to distribute and process queries across multiple nodes, ensuring high performance and scalability. This makes it an ideal choice for businesses looking to derive insights from their data without the overhead of managing hardware and software infrastructure. With features like automated backups, data encryption, and seamless integration with other AWS services, Redshift provides a robust and secure platform for data warehousing needs.

Redshift's flexibility extends to its pricing model, which is based on the amount of data stored and the compute resources used, allowing businesses to optimize costs according to their specific requirements. The service supports a wide range of data formats and can easily integrate with data lakes, enabling users to query both structured and semi-structured data. Additionally, Redshift's advanced query optimization techniques and columnar storage format enhance query performance, making it suitable for complex analytical workloads. By leveraging Redshift's capabilities, organizations can transform raw data into actionable insights, driving informed decision-making and strategic planning.

Use Cases of AWS Redshift

AWS Redshift is employed across various industries for a multitude of data-driven applications. It is particularly well suited for business intelligence and analytics tasks, where companies need to process and analyze large volumes of data quickly. Retailers use Redshift to gain insights into customer behavior and optimize inventory management. In the financial sector, it supports risk analysis and fraud detection by processing vast amounts of transactional data. Healthcare organizations leverage Redshift to analyze patient records and improve treatment outcomes. Additionally, its ability to handle real-time data makes it valuable for monitoring and operational analytics. Overall, Redshift's versatility and scalability make it a powerful tool for any organization aiming to harness the power of data.

CHAPTER 3   DATA ENGINEERING

Key Components of AWS Redshift

The key components of AWS Redshift are listed below, each playing a crucial role in its data warehousing capabilities:

1. **Cluster:** A set of nodes that work together to process queries and store data, forming the core of Redshift's architecture

2. **Leader Node:** Manages client connections and query execution plans, distributing tasks to compute nodes for processing

3. **Compute Nodes:** Execute queries and perform data storage, working in parallel to enhance performance and scalability

4. **Node Slices:** Subdivisions within compute nodes that allow parallel processing of queries, optimizing resource utilization

5. **Redshift Spectrum:** Enables querying of data stored in Amazon S3, allowing seamless integration with data lakes for broader analytics

Features of AWS Redshift

AWS Redshift offers a rich array of features that make it a powerful tool for data warehousing and analytics. Below, you'll explore some of its standout features, each contributing to its robust performance and flexibility:

1. **Columnar Storage and Data Compression:** AWS Redshift employs columnar storage, which organizes data by columns rather than rows. This approach significantly reduces the amount of I/O

required during queries, enhancing performance. Additionally, Redshift uses advanced data compression techniques, allowing it to store data more efficiently. By compressing similar data types together, it minimizes storage costs and improves query speed, making it ideal for handling large datasets with complex analytical queries.

2. **Massively Parallel Processing (MPP):** Redshift's architecture is built on massively parallel processing, which enables it to distribute data and query execution across multiple nodes. This parallelization allows Redshift to process large volumes of data rapidly, ensuring high performance even with complex queries. Each node works on a portion of the data simultaneously, significantly reducing query times. This feature is crucial for businesses that require fast, scalable analytics solutions without the need for extensive infrastructure management.

3. **Redshift Spectrum for Querying S3 Data:** Redshift Spectrum extends the capabilities of Redshift by allowing users to query data directly in Amazon S3 without needing to load it into the data warehouse. This feature provides the flexibility to analyze both structured and semi-structured data across data lakes and Redshift tables. By leveraging Spectrum, organizations can efficiently handle diverse datasets, enabling them to gain insights from their entire data landscape without additional data movement or transformation.

CHAPTER 3   DATA ENGINEERING

Advantages of AWS Redshift

AWS Redshift boasts a multitude of advantages that make it a preferred choice for data warehousing and analytics. Below, you'll see some of its key benefits, each contributing to its efficiency and appeal:

1. **High Performance for Complex Queries:** AWS Redshift is engineered to deliver exceptional performance, especially for complex analytical queries. Its architecture, based on massively parallel processing and columnar storage, ensures that queries are executed swiftly and efficiently. This high performance is crucial for organizations that need to analyze large datasets and derive insights quickly, enabling them to make timely and informed decisions. Redshift's ability to handle intricate queries with ease sets it apart in the data warehousing landscape.

2. **Seamless Integration with BI Tools:** Redshift integrates effortlessly with a wide range of business intelligence (BI) tools, allowing users to visualize and analyze data with their preferred applications. This seamless integration facilitates a smooth workflow, enabling analysts and decision-makers to access and interpret data without compatibility issues. By supporting popular BI tools like Tableau, Power BI, and Looker, Redshift empowers organizations to leverage their existing analytics ecosystems, enhancing productivity and insight generation.

3. **Cost-Effective with Reserved Instances:** One of the significant advantages of AWS Redshift is its cost-effectiveness, particularly when using reserved instances. By committing to a one- or three-year term, organizations can achieve substantial savings compared to on-demand pricing. This cost model allows businesses to optimize their budget while still accessing powerful data warehousing capabilities. The flexibility of reserved instances, combined with Redshift's efficient data storage and processing, ensures that companies can scale their analytics efforts economically.

Disadvantages of AWS Redshift

While AWS Redshift offers numerous benefits, it also has certain drawbacks that users should consider. Below, some of the key disadvantages, each impacting its usability and cost-effectiveness are highlighted:

1. **Requires Careful Schema Design for Optimal Performance:** AWS Redshift necessitates meticulous schema design to achieve optimal performance. Poorly designed schemas can lead to inefficient queries and slower performance, as Redshift relies heavily on distribution and sort keys for data organization. This requirement means that database administrators must have a deep understanding of data modeling and Redshift's architecture to ensure that data is stored and queried efficiently. Without careful planning, organizations may not fully leverage Redshift's capabilities.

2. **Potentially High Costs for Large Datasets:** While AWS Redshift can be cost-effective, especially with reserved instances, managing large datasets can lead to potentially high costs. Storage and compute resources can become expensive as data volumes grow, particularly if not optimized properly. Organizations must carefully monitor and manage their Redshift usage to avoid unexpected expenses. This includes implementing data compression, archiving unused data, and regularly reviewing resource allocation to ensure that costs remain under control while meeting analytical needs.

Practical Guide to AWS Redshift

1. Log in to the AWS Console if you haven't already.
2. Search for AWS RedShift and click Redshift, then you will redirect to the page.
3. Use the Amazon Redshift console to create your cluster with a specific name, node type, and number of nodes.
4. The configuration also includes defining how the cluster will be used and setting up the admin username and password.
5. The required number of nodes varies based on the dataset size and desired query speed. After creating the cluster, go to Properties ➤ Database configurations ➤ Port to find the port value.

6. Redshift clusters have other important features to consider. A superuser has full administrative control over a cluster and can bypass any permission restrictions. Users can connect to a Redshift cluster using a username and password, and a user group is a collection of users with the same privileges. Additionally, you can adjust the size of a cluster or assign an elastic IP address if necessary.

7. Resizing a Redshift cluster involves a few steps. First, go to "Clusters" in the navigation menu, select the cluster you want to resize, then choose "Cluster" and "Resize" from the drop-down menu. Remember that resizing a cluster should be considered based on your dataset size and desired query performance. Also, note that resizing might temporarily impact the cluster's performance.

8. Attaching an elastic IP address to a Redshift cluster involves first making the cluster private. After that, make it public and add the elastic IP address. This ensures your cluster is accessible with a static IP address, which can be helpful for certain applications. Be cautious when changing the cluster's accessibility settings, as it can have security implications.

AWS Athena

AWS Athena is a powerful serverless query service that enables users to analyze data directly in Amazon S3 using standard SQL. With no need for complex infrastructure setup or management, Athena provides a

CHAPTER 3 DATA ENGINEERING

straightforward way to run queries on large datasets. It leverages a pay-per-query model, ensuring cost-effectiveness by charging only for the amount of data scanned. This makes it particularly appealing for organizations looking to perform data analysis without the overhead of managing a traditional database system. Athena's integration with AWS Glue further simplifies the process by allowing users to create a unified metadata catalog, making data easily discoverable and queryable.

Athena is built on the open source Presto engine, which supports a wide range of data formats, including CSV, JSON, ORC, Parquet, and Avro. This flexibility allows users to work with diverse datasets without needing to convert them into a specific format. Additionally, Athena is designed to handle complex queries efficiently, making it suitable for both simple and advanced analytics tasks. Its serverless nature means that users can scale their data processing needs seamlessly, without worrying about provisioning or maintaining servers. This capability, combined with its ease of use, positions AWS Athena as an essential tool for data engineers and analysts looking to derive insights from their data stored in the cloud.

Use Cases of AWS Athena and Ad Hoc Querying

AWS Athena is ideal for various use cases, including ad hoc querying, data exploration, and business intelligence. For organizations that need quick insights from their data without setting up extensive infrastructure, Athena provides an efficient solution. It allows data scientists and analysts to perform ad hoc queries to explore datasets, test hypotheses, and generate reports on the fly. This capability is particularly useful in scenarios where data is constantly changing, and timely insights are crucial. Additionally, Athena's integration with visualization tools like Amazon QuickSight enables users to create interactive dashboards, facilitating data-driven decision-making across the organization. By offering a scalable, cost-effective, and flexible querying solution, AWS Athena empowers businesses to leverage their data more effectively.

Key Components of AWS Athena

The key components of AWS Athena are listed below, each playing a crucial role in its functionality:

1. **Query Engine:** AWS Athena uses the Presto query engine, which allows users to run SQL queries on data stored in Amazon S3. This engine is optimized for performance and supports a wide range of data formats, enabling efficient data analysis.

2. **Data Catalog:** Athena integrates with the AWS Glue Data Catalog, which acts as a centralized metadata repository. This component helps organize and manage metadata, making it easier for users to discover and query datasets stored in S3.

3. **SQL Interface:** Athena provides a standard SQL interface, allowing users to leverage their existing SQL skills to interact with data. This interface simplifies the process of querying and analyzing data without requiring specialized knowledge of new query languages.

4. **Serverless Architecture:** As a serverless service, Athena eliminates the need for infrastructure management. This component allows users to focus on data analysis without worrying about provisioning or maintaining servers, enhancing operational efficiency.

CHAPTER 3   DATA ENGINEERING

Features of AWS Athena

AWS Athena offers a range of impressive features that make it a standout choice for data analysis in the cloud. The main features are elaborated below in a detailed and engaging manner:

1. **Serverless and Pay-per-Query Pricing:** AWS Athena operates on a serverless architecture, meaning there is no need for users to manage any infrastructure. This feature eliminates the complexities of provisioning and maintaining servers, allowing users to focus solely on their data analysis tasks. The pay-per-query pricing model ensures cost efficiency, as users are billed only for the amount of data scanned by their queries. This approach makes Athena an attractive option for businesses looking to optimize costs while gaining valuable insights from their data.

2. **Integration with AWS Glue Data Catalog:** Athena seamlessly integrates with the AWS Glue Data Catalog, enabling users to maintain a centralized metadata repository. This integration simplifies data management by allowing users to easily discover and query their datasets stored in Amazon S3. The Glue Data Catalog automatically catalogs and organizes data, providing a unified view of metadata across various data sources. This feature enhances data accessibility and usability, making it easier for data engineers and analysts to perform comprehensive analyses without manual data preparation.

CHAPTER 3   DATA ENGINEERING

3. **Support for Standard SQL:** Athena supports standard SQL, providing users with a familiar and powerful query language for data analysis. This feature allows data analysts and engineers to leverage their existing SQL skills to perform complex queries on diverse datasets. Athena's SQL support includes a wide range of functions and capabilities, enabling users to perform sophisticated data transformations and aggregations. By supporting standard SQL, Athena ensures a smooth learning curve and facilitates seamless integration with existing data workflows, empowering users to extract meaningful insights from their data efficiently.

Advantages of AWS Athena

AWS Athena presents a host of compelling advantages that make it an exceptional choice for cloud-based data analysis. The primary advantages are elaborated below in a detailed and engaging manner:

1. **No Infrastructure to Manage:** One of the key advantages of AWS Athena is its serverless nature, which eliminates the need for users to manage any underlying infrastructure. This means that users can focus entirely on querying and analyzing their data without worrying about provisioning, scaling, or maintaining servers. This feature significantly reduces operational overhead and complexity, allowing organizations to streamline their data analysis processes and allocate resources more efficiently.

145

2. **Quick Setup and Ease of Use:** AWS Athena offers a straightforward setup process that allows users to start analyzing their data almost immediately. With no complex configurations or installations required, users can quickly connect Athena to their data stored in Amazon S3 and begin running queries using standard SQL. This ease of use makes Athena accessible to both technical and nontechnical users, facilitating rapid adoption and enabling teams to derive insights from their data with minimal delay.

3. **Cost-Effective for Infrequent Queries:** Athena's pay-per-query pricing model makes it particularly cost-effective for scenarios involving infrequent or ad hoc queries. Users are charged only for the amount of data scanned by their queries, allowing them to control costs based on their actual usage. This model is ideal for businesses that need to perform occasional data analysis without incurring the costs associated with maintaining a dedicated data infrastructure. By optimizing costs, Athena empowers organizations to leverage their data more strategically.

Disadvantages of AWS Athena

AWS Athena, while offering numerous benefits, also has certain limitations that users should consider. The primary disadvantages are detailed below in a comprehensive and engaging manner:

1. **Potentially High Costs for Frequent Queries:**
   Although AWS Athena is cost-effective for infrequent queries, its pay-per-query pricing model can lead to high expenses when queries are run frequently. As users are billed based on the amount of data scanned, organizations with high query volumes or large datasets may find costs accumulating quickly. This can be a concern for businesses that require constant data analysis, making it important to carefully monitor query usage and optimize query efficiency to manage expenses.

2. **Limited Support for Complex Transformations:**
   Athena's strength lies in its ability to perform straightforward SQL queries, but it may struggle with more complex data transformations. While it supports a wide range of SQL functions, certain advanced data processing tasks might require additional tools or services. This limitation can pose challenges for users needing intricate data manipulations, necessitating the integration of other AWS services or third-party tools to achieve desired outcomes. As a result, users may need to plan for additional resources and workflows.

Practical Guide to AWS Athena

1. Log in to the AWS Console if you haven't already.
2. Search for AWS Athena and click Athena, then you will redirect to the page as shown in Figure 3-10.

CHAPTER 3   DATA ENGINEERING

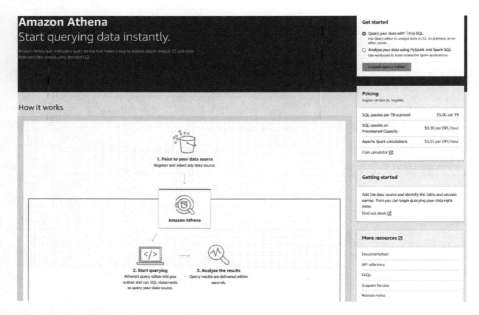

Figure 3-10. *AWS Athena landing page*

3. In the Athena console, if you're using it for the first time, click "Get Started." Then, specify the Amazon S3 location where you want to save the query results.

4. Go to the top-right corner, click the settings icon, and enter the S3 bucket path where you want to store the query results, like this: `s3://your-bucket-name/athena-results/`. Click Save to confirm the settings.

5. In the Athena Query editor, type the SQL commands "`CREATE DATABASE mydatabase`" to create a new database. After that, click "Run Query" to execute the commands.

6. You can create a table based on your S3 data using the SQL command as shown in Figure 3-11. Adjust the S3 location as necessary. After that, click "Run Query" to execute it.

```
    CREATE EXTERNAL TABLE mytable (
   id INT,
   name STRING,
   age INT
)
ROW FORMAT SERDE 'org.apache.hadoop.hive.serde2.lazy.LazySimpleSerDe'
WITH SERDEPROPERTIES (
   'serialization.format' = ','
) LOCATION 's3://your-bucket-name/data/';
```

Figure 3-11. Command to create a table for AWS Athena

7. "LOCATION" `s3://your-bucket-name/data/` – here, you can use an existing S3 bucket, or you can create a new S3 and give that location as you should have become expert now for creating S3 in AWS.

8. You can now query your data using standard SQL. For example, to retrieve all records from the table, use "`select * from mytable`".

9. Athena itself automatically saves the query results to the Amazon S3 location that is specified. You can access these results using the Amazon S3 console or AWS CLI.

Basics of Data Lake

A data lake is a centralized repository designed to store, manage, and analyze vast amounts of structured, semi-structured, and unstructured data in its native format. Unlike traditional data warehouses, data lakes allow organizations to store data without the need for a predefined schema, enabling greater flexibility and scalability. This approach supports a wide range of data types, including log files, social media feeds, images, and more, making it ideal for organizations looking to harness diverse data sources. By leveraging the ELT (extract, load, and transform) process, data lakes facilitate the storage of raw data, which can be transformed and analyzed as needed by downstream applications. This paradigm shift from the traditional ETL process allows for more efficient data processing and analysis.

In the context of AWS, data lakes are often implemented using serverless architecture, which provides several advantages. AWS services like Amazon S3, AWS Lambda, and AWS Glue are commonly used to build and manage serverless data lakes. This architecture eliminates the need for managing servers, reducing operational overhead and costs. Serverless data lakes on AWS offer scalability, flexibility, and cost-effectiveness, as resources are only utilized when needed. Additionally, AWS provides a suite of tools for data ingestion, processing, and analytics, making it easier for organizations to derive insights from their data. The serverless approach also supports rapid deployment and integration of new data sources, enabling businesses to quickly adapt to changing data requirements.

Use Cases of Data Lakes

Data lakes serve a multitude of use cases across various industries. They are particularly beneficial for organizations that need to perform advanced analytics and machine learning on large datasets. For instance, data lakes can be used to store and analyze customer behavior data, enabling companies to personalize marketing strategies and improve customer experiences. In the healthcare sector, data lakes facilitate the integration and analysis of patient records, medical images, and research data, supporting better clinical decision-making and research outcomes. Additionally, data lakes are used in financial services for risk management, fraud detection, and regulatory compliance.

The primary purpose of a data lake is to provide a flexible and scalable platform for data storage and analysis. By allowing organizations to store data in its raw form, data lakes enable data scientists and analysts to explore and analyze data without the constraints of a predefined schema. This flexibility supports a wide range of analytics, from simple reporting to complex machine learning models. Furthermore, data lakes facilitate data democratization by providing a single source of truth that can be accessed by various stakeholders within an organization. This ensures that decision-makers have access to accurate and up-to-date information, driving more informed business decisions.

Key Components of Data Lakes

The key components of a Data Lake are essential for its successful implementation and operation. Below are the main components explained briefly:

1. **Data Ingestion:** This component involves the process of importing data from various sources into the Data Lake. It ensures that data is collected in its raw form, allowing for future processing and analysis without losing any original information.

2. **Data Storage:** Data Lakes utilize scalable storage solutions to accommodate vast amounts of data in its native format. This component is crucial for maintaining flexibility and ensuring that data can be stored cost-effectively, supporting both structured and unstructured data types.

3. **Data Catalog:** A data catalog provides metadata management, helping users locate and understand the data stored within the lake. It includes data descriptions, lineage, and usage statistics, making it easier for users to find and utilize the data they need for analysis.

4. **Data Processing:** This component involves transforming and preparing data for analysis. Data processing tools and frameworks are used to clean, enrich, and organize data, enabling efficient querying and analytics.

5. **Data Security and Governance:** Ensuring data security and governance involves implementing access controls, encryption, and compliance measures. This component is vital for protecting sensitive information and ensuring that data usage adheres to organizational policies and regulatory requirements.

Features of Data Lakes

The features of Data Lakes are numerous and varied, offering a robust solution for modern data management needs. Most significant features that make Data Lakes an essential component of any data strategy are mentioned below:

1. **Scalability and Flexibility:** Data Lakes are designed to handle vast amounts of data, scaling effortlessly as data volumes grow. Their flexible architecture allows organizations to store data without a predefined schema, accommodating changes in

data structure and usage patterns. This adaptability ensures that Data Lakes can support evolving business needs and enable seamless integration with new technologies and data sources.

2. **Support for Diverse Data Types and Sources:** Data Lakes can ingest and store a wide array of data types, including structured, semi-structured, and unstructured data, from various sources. This capability allows organizations to consolidate data from disparate systems, such as databases, IoT devices, and social media platforms, into a single repository. By doing so, Data Lakes facilitate comprehensive data analysis and insight generation.

3. **Centralized Data Repository:** Acting as a centralized hub, Data Lakes provide a unified storage solution for all organizational data. This centralization eliminates data silos, ensuring that all data is accessible and available for analysis. By maintaining a single source of truth, Data Lakes enhance data governance and security, enabling better collaboration and decision-making across different departments and teams.

Advantages of Data Lakes

The advantages of Data Lakes are manifold, providing a transformative impact on data management and utilization. Some of the key advantages that highlight why Data Lakes are integral to modern data strategies are mentioned below:

1. **Cost-Effective Storage:** Data Lakes offer a cost-efficient solution for storing large volumes of data, as they utilize low-cost storage solutions to accommodate vast datasets. Unlike traditional data warehouses, which require expensive and complex infrastructure, Data Lakes allow organizations to store data in its raw form without the need for costly preprocessing. This affordability makes Data Lakes an attractive option for businesses of all sizes, enabling them to manage data growth economically.

2. **Facilitation of Advanced Analytics and Machine Learning:** By providing a centralized repository for diverse data types, Data Lakes enable organizations to perform sophisticated analytics and machine learning tasks. The ability to access raw data in its entirety allows data scientists to experiment with different models and algorithms, uncovering hidden patterns and insights. This capability supports innovation and drives data-driven decision-making, empowering businesses to gain a competitive edge through advanced analytical techniques.

3. **Easy Data Sharing and Collaboration:** Data Lakes foster a collaborative environment by making data accessible to various stakeholders within an organization. By centralizing data storage, they eliminate silos and ensure that data is readily available for analysis and sharing. This accessibility enhances teamwork and facilitates cross-departmental projects, enabling different teams to work together seamlessly. As a result, organizations can leverage collective expertise to drive innovation and improve overall efficiency.

Disadvantages of Data Lakes

The disadvantages of Data Lakes are varied, presenting challenges that organizations must navigate carefully. Some of the primary disadvantages that can impact the effectiveness of Data Lakes are listed below:

1. **Potential for Data Sprawl:** Data Lakes can lead to data sprawl, where vast amounts of unorganized data accumulate without proper management. This can result in difficulties locating and retrieving relevant data, leading to inefficiencies. Without careful oversight, the sheer volume of data can become overwhelming, diminishing the value and usability of the stored information.

2. **Challenges in Data Governance and Security:** Ensuring robust data governance and security in Data Lakes can be challenging due to the diverse and unstructured nature of the data. Implementing consistent policies and access controls is complex, potentially leading to unauthorized access and data breaches. Organizations must invest in comprehensive governance frameworks to protect sensitive information and maintain compliance with regulatory requirements.

CHAPTER 3   DATA ENGINEERING

Designing a Data Lake Architecture

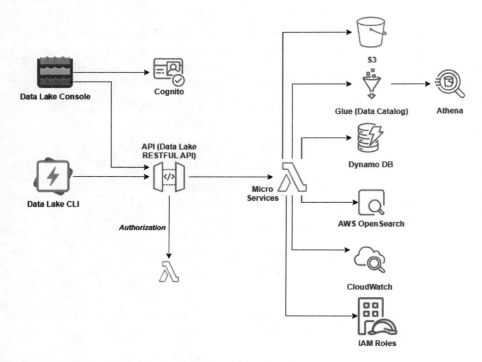

Figure 3-12. Data Lake architecture design

1. A data lake is a scalable and cost-effective solution for handling different data types as shown in Figure 3-12. It allows organizations to store raw, unprocessed data in its native format until it's needed for analysis. AWS provides several services to assist in building a data lake, including Amazon S3 for storage, AWS Glue for data cataloging and ETL, and Amazon Athena or Amazon Redshift for data querying and analysis.

156

2. The initial step in creating a data lake is bringing data in from different sources. AWS provides various options for data ingestion, including AWS Glue, AWS Data Pipeline, AWS Database Migration Service (DMS), and AWS Snowball for large-scale offline data transfer. Select the service that best suits your specific use case and data source.

3. Amazon S3 is a scalable and durable object storage service commonly used as the primary storage layer for a data lake. It provides a simple interface to store and retrieve data of any size at any time. Employ AWS S3 features such as versioning, lifecycle policies, and encryption to strengthen data security and governance. Additionally, consider partitioning and organizing data within S3 according to intended use cases to improve data management and query performance.

4. AWS Glue is a fully managed ETL service that is critical for cataloging and organizing data within a data lake. It automatically identifies and catalogs metadata about the data assets stored in various sources, enabling easy searching, querying, and analysis of the data. Utilize AWS Glue crawlers to extract schema information and keep the data catalog current.

5. Once the data is cataloged, AWS Glue can be used to transform and prepare the data. It offers a visual interface for creating ETL workflows or writing custom scripts in Python or Scala using Apache Spark. These transformations can help standardize data formats, clean and filter data, and perform aggregations or joins before loading the processed data into the data lake.

6. Data governance is essential for maintaining data quality, compliance, and security. AWS provides various security and governance features to protect your data lake, such as encryption at rest and in transit, access control through AWS Identity and Access Management (IAM) policies, and integration with AWS CloudTrail for auditing. Adhering to data lake governance best practices ensures data privacy, regulatory compliance, and appropriate data access controls.

7. AWS offers several services to analyze and explore data within the data lake. Amazon Athena provides a serverless query service that enables you to run ad hoc SQL queries directly on data stored in S3, making it easy to extract insights. For more complex analytical tasks, Amazon Redshift can be used as a highly scalable data warehouse solution.

Best Practices for Data Ingestion and Organization

The best practices for data ingestion and organization in Data Lakes are numerous and essential for maintaining a well-functioning system. Some of the key practices to ensure efficiency and effectiveness are outlined below:

1. **Strategic Planning:** Develop a clear plan for data ingestion, considering data types, sources, and use cases to prevent the data lake from becoming disorganized and ensure data accessibility.

2. **Data Visibility:** Document the ingested data, including its schema and source, to enhance transparency, prevent duplication, and support effective data governance.

3. **Data Compression and Optimization:** Apply data compression to reduce storage costs while balancing compression levels to avoid high CPU costs during querying. Organize data into partitions and use efficient file formats to improve performance.

4. **Governance and Security:** Implement strong data governance frameworks with role-based access controls and regular audits to ensure data security and compliance with regulatory standards.

Conclusion

In this conclusion, key concepts discussed in this chapter, highlighting the significance of AWS services and data lakes in the realm of data engineering are summarized here. Each point emphasizes how these tools and methodologies enhance data processing, analytics, and overall business intelligence.

1. **AWS Glue:** AWS Glue is a crucial tool in data engineering, offering a serverless ETL service that automates data preparation and integration. It simplifies workflows by efficiently handling data extraction, transformation, and loading, thus reducing processing time and effort. This flexibility allows organizations to focus on insights rather than infrastructure management.

2. **AWS Batch:** AWS Batch transforms batch processing by providing a fully managed service that runs numerous computing jobs efficiently. It dynamically allocates compute resources based on job requirements, ensuring cost-effectiveness and scalability. With seamless integration into other AWS services, AWS Batch optimizes data processing workflows without complex infrastructure management.

3. **AWS Redshift and Athena:** AWS Redshift and Athena provide robust solutions for data warehousing and analytics. Redshift offers a managed, scalable data warehouse for fast querying, while Athena allows serverless querying of data in Amazon S3 using SQL. Together, they enable efficient data analysis, supporting strategic decision-making and unlocking valuable business insights.

4. **Data Lakes:** Data lakes are essential in modern data engineering, offering a centralized repository for both structured and unstructured data. They facilitate the integration and analysis of diverse data types, supporting advanced analytics and real-time processing. By implementing data lakes, businesses can transform raw data into insights, driving informed decision-making and innovation.

CHAPTER 4

Backend Development

Introduction

In the dynamic realm of cloud computing, AWS serverless applications have emerged as a game-changing paradigm for backend development. This chapter delves into the intricate world of serverless backend architecture, unveiling a suite of powerful AWS services that empower developers to create robust, scalable, and efficient systems. At the core of this approach lies AWS Lambda Functions, enabling code execution in response to events without the burden of server management. These functions work in tandem with state machines, which orchestrate complex workflows, allowing developers to implement sophisticated processes with ease. To ensure optimal performance and resource utilization, Load Balancers play a crucial role in distributing incoming traffic across multiple instances. Security, a paramount concern in the digital landscape, is addressed through services like Certificate Manager for SSL/TLS certificate handling and Secrets Manager for safeguarding sensitive information. The chapter also explores the vital communication tools offered by AWS, including SNS (Simple Notification Service) for message fan-out and SQS (Simple Queue Service) for reliable asynchronous processing. Data management solutions are thoroughly examined, contrasting the flexibility of NoSQL databases with the structured environment of RDS (Relational Database Service). Performance optimization is further enhanced through

CHAPTER 4   BACKEND DEVELOPMENT

ElastiCache, which leverages in-memory caching to reduce latency and boost throughput. Lastly, you'll be introduced to the containerization capabilities of AWS through ECS (Elastic Container Service) and EKS (Elastic Kubernetes Service), showcasing how these tools facilitate the deployment and management of containerized applications at scale. This comprehensive exploration equips developers with the knowledge and tools necessary to harness the full potential of AWS serverless technologies in creating cutting-edge backend systems.

AWS Lambda Functions

AWS Lambda functions are a cornerstone of serverless architecture, revolutionizing the way developers approach backend development. These event-driven, scalable compute services allow you to run code without provisioning or managing servers as shown in Figure 4-1. Lambda functions execute your code only when needed and scale automatically, from a few requests per day to thousands per second. This paradigm shift enables developers to focus on writing code that delivers business value, rather than worrying about infrastructure management and scalability concerns.

In the realm of serverless applications, Lambda functions serve as the execution environment for your code. They can be triggered by various AWS services, HTTP requests via API Gateway, or custom events from your application. Lambda supports multiple programming languages, including Node.js, Python, Java, Go, and .NET, providing flexibility for developers to work in their preferred language. The service automatically handles all the underlying infrastructure, including server and operating system maintenance, capacity provisioning, automatic scaling, and logging. This abstraction of infrastructure management allows for rapid development and deployment of backend services.

CHAPTER 4 BACKEND DEVELOPMENT

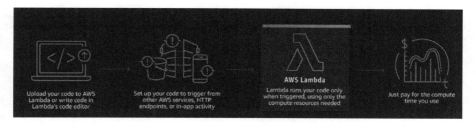

Figure 4-1. *Lambda architecture*

Use Cases for AWS Lambda Functions

AWS Lambda functions excel in scenarios that require event-driven, short-lived computations. They are particularly well suited for tasks such as real-time file processing, where Lambda can automatically process files as soon as they're uploaded to S3. Other ideal use cases include building serverless APIs, where Lambda functions handle HTTP requests, and creating scalable data processing pipelines. AWS Lambda is also excellent for automating cloud infrastructure tasks, handling scheduled jobs, and powering chatbots or voice assistants. Its ability to scale instantly makes it perfect for handling unpredictable or bursty workloads.

Key Components of AWS Lambda Functions

AWS Lambda functions consist of several essential components that work together to create a powerful serverless execution environment. Understanding these components is crucial for effectively developing and deploying Lambda-based applications. Let's explore the key building blocks that make up a Lambda function:

1. **Handler Function:** This is the heart of your Lambda function, serving as the entry point for execution. It's a method in your code that processes incoming events and returns responses. The handler function receives context about the invocation, such as the event data and runtime information. It's where you implement your core business logic, process inputs, and generate outputs. Proper structuring of the handler function is essential for optimal performance and maintainability.

2. **Event Source:** Event sources are the triggers that initiate the execution of your Lambda function. These can be diverse, ranging from HTTP requests via API Gateway to changes in your AWS resources like S3 bucket events, DynamoDB streams, or custom events from your applications. Each event source provides specific data to your function, allowing you to create event-driven architectures. Understanding and configuring event sources correctly is key to building responsive and efficient serverless applications.

3. **Execution Environment:** The execution environment is a secure and isolated runtime where your Lambda function operates. It includes the chosen programming language runtime (e.g., Node.js, Python, Java) and any additional libraries or dependencies your function requires. AWS manages this environment, ensuring it's up to date and secure. The execution environment also provides a temporary file system and environment variables, allowing you to customize the runtime behavior of your function.

4. **Configuration Settings:** These are the parameters that define how your Lambda function behaves and interacts with its environment. Key settings include memory allocation, which also affects CPU power, timeout duration to prevent long-running executions, environment variables for storing configuration data, and IAM roles for defining permissions. Proper configuration is crucial for optimizing performance, controlling costs, and ensuring your function has the necessary resources and permissions to operate effectively.

Features of AWS Lambda Functions

The key features of AWS Lambda functions are explained below:

1. **Automatic Scaling:** AWS Lambda automatically scales your application by running code in response to each trigger. Your code runs in parallel and processes each trigger individually, scaling precisely with the size of the workload, from a few requests per day to hundreds of thousands per second.

2. **Pay-per-Use Model:** With AWS Lambda, you are charged based on the number of requests for your functions and the time it takes for your code to execute. This pricing model allows for cost-effective solutions, especially for applications with variable usage patterns.

3. **Integration with AWS Services:** AWS Lambda seamlessly integrates with other AWS services, allowing you to extend other AWS services with custom logic or create full-featured backend applications. This integration enables powerful, event-driven architectures.

4. **Stateless Execution:** AWS Lambda functions are stateless by design, meaning each invocation is independent. This architecture promotes scalability and reliability, as each function execution starts with a clean slate.

Advantages of AWS Lambda Functions

The key advantages of AWS Lambda functions are explained below:

1. **Reduced Operational Complexity:** AWS Lambda eliminates the need for traditional server management tasks such as operating system maintenance, security patching, and capacity planning. This reduction in operational overhead allows developers to focus more on writing code and less on infrastructure management.

2. **Cost Efficiency:** With AWS Lambda's pay-per-use model, you only pay for the compute time you consume. There are no charges when your code isn't running, making it highly cost-effective for applications with variable traffic or intermittent processing needs.

3. **Rapid Scaling and High Availability:** AWS Lambda functions can scale almost instantaneously to match incoming request rates, handling traffic spikes effortlessly. AWS also ensures high availability by running your functions across multiple Availability Zones in a region.

4. **Ecosystem and Language Support:** AWS Lambda supports a wide range of programming languages and integrates seamlessly with numerous AWS services. This extensive ecosystem allows developers to build complex, feature-rich applications using their preferred tools and languages.

Disadvantages of AWS Lambda Functions

The major disadvantages of AWS Lambda functions are explained below:

1. **Cold Start Latency:** When a Lambda function hasn't been used recently, it may experience a "cold start," resulting in increased latency for the first invocation. This can be problematic for latency-sensitive applications.

2. **Limited Execution Duration:** AWS Lambda functions have a maximum execution time of 15 minutes. This limitation can be challenging for long-running tasks or complex processing jobs that require extended execution times.

3. **Limited Local Storage:** AWS Lambda provides limited ephemeral storage, which may be insufficient for applications requiring large amounts of local storage or those processing large files.

4. **Complexity in Managing State:** Due to their stateless nature, managing application state with Lambda can be challenging, often requiring external services like DynamoDB for state persistence.

CHAPTER 4   BACKEND DEVELOPMENT

Practical Guide to AWS Lambda Functions

1. Log in to the AWS Console if you haven't already.

2. In the search bar, type "AWS Lambda." Click the "AWS Lambda" result to access the Lambda Console.

Figure 4-2. *Lambda Console page*

3. To create a new Lambda function, click the "Create a function" button as shown in Figure 4-2. In the next step, provide a name for your Lambda function, such as "ApressFirst," and select the desired programming language and its specific version, as illustrated in Figure 4-3.

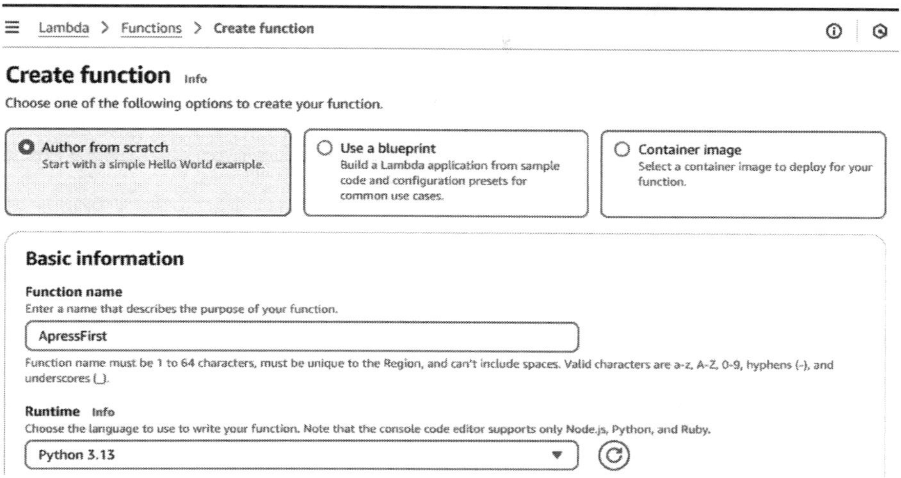

CHAPTER 4   BACKEND DEVELOPMENT

Figure 4-3.   Creating first Lambda function

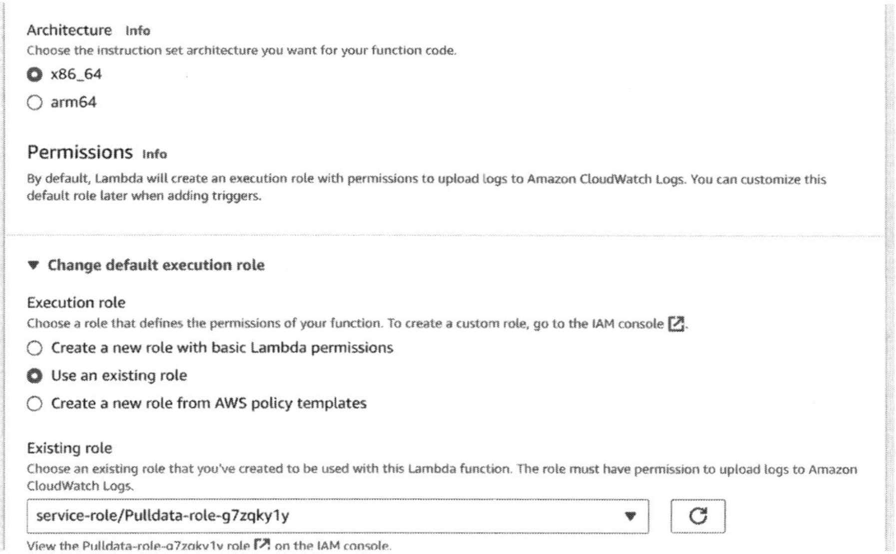

Figure 4-4.   Lambda role selection

169

CHAPTER 4 BACKEND DEVELOPMENT

4. As illustrated in Figure 4-4, you can choose the desired architecture type for your Lambda function. Additionally, you have the option to either create a new IAM role specifically for your Lambda function or select an existing role that has the necessary permissions.

5. Then click the Create function.

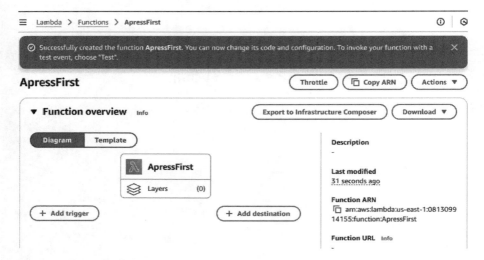

Figure 4-5. *Successful creation of a Lambda function*

6. As depicted in Figure 4-5, the system will either redirect you to a success page upon successful execution or display an error message if any issues arise.

7. In the code source section, as shown in Figure 4-6, you can write your desired code. After making your changes, deploy the updated code and then click the "Test" button to execute it. You can create a test event to test the deployed Lambda. Output of Lambda code is shown in Figure 4-7.

170

CHAPTER 4   BACKEND DEVELOPMENT

Figure 4-6. *Lambda code source console*

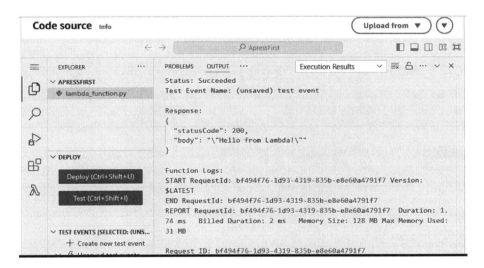

Figure 4-7. *Output of Lambda code*

171

CHAPTER 4   BACKEND DEVELOPMENT

AWS Step Functions

AWS Step Functions is a powerful serverless workflow service that enables developers to coordinate multiple AWS services into sophisticated applications. It provides a visual interface to design and run a series of interconnected steps, allowing you to create complex, multi-step processes with ease. Step Functions uses state machines, which are based on the Amazon States Language, to define your workflow as a series of states that perform specific tasks, make decisions, or handle errors.

By leveraging Step Functions, developers can build robust, scalable applications that orchestrate various AWS services, including Lambda functions, ECS tasks, and API Gateway endpoints. This service simplifies the process of managing distributed systems, handling long-running processes, and implementing complex business logic. Step Functions automatically manages state transitions, checkpoints, and restarts, ensuring that your application executes reliably and consistently, even in the face of errors or unexpected events.

Use Cases for AWS Step Functions

Step Functions excel in orchestrating complex, multi-step processes such as data processing pipelines, order fulfillment systems, and customer onboarding workflows. They are ideal for implementing long-running business processes, coordinating microservices, and managing distributed transactions across multiple AWS services. Additionally, Step Functions are valuable for error handling and retry logic in serverless architectures, as well as for implementing human-in-the-loop workflows that require manual approval or intervention steps.

Key Components of AWS Step Functions

The following are the essential components of AWS Step Functions:

1. **State Machines:** These are the core of Step Functions, defining the series of steps and logic flow of your workflow. State machines are created using Amazon States Language, a JSON-based language that describes each state, its purpose, and how it connects to other states. They can include various state types such as Task, Choice, Parallel, and more.

2. **Tasks:** These are the individual units of work within a state machine. Tasks can invoke AWS Lambda functions, run Amazon ECS tasks, call API Gateway endpoints, or interact with other AWS services. They represent the actual actions performed during the execution of your workflow.

3. **Transitions:** Defining the flow between states, transitions dictate how a workflow progresses from one stage to the next. Transitions can be based on the result of a task, a choice made in the workflow, or a predefined sequence. They control the flow of your application and determine which state is executed next.

4. **Executions:** An execution is an instance of your state machine running with specific input data. Each execution has a unique ID and maintains its own state, allowing you to track and manage multiple concurrent workflows. Executions can be started manually or triggered by events from other AWS services.

CHAPTER 4   BACKEND DEVELOPMENT

Features of AWS Step Functions

AWS Step Functions offers several key features that enhance serverless application development:

1. **Visual Workflow Designer:** Step Functions provides an intuitive, drag-and-drop interface for creating and editing state machines. This visual tool allows developers to design complex workflows without writing code, making it easier to understand and modify the application logic. The designer also generates the corresponding Amazon States Language JSON automatically, streamlining the development process.

2. **Error Handling and Retry Mechanisms:** Step Functions offers robust error handling capabilities, allowing you to define custom error states and implement retry logic. You can configure automatic retries with exponential backoff for transient errors, set up fallback states for graceful degradation, and implement catch-all error handlers to ensure your workflows are resilient and fault-tolerant.

3. **Integration with AWS Services:** Step Functions seamlessly integrates with a wide range of AWS services, enabling you to build comprehensive serverless applications. You can easily incorporate Lambda functions, ECS tasks, DynamoDB operations, and many other AWS services directly into your workflows. This tight integration simplifies the process of orchestrating complex, distributed systems across the AWS ecosystem.

4. **Parallel Execution and Branching:** Step Functions supports parallel execution of tasks and conditional branching within workflows. This allows you to design complex, multi-path processes that can execute multiple tasks simultaneously or make decisions based on the results of previous steps. Parallel execution can significantly improve the performance and efficiency of your serverless applications.

Advantages of AWS Step Functions

AWS Step Functions offers several benefits for serverless application development:

1. **Simplified Orchestration:** Step Functions streamlines the process of coordinating multiple AWS services and microservices, reducing complexity in distributed systems. It provides a centralized way to manage and monitor complex workflows, making it easier to build and maintain large-scale serverless applications.

2. **Improved Reliability:** With built-in error handling, retry mechanisms, and state management, Step Functions enhances the reliability of your serverless applications. It automatically handles failures and retries, ensuring that your workflows are resilient and can recover from transient errors without manual intervention.

3. **Visual Debugging and Monitoring:** Step Functions offers comprehensive visual tools for debugging and monitoring workflow executions. The visual interface allows developers to trace the execution path, inspect the state of each step, and quickly identify and resolve issues in complex workflows.

4. **Scalability and Cost-Effectiveness:** As a fully managed service, Step Functions automatically scales to handle varying workloads without requiring infrastructure management. You only pay for the state transitions you use, making it a cost-effective solution for orchestrating serverless applications of any size.

Disadvantages of AWS Step Functions

Despite its benefits, AWS Step Functions has some limitations:

1. **Learning Curve:** The Amazon States Language and the concept of state machines can be challenging for developers new to workflow orchestration. It may require time and effort to become proficient in designing efficient and complex workflows.

2. **Limited Language Support:** Step Functions primarily uses JSON for defining state machines, which can be verbose and less expressive than general-purpose programming languages. This may make it less flexible for implementing certain types of complex logic.

CHAPTER 4   BACKEND DEVELOPMENT

3. **Potential Costs:** While cost-effective for many scenarios, Step Functions charges per state transition. For workflows with a high number of steps or frequent executions, costs can accumulate quickly, potentially making it expensive for certain use cases.

4. **Execution Time Limits:** Step Functions has a maximum execution time of one year for standard workflows. This limitation may be problematic for extremely long-running processes that require longer execution times.

Practical Guide to AWS Step Functions

1. Log in to your AWS account using the Console.

2. In the search bar, type "Step Function." Click the "Step Function" result to access the Step Function Console as shown in Figure 4-8.

Figure 4-8. *Step Function console page*

CHAPTER 4   BACKEND DEVELOPMENT

3. To begin creating your first Step Function, click the "Get Started" button. This will take you to the page shown in Figure 4-9.

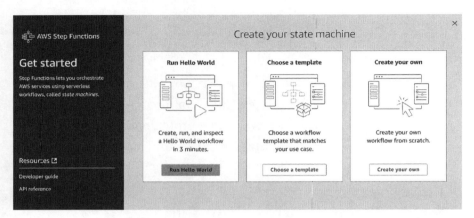

Figure 4-9. *Creating Step Function*

4. Figure 4-9 illustrates the three ways to create a Step Function: running a sample, using CF templates, or building in the console.

5. Please select "Run Hello World," which will take you to the page shown in Figure 4-10.

CHAPTER 4   BACKEND DEVELOPMENT

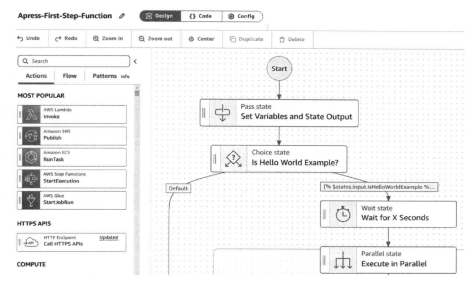

Figure 4-10. *Step Function Hello World*

6. To modify the name of your Step Function, you can either click the edit symbol or use the Config button.

7. As illustrated in Figure 4-10, you have two options for creating a Step Function: you can use the visual interface to design your workflow, or you can write the code manually. Once you've finished designing or coding your Step Function, click the "Create" button to generate the workflow.

8. Once you create successfully your Step Function, you need to start executing it as shown in Figure 4-11.

179

CHAPTER 4   BACKEND DEVELOPMENT

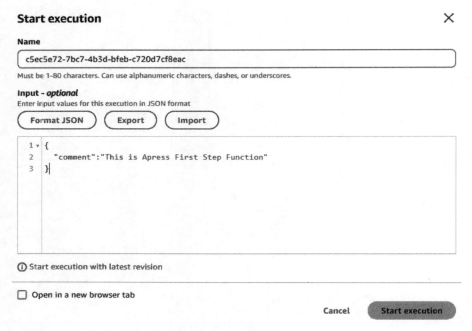

Figure 4-11. *Execution of Step Function*

9. Once you click the Start Execution, it will redirect to the Output Screen as shown in Figures 4-12 and 4-13.

CHAPTER 4 BACKEND DEVELOPMENT

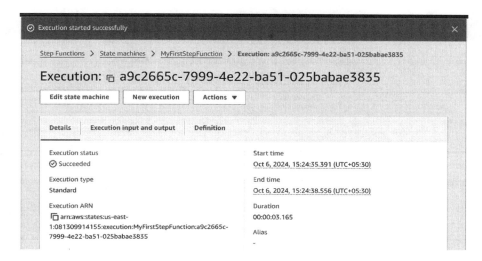

Figure 4-12. *Successful execution of Step Function*

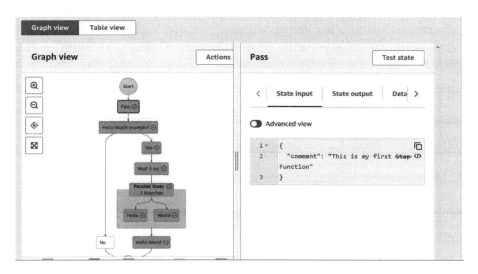

Figure 4-13. *Graph view of my Step Function*

CHAPTER 4   BACKEND DEVELOPMENT

10. In addition to the graphical view, you can also view the Step Function execution details in a table format. Furthermore, the output of each state within the workflow is displayed in the right panel, as shown in Figure 4-13.

11. You can also view each state or event details in the same page as shown in Figure 4-14.

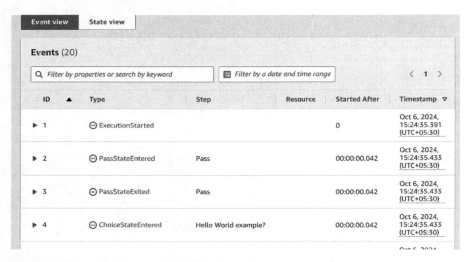

Figure 4-14. *Event view of Step Function*

12. Figure 4-15 shows the "State Machines" section where you can find your Step Functions.

182

CHAPTER 4   BACKEND DEVELOPMENT

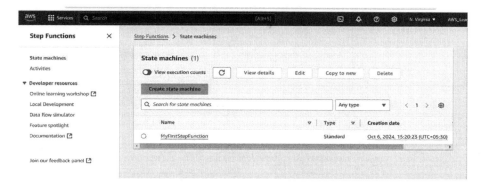

Figure 4-15. State machines list

AWS Elastic Load Balancer

In the realm of serverless applications, AWS Elastic Load Balancers (ELB) play a crucial role in ensuring efficient distribution of incoming traffic across multiple targets, such as Amazon EC2 instances, containers, and IP addresses. As a fully managed service, ELB automatically scales to meet the demands of your application traffic, providing high availability and fault tolerance as shown in Figure 4-16. By intelligently routing requests, ELB enhances the performance and reliability of your serverless architecture, allowing you to focus on developing and optimizing your application logic rather than worrying about infrastructure management.

ELB encompasses a diverse array of load balancing solutions, including Application Load Balancer (ALB), Network Load Balancer (NLB), and Classic Load Balancer (CLB). Each type is designed to cater to specific use cases and requirements, offering features like content-based routing, WebSocket support, and TCP/UDP load balancing, which is explained in detail in the next section. By leveraging ELB in your serverless applications, you can ensure seamless scalability, improved security through integration with AWS WAF (Web Application Firewall), and enhanced monitoring capabilities via Amazon CloudWatch.

183

CHAPTER 4   BACKEND DEVELOPMENT

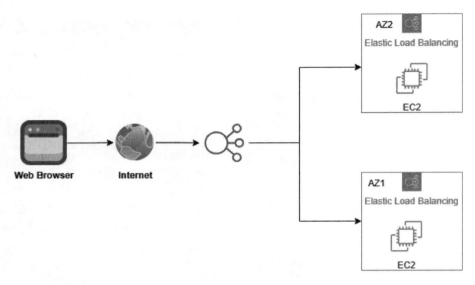

Figure 4-16. *AWS ELB architecture*

Types of AWS Elastic Load Balancers

AWS offers a diverse range of Elastic Load Balancers to cater to various application needs and architectures. Here are the three primary types:

1. **Application Load Balancer (ALB):** This advanced load balancer operates at the application layer (Layer 7) of the OSI model. ALB excels in routing HTTP/HTTPS traffic, making it ideal for modern web applications and microservices architectures. It offers content-based routing, supports WebSocket and HTTP/2 protocols, and provides enhanced metrics and access logs. ALB's ability to route requests based on URL paths, host headers, and query string parameters makes it highly flexible for complex routing scenarios.

2. **Network Load Balancer (NLB):** Designed to handle TCP, UDP, and TLS traffic at the transport layer (Layer 4), NLB is optimized for extreme performance and low latency. It can handle millions of requests per second while maintaining ultra-low latencies. NLB is particularly useful for applications that require static IP addresses for their load balancer and those that need to handle sudden, volatile traffic patterns. It's well suited for gaming applications, IoT services, and other use cases requiring high throughput.

3. **Classic Load Balancer (CLB):** As the original Elastic Load Balancer offering, CLB provides basic load balancing across multiple EC2 instances. It operates at both the application (Layer 7) and transport (Layer 4) layers. While less feature-rich compared to ALB and NLB, CLB remains a viable option for applications built within the EC2-Classic network. It's simpler to set up and manage, making it suitable for straightforward load balancing needs in legacy applications.

Use Cases for AWS Elastic Load Balancers

AWS Elastic Load Balancers are well suited for a variety of scenarios in serverless applications. They excel in distributing traffic across multiple Availability Zones, making them ideal for high-availability architectures. ELBs are particularly useful for microservices-based applications, where they can route requests to different services based on URL paths or host headers. In ecommerce platforms, ELBs can handle sudden traffic spikes during sales events, ensuring a smooth user experience. For content delivery networks, ELBs can efficiently distribute requests to the nearest content servers. Additionally, they're valuable in blue-green deployments, facilitating seamless version updates by gradually shifting traffic between old and new application versions.

Key Components of AWS Elastic Load Balancers

The following are the essential components of AWS Elastic Load Balancers:

1. **Listeners:** These components check for connection requests from clients using the configured protocol and port. Listeners define how incoming requests are evaluated and routed to the appropriate target groups based on rules, ensuring efficient traffic distribution and enabling advanced routing capabilities for your serverless applications.

2. **Target Groups:** These are logical groupings of targets, such as EC2 instances, IP addresses, or Lambda functions, to which the load balancer routes requests. Target groups allow you to configure health checks, stickiness, and load balancing algorithms, providing flexibility in managing and scaling your backend resources.

3. **Rules:** Applied to listeners, rules determine how the load balancer routes requests to the registered targets. They consist of conditions and actions, allowing you to implement complex routing logic based on various criteria such as path patterns, HTTP headers, or query string parameters, enhancing the flexibility of your serverless architecture.

Features of AWS Elastic Load Balancers

AWS Elastic Load Balancers offer several key features:

1. **Automatic Scaling:** ELBs automatically scale their capacity to handle varying levels of incoming traffic without manual intervention. This feature ensures that your serverless applications can handle sudden spikes in demand without performance degradation. The load balancer continuously monitors traffic patterns and adjusts its resources accordingly, providing a seamless experience for your users and eliminating the need for manual capacity planning.

2. **Health Checks:** ELBs perform regular health checks on registered targets to ensure they're functioning correctly. If a target becomes unhealthy, the load balancer automatically routes traffic away from it to healthy targets. This feature enhances the reliability and fault tolerance of your serverless applications by preventing requests from being sent to malfunctioning instances or services.

3. **SSL/TLS Termination:** ELBs can handle SSL/TLS encryption and decryption, offloading this computationally intensive task from your backend servers. This feature simplifies the management of SSL certificates and improves the overall performance of your serverless applications. It also enables centralized security management, allowing you to implement and update security policies at the load balancer level.

4. **Content-Based Routing:** Application Load Balancers support content-based routing, allowing you to direct traffic based on the content of the request. This feature enables advanced routing scenarios, such as routing requests to different microservices based on URL paths or implementing A/B testing. It provides greater flexibility in designing and evolving your serverless architecture without changing your backend application code.

Advantages of AWS Elastic Load Balancers

AWS Elastic Load Balancers offer several benefits:

1. **High Availability:** ELBs distribute traffic across multiple Availability Zones, ensuring your application remains accessible even if one zone experiences issues.

2. **Scalability:** They automatically scale to handle varying traffic loads, eliminating the need for manual intervention and ensuring optimal performance.

3. **Security:** ELBs integrate with AWS security features like WAF and Shield, providing robust protection against common web exploits and DDoS attacks.

4. **Simplified Management:** As a fully managed service, ELBs reduce operational overhead, allowing you to focus on application development rather than infrastructure management.

Disadvantages of AWS Elastic Load Balancers

Despite their benefits, ELBs have some drawbacks:

1. **Cost:** ELBs can be expensive for low-traffic applications, as you're charged for both running time and data transfer.

2. **Limited Customization:** While feature-rich, ELBs may not offer the level of customization required for some specialized use cases.

3. **Complexity:** Managing multiple load balancer types and configurations can be complex, especially for newcomers to AWS.

4. **Latency:** In some scenarios, ELBs may introduce a slight latency overhead, which could impact extremely time-sensitive applications.

Practice Guide to AWS Elastic Load Balancers

1. Log in to your AWS account using the Console.

2. Create at least two EC2 instances and install web server software like Apache or Nginx on each. Make sure these instances are part of the same security group, allowing inbound traffic on the port used by your web server (usually port 80 for HTTP).

3. In the AWS Management Console, go to the EC2 service. Create a target group, specifying the target type as instances, and choose the protocol and port (e.g., HTTP on port 80). Finally, register your EC2 instances with this target group. A sample dashboard is shown in Figure 4-17.

CHAPTER 4 BACKEND DEVELOPMENT

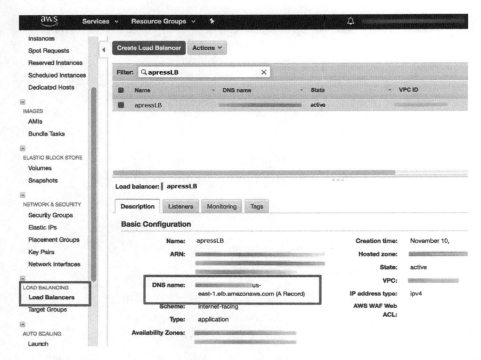

Figure 4-17. *Sample AWS ELB configuration dashboard*

4. Create an Application Load Balancer (ALB): In the AWS Management Console, go to the EC2 service. Create an Application Load Balancer (ALB) and set up listeners, such as HTTP on port 80.

5. Configure Listener Rules: Define listener rules to route incoming traffic to the target group.

6. To test your Elastic Load Balancer (ELB), open a web browser and enter the DNS name associated with your ALB. Your web application should load successfully. Additionally, check that traffic is being distributed evenly across your EC2 instances.

7. Configure health checks within the target group to monitor the health of your EC2 instances. The Elastic Load Balancer (ELB) will automatically direct traffic to instances that are deemed healthy.

8. Monitoring: Employ AWS CloudWatch to track the performance and health of your Elastic Load Balancer (ELB) and EC2 instances. Create CloudWatch alarms to enable proactive monitoring and receive notifications when specific thresholds are breached.

AWS Certificate Manager

AWS Certificate Manager (ACM) is a crucial service for securing serverless applications in the AWS ecosystem. It simplifies the process of obtaining, managing, and deploying SSL/TLS certificates, which are essential for encrypting data in transit and establishing secure connections between clients and servers. ACM integrates seamlessly with various AWS services, including API Gateway, Elastic Load Balancing, and CloudFront, making it an indispensable tool for developers building secure serverless architectures. By automating certificate management tasks, ACM reduces the complexity and potential for human error associated with manual certificate handling.

In the context of serverless applications, ACM plays a vital role in ensuring data privacy and maintaining compliance with security standards. It supports both public and private certificates, allowing developers to secure both external-facing endpoints and internal communications within their AWS infrastructure. ACM's ability to automatically renew certificates before expiration eliminates the risk of service disruptions due to expired certificates, a common issue in traditional certificate management approaches. This automated renewal process aligns perfectly with the serverless philosophy of reducing operational overhead and focusing on core application logic.

CHAPTER 4   BACKEND DEVELOPMENT

Use Cases for AWS Certificate Manager

AWS Certificate Manager is particularly well suited for several scenarios in serverless architectures. One primary use case is securing API endpoints created with Amazon API Gateway, where ACM can provide and manage SSL/TLS certificates for custom domain names. It's also ideal for securing serverless web applications hosted on AWS services like S3 and CloudFront, ensuring encrypted connections for end users. ACM shines in microservices architectures, where it can secure inter-service communications using private certificates. For serverless applications that handle sensitive data or need to comply with regulations like GDPR or HIPAA, ACM's automated certificate management ensures consistent encryption and reduces the risk of compliance violations due to expired or misconfigured certificates.

Key Components of AWS Certificate Manager

The following are the essential components of AWS Certificate Manager:

1. **Certificate Authority (CA):** ACM acts as a trusted Certificate Authority, capable of issuing both public and private certificates. For public certificates, ACM utilizes Amazon's public CA, while for private certificates, it leverages AWS Private CA. This dual capability allows for securing both public-facing and internal resources within your AWS environment.

2. **Certificate Request and Issuance:** This component handles the process of requesting and obtaining SSL/TLS certificates. For public certificates, ACM automates domain validation through DNS or email. For private certificates, it manages the entire lifecycle within your AWS account, including issuance, renewal, and revocation.

3. **Certificate Store:** ACM provides a secure, centralized repository for storing and managing your SSL/TLS certificates. This store ensures that certificates are easily accessible for use with various AWS services while maintaining strict security controls to protect sensitive certificate information.

4. **Integration Layer:** This component enables seamless integration between ACM and other AWS services. It allows services like Elastic Load Balancing, CloudFront, and API Gateway to automatically retrieve and use certificates managed by ACM, simplifying the process of securing your serverless applications.

Features of AWS Certificate Manager

AWS Certificate Manager offers several key features that enhance the security and management of SSL/TLS certificates:

1. **Automated Certificate Renewal:** ACM automatically renews public certificates issued through Amazon's public Certificate Authority before they expire. This feature eliminates the risk of service disruptions due to expired certificates and reduces the operational overhead associated with manual certificate management. For private certificates, ACM provides notifications and tools to facilitate timely renewals.

2. **Integration with AWS Services:** ACM seamlessly integrates with various AWS services, including Elastic Load Balancing, CloudFront, and API Gateway. This integration allows these services to automatically provision and use SSL/TLS certificates managed by ACM, simplifying the process of securing your serverless applications and ensuring consistent encryption across your AWS infrastructure.

3. **Support for Public and Private Certificates:** ACM can issue and manage both public and private SSL/TLS certificates. Public certificates are used for securing publicly accessible resources, while private certificates are ideal for securing internal communications within your AWS environment. This dual capability provides flexibility in addressing different security requirements within your serverless architecture.

4. **Managed Certificate Rotation:** For services that support it, ACM can automatically rotate certificates without causing downtime or requiring manual intervention. This feature ensures that your serverless applications always use up-to-date certificates, enhancing security and reducing the risk of vulnerabilities associated with outdated encryption.

5. **Centralized Certificate Management:** ACM provides a centralized console for managing all your SSL/TLS certificates across different AWS regions and accounts. This consolidated view simplifies certificate lifecycle management, allowing you to easily monitor expiration dates, track certificate usage, and manage renewals from a single interface.

Advantages of AWS Certificate Manager

AWS Certificate Manager offers several benefits for serverless applications:

1. **Cost-Effective:** ACM provides public SSL/TLS certificates at no additional cost, reducing expenses associated with certificate procurement and management.

2. **Time-Saving:** Automated certificate issuance, renewal, and integration with AWS services significantly reduce the time spent on manual certificate management tasks.

3. **Enhanced Security:** ACM's automated processes minimize human errors in certificate management, improving overall security posture.

4. **Simplified Compliance:** Automated certificate management helps maintain compliance with security standards and regulations by ensuring up-to-date encryption.

Disadvantages of AWS Certificate Manager

Despite its benefits, ACM has some limitations:

1. **AWS Specific:** ACM Certificates can only be used with AWS services, limiting flexibility for hybrid or multi-cloud architectures.

2. **Regional Restrictions:** Certificates are region specific, requiring separate management for multi-region deployments.

3. **Limited Certificate Types:** ACM primarily supports standard SSL/TLS certificates, lacking options for specialized certificate types.

Practical Guide to AWS Certificate Manager

1. ACM Certificates are digital certificates based on the X.509 version 3 standard. They are valid for 13 months. When requesting an ACM Certificate, you need to prove control over all included domain names.

2. Every ACM Certificate requires at least one fully qualified domain name (FQDN). You can add additional names for broader coverage. Wildcard certificates (*.example.com) protect all subdomains within a specific domain.

3. You cannot download the private key associated with an ACM Certificate. It's encrypted using an AWS-managed key for security. This key is unique per account and region within AWS Key Management Service (KMS).

4. Changing domain names in an existing certificate isn't possible. You need to request a new one with the desired domain. Deleting a certificate used by another AWS service requires unlinking it first.

5. Public certificates are automatically trusted by browsers and applications.

6. Private certificates require manual configuration by an administrator to establish trust.

CHAPTER 4   BACKEND DEVELOPMENT

7. Before AWS Certificate Manager (ACM) can issue a certificate for your website, it needs to confirm that you own or control the specified domain names. You can choose either email or DNS validation.

8. ACM uses CNAME records to verify domain ownership. The validation console will provide a CNAME record you need to add to your DNS settings (like Route 53).

9. ACM sends verification emails to WHOIS contacts and common system addresses for each domain. One recipient needs to click the approval link to validate.

AWS Secrets Manager

AWS Secrets Manager is a crucial service in the realm of cloud security, offering a robust solution for managing sensitive information such as database credentials, API keys, and other confidential data. This service eliminates the need for hardcoding secrets in application code or storing them in configuration files, significantly reducing the risk of unauthorized access and data breaches. By centralizing the storage and management of secrets, AWS Secrets Manager enables developers to implement best practices for security and compliance while also streamlining the process of secret rotation and access control.

The service integrates seamlessly with other AWS services and supports various types of secrets, including those for databases, APIs, and third-party applications. With features like automatic secret rotation, fine-grained access control, and encryption at rest and in transit, AWS Secrets Manager provides a comprehensive solution for organizations looking to enhance their security posture in cloud environments. This chapter will delve into the key aspects of AWS Secrets Manager, exploring its use cases, components, features, advantages, and potential drawbacks.

Use Cases of AWS Secrets Manager

AWS Secrets Manager is well suited for a variety of scenarios where secure management of sensitive information is paramount. Database credential management is a prime example, where Secrets Manager can securely store and automatically rotate database passwords, reducing the risk of unauthorized access. API key management is another critical use case, allowing developers to store and retrieve API keys securely without exposing them in code repositories. Additionally, Secrets Manager is ideal for managing credentials for microservices and serverless applications, ensuring that each component can access only the secrets it needs. It's also valuable for compliance requirements, helping organizations meet regulatory standards by providing auditable access logs and encrypted storage for sensitive data.

Key Components of AWS Secrets Manager

The key components of AWS Secrets Manager include

1. **Secret:** This is the core entity in Secrets Manager, representing the sensitive information that needs to be protected. A secret can contain multiple key-value pairs, allowing for the storage of complex credentials or configuration data. Secrets are encrypted at rest using AWS Key Management Service (KMS) and can be versioned to maintain a history of changes.

2. **Rotation:** This component enables automatic updates of secrets at regular intervals. Rotation helps maintain security by regularly changing credentials, reducing the risk of compromised secrets. AWS provides built-in rotation functions for some services, but custom rotation functions can also be implemented using AWS Lambda.

3. **Access Policy:** This component controls who can access the secrets and what actions they can perform. Access policies are defined using AWS Identity and Access Management (IAM) and can be fine-tuned to grant or restrict access based on specific conditions, ensuring the principle of least privilege.

4. **Encryption:** All secrets in AWS Secrets Manager are encrypted at rest using AWS KMS (Key Management System). This component ensures that sensitive data remains protected even if unauthorized access to the storage system occurs. The encryption keys can be managed by AWS or can be customer-managed for additional control.

Features of AWS Secrets Manager

AWS Secrets Manager offers several key features that enhance security and simplify secret management:

1. **Automatic Secret Rotation:** This feature allows for the automatic updating of secrets at regular intervals without manual intervention. It supports built-in rotation for Amazon RDS, Amazon Redshift,

and Amazon DocumentDB and allows custom rotation using Lambda functions for other types of secrets. This feature significantly reduces the risk of compromised credentials by ensuring they are regularly updated.

2. **Fine-Grained Access Control:** Secrets Manager integrates with AWS Identity and Access Management (IAM) to provide granular control over who can access secrets and what actions they can perform. This feature allows organizations to implement the principle of least privilege, ensuring that users and applications have access only to the secrets they need.

3. **Encryption and Secure Storage:** All secrets are encrypted at rest using AWS Key Management Service (KMS) and in transit using TLS. This feature ensures that sensitive information remains protected throughout its lifecycle, from storage to retrieval. Organizations can use AWS-managed keys or their own customer-managed keys for added control.

4. **Centralized Auditing and Monitoring:** Secrets Manager integrates with AWS CloudTrail to provide a comprehensive audit trail of all API calls made to the service. This feature enables organizations to monitor and track access to secrets, helping with compliance requirements and security investigations.

Advantages of AWS Secrets Manager

AWS Secrets Manager offers several key advantages:

1. **Enhanced Security:** By centralizing secret management and implementing automatic rotation, Secrets Manager significantly reduces the risk of credential exposure and unauthorized access. This centralized approach makes it easier to implement and maintain robust security practices across an organization.

2. **Simplified Compliance:** With built-in auditing and encryption features, Secrets Manager helps organizations meet various compliance requirements. It provides a clear audit trail of secret access and usage, simplifying the process of demonstrating compliance during audits.

3. **Improved Developer Productivity:** By eliminating the need for manual secret management and rotation, Secrets Manager allows developers to focus on building applications rather than managing credentials. This helps in faster development cycles which in turn reduce operational overhead.

4. **Seamless Integration:** Secrets Manager integrates well with other AWS services and third-party tools, making it easy to incorporate into existing workflows and applications. This integration capability enhances its utility across various cloud-based scenarios.

Disadvantages of AWS Secrets Manager

Despite its benefits, AWS Secrets Manager has some potential drawbacks:

1. **Cost:** For organizations with a large number of secrets, the per-secret pricing model can become expensive, especially when compared to simpler alternatives.

2. **Complexity:** The service's advanced features may introduce complexity for small projects or teams unfamiliar with AWS services, potentially leading to a steeper learning curve.

3. **AWS Dependency:** Relying heavily on Secrets Manager can increase dependency on AWS, potentially making it challenging to migrate to other cloud providers or hybrid environments.

4. **Performance Overhead:** Frequent API calls to retrieve secrets can introduce latency, which might impact application performance in scenarios requiring high-frequency secret access.

Practice Guide to AWS Secrets Manager

1. Log in to your AWS account using the Console.
2. In the search bar, type "Secrets Manager." Click the "Secrets Manager" result to access the Secrets Manager Console as shown in Figure 4-18.

CHAPTER 4　BACKEND DEVELOPMENT

Figure 4-18. *AWS Secrets Manager Console*

3. To create a new secret, click the Store a new secret button, then it will redirect to the page as shown in Figure 4-19.

Figure 4-19. *Choose secret type*

4. For Amazon RDS, Amazon Redshift, and Amazon DocumentDB credentials, choose the matching secret type. For other types of databases, choose Credentials for other databases. For any other type of secret, choose Other type of secret.

203

CHAPTER 4 BACKEND DEVELOPMENT

5. Enter the username and password that grant access to the database. These are the credentials to store in Secrets Manager as shown in Figure 4-20.

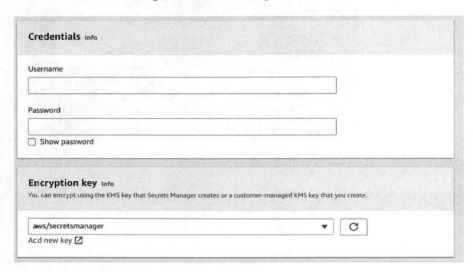

Figure 4-20. *Username and password screen*

6. If you selected the Other type of secret, then you have to provide a key-value pair as shown in Figure 4-21.

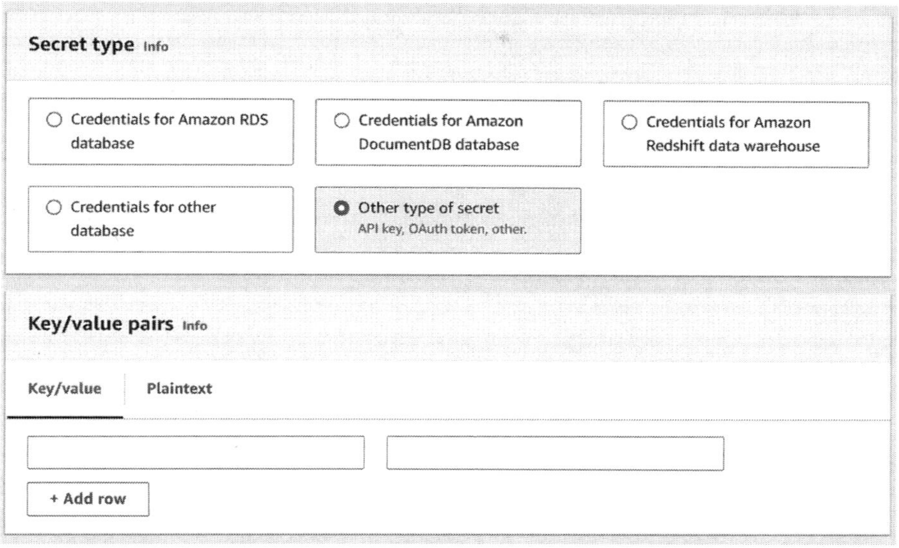

CHAPTER 4   BACKEND DEVELOPMENT

Figure 4-21.   Other type of secret

7. Next, you have to configure the secret as shown in Figures 4-22 and 4-23.

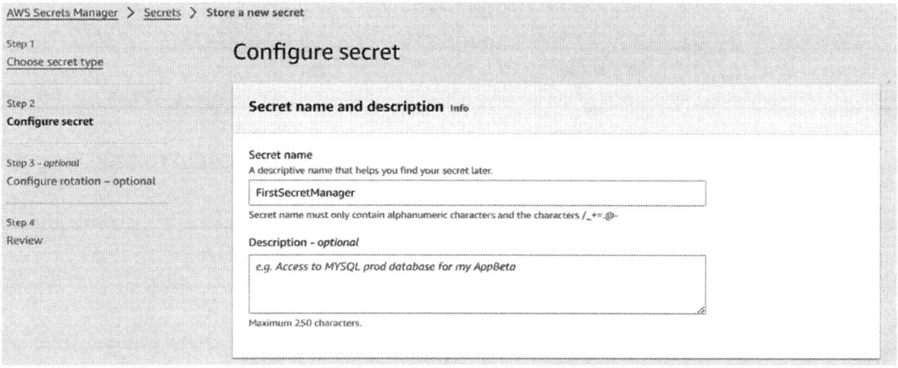

Figure 4-22.   Configure secret

205

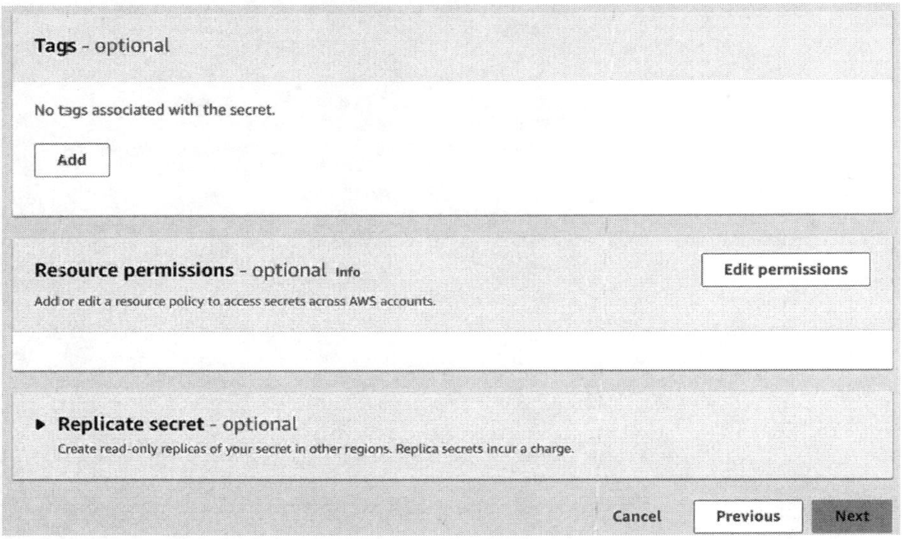

CHAPTER 4   BACKEND DEVELOPMENT

Figure 4-23. *Other options to configure secret*

8. Once you click Next, then it will redirect to the page as shown in Figure 4-24.

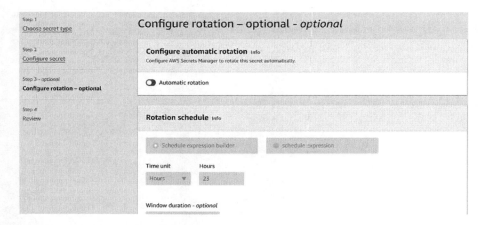

Figure 4-24. *Configure rotation*

CHAPTER 4   BACKEND DEVELOPMENT

9. Review the configuration and store the secrets as shown in Figure 4-25.

Figure 4-25. Sample code of secret

AWS Simple Notification Service

AWS's Simple Notification Service (SNS) is a crucial component in the AWS serverless ecosystem, offering a fully managed pub/sub messaging service. It enables decoupled communication between distributed systems, microservices, and serverless applications. SNS facilitates the seamless dissemination of messages to multiple subscribers, including AWS Lambda functions, HTTP/S endpoints, email addresses, and mobile push notifications. This versatility makes it an indispensable tool for building scalable, event-driven architectures in the cloud.

CHAPTER 4   BACKEND DEVELOPMENT

SNS operates on a publisher-subscriber model, where publishers send messages to topics, and subscribers receive these messages based on their subscriptions. This model allows for efficient, asynchronous communication between various components of a serverless application. By leveraging SNS, developers can create robust, loosely coupled systems that can easily adapt to changing requirements and scale effortlessly.

Use Cases for AWS Simple Notification Service

SNS finds its niche in a variety of scenarios within serverless architectures. It excels in event-driven workflows, where real-time notifications are crucial. For instance, it's ideal for sending alerts about critical system events, coordinating tasks across distributed systems, or triggering serverless functions in response to specific events. SNS is also well suited for mobile push notifications, enabling applications to engage users with timely updates. Additionally, it serves as a backbone for fan-out architectures, where a single message needs to be broadcast to multiple endpoints simultaneously, making it perfect for content distribution or multi-channel communication systems.

Key Components of Simple Notification Service

The following are the essential elements of Amazon SNS:

1. **Topics:** These are the communication channels in SNS, acting as logical access points for publishing messages. Topics allow for the organization and categorization of different message streams, enabling efficient message routing and management within the service.

2. **Publishers:** These entities send messages to SNS topics. Publishers can be various AWS services, applications, or external systems that generate events or notifications requiring distribution to multiple subscribers.

3. **Subscribers:** These are the endpoints that receive messages from SNS topics. Subscribers can include AWS Lambda functions, SQS queues, HTTP/S endpoints, email addresses, SMS numbers, and mobile push notifications, providing diverse integration options.

4. **Messages:** These are the units of data transmitted through SNS. Messages can contain any type of content, including JSON, XML, or plain text, and are delivered to all subscribed endpoints associated with the topic.

Features of Simple Notification Service

Amazon SNS offers several key features that enhance its functionality:

1. **Message Filtering:** SNS provides advanced message filtering capabilities, allowing subscribers to receive only the messages that match specific attributes or content. This feature enables fine-grained control over message delivery, reducing unnecessary processing and improving overall system efficiency. Subscribers can define filter policies using JSON, specifying conditions for message attributes.

CHAPTER 4   BACKEND DEVELOPMENT

2. **Message Attributes:** SNS supports the inclusion of metadata with messages in the form of message attributes. These attributes can carry additional information about the message, such as its priority, type, or any custom data. Message attributes are useful for implementing routing logic, filtering, and providing context to subscribers.

3. **Dead Letter Queues:** SNS integrates with Amazon SQS (Simple Queue Service) to support dead letter queues (DLQs) for undeliverable messages. If a message fails to be delivered to a subscriber after a specified number of attempts, it can be sent to a DLQ for further analysis or reprocessing, ensuring no critical information is lost.

A dead letter queue (DLQ) is a type of message queue used to store messages that cannot be processed or delivered due to errors. This helps in isolating problematic messages for further analysis and troubleshooting.

---

4. **Cross-Region Delivery:** SNS facilitates message delivery across different AWS regions, enabling the creation of globally distributed applications. This feature allows for improved disaster recovery, reduced latency for geographically dispersed users, and compliance with data residency requirements in multi-region architectures.

Advantages of Simple Notification Service

Amazon SNS offers several benefits for serverless applications:

1. **Scalability:** SNS automatically scales to handle varying message volumes, from a few messages per day to millions per second. This elasticity ensures that your application can handle sudden spikes in traffic without manual intervention or capacity planning.

2. **Reliability:** With built-in redundancy across multiple Availability Zones, SNS provides high availability and durability for your messages. It also offers at-least-once delivery semantics, ensuring that messages are not lost in transit.

3. **Ease of Integration:** SNS seamlessly integrates with various AWS services and external endpoints, making it simple to incorporate into existing architectures. This integration capability facilitates the creation of complex, event-driven workflows across different services.

4. **Cost-Effectiveness:** With a pay-as-you-go pricing model, SNS is cost-effective for both small- and large-scale applications. You only pay for the messages you publish and the deliveries made, without any upfront costs or long-term commitments.

Disadvantages of Simple Notification Service

Despite its advantages, SNS has some limitations:

1. **Message Size Limit:** SNS imposes a 256KB limit on message size, which may be restrictive for certain use cases requiring larger payloads.

2. **No Message Persistence:** Unlike queue services, SNS doesn't persist messages. If a subscriber is offline, it may miss messages published during that time.

3. **Limited Ordering Guarantees:** While SNS attempts to preserve message order, it doesn't provide strict ordering guarantees, which may be problematic for some applications.

4. **Potential for Message Duplication:** In rare cases, subscribers might receive duplicate messages, requiring idempotent processing on the receiver's end to handle this scenario.

Practical Guide to AWS Simple Notification Service

1. Log in to your AWS account using the Console.

2. In the search bar, type "Simple Notification Service." Click the "Simple Notification Service" result to access the Simple Notification Service Console.

3. Then give a topic name and click the Next Step, then it will redirect to the page as shown in Figure 4-26.

CHAPTER 4 BACKEND DEVELOPMENT

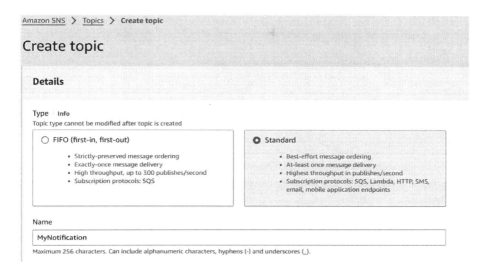

Figure 4-26. Creating topic for notification

4. Once you have created a topic in Amazon SNS, you can publish messages to that topic, and you can receive messages from a topic in Amazon SNS.

AWS Simple Queue Service

Amazon Simple Queue Service (AWS SQS) is also a fully managed message queuing service that enables decoupling and scaling of microservices, distributed systems, and serverless applications. It provides a secure, durable, and available queue for storing messages as they travel between different components of a distributed application. SQS streamlines the process of handling message-oriented communication by removing the intricacies and resource demands typically associated with maintaining such systems. This allows developers to channel their efforts toward crafting unique and valuable application features that set their products apart.

SQS offers two types of message queues: standard queues for maximum throughput and at-least-once delivery and FIFO (First-In-First-Out) queues for exact-once processing and strict message ordering. With its seamless integration with other AWS services and pay-per-use pricing model, SQS has become an essential building block for creating resilient and scalable serverless architectures. It supports various message sizes, retention periods, and encryption options, making it suitable for a wide range of use cases across different industries and application domains.

Use Cases for AWS Simple Queue Service

AWS SQS shines in scenarios where asynchronous processing, workload distribution, and system decoupling are crucial. It excels in handling traffic spikes, buffering requests, and ensuring smooth communication between application components. Common use cases include order processing systems, where SQS can queue customer orders for reliable fulfillment, even during high-traffic periods. In content management systems, SQS can manage media transcoding tasks, allowing for efficient processing of uploaded files. For IoT applications, SQS can buffer and process device data, ensuring no information is lost during peak times. Additionally, SQS is ideal for implementing job queues in distributed systems, enabling efficient task distribution among worker nodes and improving overall system scalability and fault tolerance.

Key Components of AWS Simple Queue Service

The following are the essential components of AWS SQS:

1. **Queue:** The fundamental entity in SQS, serving as a temporary repository for messages. It acts as a buffer between message producers and consumers, allowing for asynchronous communication and providing a reliable message storage mechanism.

2. **Message:** The unit of data transmitted through SQS. Messages can contain up to 256KB of text in any format, including XML, JSON, and unformatted text, allowing for versatile data exchange between application components.

3. **Producer:** The component responsible for sending messages to the queue. Producers can be various parts of an application, such as web servers, microservices, or other AWS services, that generate data to be processed asynchronously.

Features of AWS Simple Queue Service

AWS SQS offers several key features that make it a powerful tool for building distributed systems:

1. **Message Retention:** SQS can store messages for up to 14 days, ensuring that data is not lost even if consumers are temporarily unavailable. This feature enhances system reliability by providing a buffer for message processing, allowing applications to handle intermittent failures or maintenance periods without data loss.

2. **Visibility Timeout:** This feature prevents multiple consumers from processing the same message simultaneously. When a consumer retrieves a message, it becomes invisible to other consumers for a specified period, allowing the initial consumer to process and delete the message before it becomes visible again.

3. **Dead Letter Queues:** SQS supports the creation of dead letter queues to handle messages that fail to be processed after a specified number of attempts. This feature helps in isolating problematic messages for further analysis and prevents them from blocking the main queue.

4. **Batch Operations:** SQS allows sending, receiving, and deleting messages in batches, which can significantly improve throughput and reduce costs. This feature is particularly useful for high-volume applications that need to process large numbers of messages efficiently.

Advantages of AWS Simple Queue Service

AWS SQS offers several benefits that make it an attractive choice for developers:

1. **Scalability:** SQS automatically scales to handle any volume of messages without requiring manual intervention. This elasticity ensures that the service can accommodate sudden spikes in traffic or gradual increases in workload over time.

2. **Reliability:** With its distributed architecture and multiple availability zones, SQS provides high availability and durability for messages. This ensures that data is not lost even in the event of hardware failures or network issues.

3. **Cost-Effectiveness:** SQS follows a pay-per-use model, eliminating the need for upfront investments in infrastructure. Users only pay for the resources they consume, making it an economical choice for businesses of all sizes.

CHAPTER 4 BACKEND DEVELOPMENT

4. **Easy Integration:** SQS seamlessly integrates with other AWS services and supports various programming languages. This simplifies the process of incorporating message queuing into existing applications and workflows.

Disadvantages of AWS Simple Queue Service

While AWS SQS is a powerful service, it does have some limitations:

1. **Message Size Limit:** SQS has a maximum message size of 256KB, which may be insufficient for applications dealing with large payloads or complex data structures.

2. **No Message Prioritization:** Standard SQS queues do not support message prioritization, which can be a drawback for applications requiring preferential treatment of certain messages.

3. **Potential for Duplicate Messages:** In rare cases, SQS may deliver duplicate messages, requiring consumers to implement idempotent processing to handle this scenario effectively.

Practical Guide to AWS Simple Queue Service

1. Log in to your AWS account using the Console.

2. In the search bar, type "Simple Queue Service." Click the "Simple Queue Service" result to access the Simple Queue Service Console.

3. Then click the Create Queue; it will land to the page as shown in Figure 4-27.

217

CHAPTER 4 BACKEND DEVELOPMENT

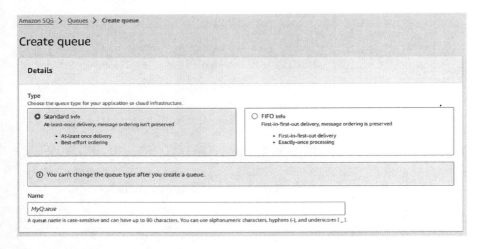

Figure 4-27. *Creating queue*

4. Give the name to your queue and then the configuration section is prefilled with default values that are suitable for basic queue operation.

5. Then select the Encryption type. When you enable server-side encryption (SSE), Amazon SQS encrypts all messages that are sent to this queue. The messages are stored in encrypted form, and Amazon SQS decrypts a message only when it is sent to an authorized consumer. SSE encrypts the body of the message, but doesn't encrypt the following fields: queue metadata (queue name and attributes), message metadata (message ID, timestamp, and attributes), and per-queue metrics.

6. Then select the access policy: The access policy defines the accounts, users, and roles that can access this queue and the actions that are allowed. You can configure basic and advanced settings.

CHAPTER 4 BACKEND DEVELOPMENT

7. The remaining configurations are optional like tags.

8. Click Create Queue.

When deciding between AWS SQS and SNS, consider the primary purpose of your messaging needs. SQS is ideal for decoupling application components and implementing asynchronous processing, where messages need to be reliably stored and processed by a single consumer. It's best suited for scenarios where you need a queue-based system for workload distribution.

On the other hand, SNS is designed for broadcast communication, where a single message needs to be distributed to multiple subscribers simultaneously. Choose SNS when you need a publish-subscribe model, such as for sending notifications or triggering multiple workflows in parallel based on a single event.

Introduction to Databases

In the realm of AWS serverless applications, databases play a crucial role in storing, retrieving, and managing data efficiently. AWS offers a diverse range of database solutions tailored to meet various application requirements, from traditional relational databases to modern NoSQL options. These services are designed to seamlessly integrate with serverless architectures, providing scalability, high availability, and performance.

When developing serverless applications on AWS, choosing the right database is essential for optimal performance and cost-effectiveness. Factors such as data structure, query patterns, scalability needs, and consistency requirements influence the selection process.

CHAPTER 4   BACKEND DEVELOPMENT

In this section, you'll explore two main categories of databases: SQL and NoSQL, each offering unique advantages for different use cases in serverless environments. In the following subsections, you'll delve into the specifics of SQL and NoSQL databases in AWS, examining their characteristics, use cases, features, advantages, and potential drawbacks.

SQL

SQL databases, also known as relational databases, utilize structured query language (SQL) for defining and manipulating data. These databases organize information into tables with predefined schemas, establishing relationships between different data entities. In AWS, SQL databases offer robust solutions for applications requiring complex queries, transactions, and strict data consistency. They excel in scenarios where data integrity and ACID (Atomicity, Consistency, Isolation, Durability) properties are paramount.

Amazon RDS (Relational Database Service) and Amazon Aurora are the primary AWS services for SQL databases, providing managed solutions for various database engines like MySQL, PostgreSQL, and Oracle.

Use Cases for SQL Databases

SQL databases in AWS are ideal for applications that demand structured data models and complex relationships. They excel in scenarios such as financial systems, ecommerce platforms, and content management systems. These databases are particularly well suited for applications requiring join operations, transactions across multiple tables, and adherence to strict data integrity rules.

Features of SQL Databases

SQL databases in AWS offer several key features:

1. **ACID Compliance:** SQL databases ensure data integrity through ACID properties, guaranteeing that transactions are processed reliably even in the event of system failures or errors.

2. **Complex Query Capabilities:** These databases support sophisticated queries, including joins across multiple tables, aggregations, and subqueries, enabling efficient data retrieval and analysis for complex data relationships.

3. **Scalability Options:** AWS provides features like read replicas and multi-AZ deployments, allowing SQL databases to scale horizontally and vertically to accommodate growing data and traffic demands.

4. **Managed Services:** AWS offers fully managed SQL database services, handling routine database tasks such as backups, patching, and high availability, reducing the operational overhead for developers.

Advantages of SQL Databases

SQL databases in AWS provide several benefits:

1. Strong data consistency and integrity, ensuring accurate and reliable data storage and retrieval for critical applications

2. Powerful querying capabilities, enabling complex data analysis and reporting through standardized SQL language

3. Mature ecosystem with extensive tools, frameworks, and community support, facilitating easier development and troubleshooting

CHAPTER 4　BACKEND DEVELOPMENT

Disadvantages of SQL Databases

Despite their strengths, SQL databases have some limitations:

1. Limited flexibility in handling unstructured or rapidly changing data models, which can be challenging for certain types of applications

2. Potential performance bottlenecks when dealing with extremely large datasets or high write throughput scenarios

3. Scaling challenges in distributed systems, as maintaining ACID properties across multiple nodes can be complex and impact performance

Practical Guide

1. `"CREATE TABLE table_name (column_name column_type constraints);"`
   column_name: Name of the particular column with any space.
   column_type: Data type of the column. A data type depends upon the data of the reference column. A data type can be char(), varchar(), int(), float(), etc.
   constraints: In order to give restrictions to a particular column, constraints are used. Constraints can be not null, primary key, foreign key, etc. These are the keywords which give a set of restrictions to the particular column.

2. `"Select * from table_name"`: To select the values from the table.

CHAPTER 4   BACKEND DEVELOPMENT

3. **Alter Table Command:** This is the DDL command (Data Definition Language) used to change the structure of the table.

   `"Alter table table_name modify column_name varchar(50) not null; "`

4. **Update Table Command:** This is the DML command (Data Manipulating Language) used to alter the records.

   `"Update table_name set column_name = 100 where column_name = "Employee_Name";"`

5. **Delete Command:** (DML command) works on the records of the table.

6. **Drop Command:** (DDL command) works on the structure of the table.

   `"delete from table_name  where column_name  = 100;"`
   `"drop table table_name;"`

NoSQL

NoSQL databases represent a departure from traditional relational models, offering flexible schemas and horizontal scalability. These databases are designed to handle large volumes of unstructured or semi-structured data, making them ideal for modern web and mobile applications. NoSQL databases in AWS provide high performance, low latency, and the ability to scale effortlessly, catering to the dynamic needs of serverless architectures.

CHAPTER 4　BACKEND DEVELOPMENT

Amazon DynamoDB is the flagship NoSQL database service in AWS, offering a fully managed, serverless database solution with seamless scalability and single-digit millisecond performance.

Use Cases for NoSQL Databases

NoSQL databases in AWS excel in scenarios requiring high scalability and flexibility. They are particularly well suited for real-time big data applications, content management systems, mobile apps, and IoT data storage. NoSQL databases shine in use cases where data models evolve rapidly, and applications need to handle diverse data types or require low-latency access to large datasets.

Features of NoSQL Databases

NoSQL databases in AWS offer several distinctive features:

1. **Flexible Schema:** NoSQL databases allow for dynamic and evolving data models, enabling developers to store and retrieve diverse data types without the constraints of predefined schemas.

2. **Horizontal Scalability:** These databases can easily distribute data across multiple servers, allowing for seamless scaling to handle increasing loads and data volumes without compromising performance.

3. **High Performance:** NoSQL databases are optimized for specific data models and access patterns, delivering low-latency reads and writes, even at scale.

4. **Serverless Operations:** AWS NoSQL services like DynamoDB offer fully managed, serverless experiences, automatically handling scaling, patching, and backups without manual intervention.

Advantages of NoSQL Databases

NoSQL databases in AWS provide several key benefits:

1. Exceptional scalability and performance for handling large volumes of data and high-velocity workloads in distributed environments

2. Flexibility in data modeling, allowing for rapid application development and easy adaptation to changing requirements

3. Cost-effective solutions for many use cases, with pay-per-use pricing models and reduced operational overhead

Disadvantages of NoSQL Databases

Despite their strengths, NoSQL databases have some limitations:

1. Limited support for complex queries and joins compared to traditional SQL databases, which can complicate certain data analysis tasks

2. Potential data consistency issues in distributed systems, as some NoSQL databases prioritize availability and partition tolerance over strong consistency

3. Lack of standardization across different NoSQL systems, which can lead to vendor lock-in and challenges in migrating between platforms

CHAPTER 4   BACKEND DEVELOPMENT

Practical Guide

1. **Create:** The Create operation enables users to insert new records into the database. It is the same as the functioning of the INSERT function in the SQL relational database application. Only an admin can add new attributes to the table, whereas a user can create rows and populate them with data corresponding to each attribute.

   For example, the dynamodb.create_table() function is used to create a table in DynamoDB.

2. **Read:** Similar to the search function, Read enables users to look up particular records in the table and access their values. Users can look for keywords or filter the data based on customized criteria to find records.

   For example, the dynamodb.get_item() function is used to read data from DynamoDB.

3. **Update:** The Update operation modifies existing records in the database. It is useful when an existing record in the database must be changed along with all the attribute values. You can update one or more existing records into the new record by using the *updateOne()* or *updateMany()* functions.

   For example, the dynamodb.update_item() function is used to update a record from DynamoDB.

4. **Delete:** Users can delete values with the Delete operation to remove records that are no longer needed. Users can delete one or more records at

a time by specifying the right functions, that is, *deleteOne()* or *deleteMany()*.

For example, the dynamodb.delete_item() function is used to delete a record from DynamoDB.

AWS ElastiCache

Amazon ElastiCache is a fully managed, in-memory caching service that seamlessly integrates with serverless architectures. It provides a high-performance, scalable, and cost-effective solution for enhancing the speed and responsiveness of applications. By storing frequently accessed data in memory, ElastiCache significantly reduces the load on backend databases and improves overall system performance.

In serverless environments, ElastiCache plays a crucial role in optimizing data retrieval and processing. It supports popular open source engines like Redis and Memcached, allowing developers to leverage familiar tools and technologies. ElastiCache's ability to handle millions of requests per second with sub-millisecond latency makes it an ideal choice for applications that require real-time data access. Moreover, its seamless integration with other AWS services, such as Lambda and API Gateway, enables the creation of highly efficient and scalable serverless architectures.

Use Cases for AWS ElastiCache

AWS ElastiCache is particularly well suited for scenarios that demand rapid data access and processing. Common use cases include session management for web applications, where user data needs to be quickly retrieved across multiple servers. It excels in caching database query results, reducing the load on primary databases and improving response times. Real-time analytics and leaderboard systems benefit from

ElastiCache's ability to handle high-velocity data streams. Additionally, it's ideal for implementing distributed locking mechanisms in microservices architectures and for storing temporary data in IoT applications. ElastiCache's versatility makes it a valuable asset in various serverless scenarios where low-latency data access is critical.

Key Components of AWS ElastiCache

The following are the essential components of AWS ElastiCache:

1. **Cache Node:** The smallest building block of ElastiCache, a cache node is a fixed-size chunk of secure, network-attached RAM. Each node runs an instance of the Redis or Memcached engine and has its own DNS name and port.

2. **Cache Cluster:** A logical grouping of one or more cache nodes. For Redis, a cluster can contain up to 500 nodes, while for Memcached, it can have up to 40 nodes.

3. **Replication Group (Redis Only):** A collection of cache clusters, with one primary cluster and up to five read replica clusters. It enables high availability and improved read performance.

4. **Parameter Group:** A named set of engine-specific parameters that can be applied to a cache cluster. It allows customization of cache behavior and performance.

Features of AWS ElastiCache

AWS ElastiCache offers several key features that enhance its functionality:

1. **Auto Discovery:** This feature automatically identifies and tracks all nodes in a cache cluster. It simplifies client configurations by eliminating the need to manually manage connection information for individual cache nodes. Auto Discovery adapts to changes in the cluster, such as node additions or removals, ensuring seamless scalability and high availability.

2. **Data Tiering (Redis):** ElastiCache for Redis supports data tiering, allowing you to store data across memory and SSD. This feature enables larger datasets to be managed cost-effectively by automatically moving less frequently accessed data to SSD storage while keeping hot data in memory for quick access.

3. **Global Datastore (Redis):** This feature enables cross-region replication, allowing you to create read replicas of your Redis cluster in different AWS regions. It provides low-latency reads and disaster recovery capabilities across geographical locations, enhancing the global reach and resilience of your applications.

4. **Encryption and Compliance:** ElastiCache offers encryption at rest and in transit, ensuring data security. It complies with various standards such as HIPAA, PCI DSS, and FedRAMP, making it suitable for applications handling sensitive data. The service also integrates with AWS Key Management Service for enhanced key management.

CHAPTER 4   BACKEND DEVELOPMENT

Advantages of AWS ElastiCache

AWS ElastiCache offers several significant benefits:

1. **Performance Boost:** ElastiCache dramatically improves application performance by reducing database load and minimizing latency. It can handle millions of requests per second with sub-millisecond response times, significantly enhancing user experience.

2. **Scalability:** The service easily scales to accommodate growing workloads, allowing you to add or remove nodes as needed without downtime.

3. **Cost-Effectiveness:** By offloading frequent queries from your primary database to ElastiCache, you can reduce the need for expensive database scaling. This not only improves performance but also leads to substantial cost savings, especially for read-heavy workloads. ElastiCache's pay-as-you-go pricing model ensures you only pay for the resources you actually use, making it an economical choice for both small- and large-scale applications.

4. **Managed Service:** As a fully managed service, ElastiCache handles time-consuming tasks such as hardware provisioning, software patching, setup, configuration, and failure recovery. This allows development teams to focus on building applications rather than managing infrastructure, significantly reducing operational overhead and accelerating development cycles.

Disadvantages of AWS ElastiCache

While AWS ElastiCache offers numerous benefits, it also has some limitations:

1. **Learning Curve:** For teams new to caching or specific engines like Redis or Memcached, there can be a significant learning curve. Understanding caching strategies and optimizing cache usage requires time and expertise.

2. **Cost for Large Datasets:** For very large datasets, the cost can escalate quickly, especially when using memory-optimized node types.

3. **Limited Customization:** As a managed service, ElastiCache restricts some levels of customization. Users cannot access the underlying EC2 instances, which may limit certain advanced configurations or optimizations that might be possible with self-managed caching solutions.

Practical Guide to ElastiCache

1. Log in to your AWS account using the Console.

2. In the search bar, type "ElastiCache." Click the "ElastiCache" result to access the "ElastiCache Console." Refer to Figure 4-28.

CHAPTER 4   BACKEND DEVELOPMENT

Figure 4-28. *ElastiCache Console*

3. Select which type of cache you want to create as shown in Figure 4-29.

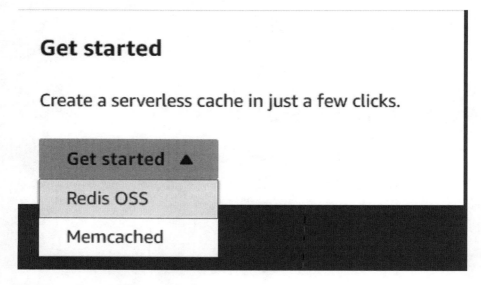

Figure 4-29. *Cache type selection*

CHAPTER 4   BACKEND DEVELOPMENT

4. If you want to create Redis, then it will land to the page as shown in Figure 4-30.

Figure 4-30. *Creating Redis cache*

5. You can configure your ElastiCache cache in two ways: create a serverless cache or design your own cache.

6. You are recommended starting with the serverless option, which simplifies creating, managing, and using a cache inside your applications. You can create a highly available cache that scales to meet your application demands in under a minute. Serverless caches are compatible with Redis 7.0 and later.

7. You can also choose to design your own cluster by selecting cache node types and sizes. When designing your own cluster, you can choose from Redis 4.0 and later.

233

CHAPTER 4 BACKEND DEVELOPMENT

8. Provide the necessary details and create the Redis cache.

9. If you select the "Memcached" option, then it will land to the page as shown in Figure 4-31.

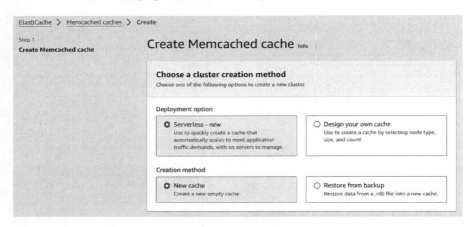

Figure 4-31. *Memcached creation page*

10. You are recommended starting with the serverless option, which simplifies creating, managing, and using a cache inside your applications.

11. You also have the option to customize your cache by selecting the configuration, entering cluster information, and specifying connectivity details.

12. Add the tags if required and then click the Create button.

CHAPTER 4   BACKEND DEVELOPMENT

Introduction to ECS and EKS in AWS

Amazon Web Services (AWS) offers two powerful container orchestration services: Elastic Container Service (ECS) and Elastic Kubernetes Service (EKS). These services provide robust solutions for deploying, managing, and scaling containerized applications in the cloud. ECS and EKS cater to different needs and preferences, allowing developers to choose the most suitable option for their serverless backend development projects.

Both ECS and EKS offer unique advantages and features that can significantly enhance the development and deployment of serverless applications. While ECS provides a simpler, more AWS-integrated approach, EKS offers the flexibility and extensive ecosystem of Kubernetes. In the following sections, you'll explore each service on a high level, discussing their ideal use cases for serverless backend development.

It's important to note that ECS and EKS are covered on a high level in this section. These services are extensive topics that could each warrant a dedicated book. For more comprehensive information and detailed documentation, please refer to the official AWS online documentation.

Amazon Elastic Container Service (ECS)

Amazon ECS is a fully managed container orchestration service that simplifies the process of running, stopping, and managing containers on a cluster. It integrates seamlessly with the AWS ecosystem, providing a secure and scalable environment for deploying containerized applications. ECS offers a user-friendly interface and streamlined workflows, making it an excellent choice for teams new to containerization or those seeking a more straightforward container management solution.

ECS supports various deployment options, including AWS Fargate for serverless container management, EC2 instances for more control over the underlying infrastructure, and ECS Anywhere for on-premises deployments. This flexibility allows developers to choose the most suitable approach for their specific backend development needs.

235

CHAPTER 4   BACKEND DEVELOPMENT

Use Cases for ECS

ECS is well suited for a variety of serverless backend development scenarios. Here are some key use cases:

1. **Microservices Architectures:** ECS excels in deploying and managing microservices-based applications, allowing easy scaling and updates of individual components.

2. **Batch Processing:** It efficiently handles batch jobs and scheduled tasks, making it ideal for data processing and analytics workloads.

3. **Web Applications:** ECS supports the deployment of scalable web applications, integrating seamlessly with other AWS services for load balancing and auto-scaling.

4. **CI/CD Pipelines:** It facilitates continuous integration and deployment workflows, enabling rapid and reliable application updates.

Amazon Elastic Kubernetes Service (EKS)

Amazon EKS is a managed Kubernetes service that simplifies the deployment, management, and scaling of containerized applications using Kubernetes. It provides a fully managed control plane, eliminating the need for users to install, operate, and maintain their own Kubernetes clusters. EKS offers the power and flexibility of Kubernetes, combined with the security, reliability, and scalability of AWS infrastructure.

EKS integrates with various AWS services, including IAM for authentication, Elastic Load Balancing for load distribution, and VPC for networking. It also supports EKS Anywhere for on-premises Kubernetes deployments and EKS on AWS Outposts for hybrid cloud scenarios.

Use Cases for EKS

EKS is particularly well suited for certain serverless backend development scenarios. Here are some primary use cases:

1. **Complex, Large-Scale Applications:** EKS excels in managing intricate, multi-component applications that require advanced orchestration capabilities.

2. **Hybrid and Multi-cloud Deployments:** It offers consistency across different environments, making it ideal for applications that span multiple clouds or on-premises infrastructure.

3. **Machine Learning Workloads:** EKS efficiently handles resource-intensive ML tasks, integrating well with GPU-enabled instances and specialized hardware.

4. **Open Source Ecosystem Integration:** It allows easy incorporation of various open source tools and frameworks from the Kubernetes ecosystem.

Conclusion

As this chapter wrap up your journey through the realm of AWS serverless backend development, let's recap the key takeaways:

1. AWS Lambda functions and state machines form the backbone of serverless architecture, enabling developers to focus on code logic rather than infrastructure management. These tools synergize to create dynamic, event-driven applications that can handle complex workflows efficiently.

CHAPTER 4   BACKEND DEVELOPMENT

2. Load Balancers, Certificate Manager, and Secrets Manager work in concert to ensure application resilience, security, and efficient resource utilization. These services are crucial for maintaining high availability and protecting sensitive data in cloud-based environments.

3. SNS and SQS provide robust messaging capabilities, facilitating seamless communication between various components of a serverless application. These services enable developers to build loosely coupled, scalable systems that can handle high volumes of data and events.

4. Data storage solutions, including NoSQL databases and RDS, offer flexibility and structure, respectively, catering to diverse application needs. ElastiCache further enhances performance by reducing data access times through in-memory caching.

5. ECS and EKS represent the next frontier in containerization, allowing for efficient deployment and management of containerized applications. These services exemplify AWS's commitment to providing cutting-edge tools for modern application development.

In conclusion, mastering these AWS serverless technologies empowers developers to create highly efficient, scalable, and secure backend systems that can adapt to the ever-evolving demands of modern cloud computing.

CHAPTER 5

Cloud DevOps

Introduction

In the realm of serverless applications on AWS, Cloud DevOps plays a pivotal role in streamlining development, deployment, and monitoring processes. This chapter delves into the core AWS services that form the backbone of a robust DevOps pipeline for serverless architectures. You'll explore AWS CodeCommit, a fully managed source control service that securely hosts Git repositories, enabling seamless collaboration among development teams. Next, you'll examine AWS CodeBuild, which automates the build and testing phases, ensuring code quality and consistency. The chapter then focuses on AWS CodePipeline, a continuous delivery service that orchestrates the entire software release process. You'll also investigate the power of Amazon CloudWatch, discussing its Alarms, Monitoring, and Dashboards features. CloudWatch Alarms provide real-time notifications for critical events, while CloudWatch Monitoring offers comprehensive insights into application performance. Finally, you'll explore how CloudWatch Dashboards enable teams to visualize and analyze key metrics at a glance. By mastering these tools, developers can create efficient, reliable, and scalable serverless applications on AWS.

CHAPTER 5   CLOUD DEVOPS

AWS CodeCommit

AWS CodeCommit is a fully managed source control service that securely hosts private Git repositories. It eliminates the need for developers to manage their own source control systems or worry about scaling infrastructure. CodeCommit seamlessly integrates with existing Git-based tools, making it a powerful addition to the AWS ecosystem for DevOps practices.

As part of the AWS suite of developer tools, CodeCommit offers high availability, durability, and scalability. It supports standard Git functionality, allowing teams to store anything from code to binaries. With features like encryption at rest and in transit, pull requests, and integration with other AWS services, CodeCommit provides a robust platform for collaborative development. Its pay-as-you-go model and automatic scaling make it an attractive option for organizations of all sizes looking to streamline their development workflows.

AWS announced that CodeCommit will no longer be available to new customers starting July 25, 2024. Existing CodeCommit users can continue using the service, but AWS does not plan to introduce new features beyond security and availability updates. For those looking to migrate away from CodeCommit, AWS recommends using alternative Git providers such as GitHub or GitLab.

AWS CodeBuild

AWS CodeBuild is a fully managed continuous integration service that streamlines the process of compiling source code, running tests, and producing deployment-ready software packages. As an integral part of modern DevOps practices, CodeBuild eliminates the need for developers to manage their own build servers, allowing them to focus on writing code and delivering features.

CHAPTER 5   CLOUD DEVOPS

This powerful service automatically scales to meet the demands of any project size, processing multiple builds concurrently to prevent bottlenecks in the development pipeline. It supports a wide range of programming languages and build environments, making it a versatile tool for teams of all sizes. By automating the build and test processes as shown in Figure 5-1, CodeBuild helps ensure consistent, reliable software releases while reducing the operational overhead associated with traditional build systems.

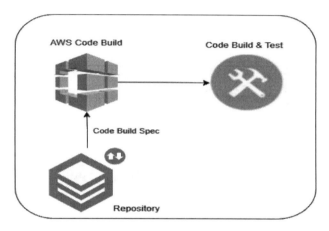

Figure 5-1. *CodeBuild architecture*

AWS CodeBuild is a build service that seamlessly integrates well with other AWS services, offering high scalability and eliminating the need to manage build servers. However, it can be complex to configure, especially with multiple AWS accounts and cross-account permissions. Jenkins, an open source automation server, provides extensive plug-in support and flexibility but requires more effort for setup and server maintenance. GitHub Actions offers an integrated experience for GitHub users, with workflows defined directly in the repository, making setup and maintenance easier. It supports multiple environments and is highly customizable.

When comparing advantages, CodeBuild is ideal for AWS-centric environments due to its seamless integration and scalability, though it may lack the flexibility of Jenkins and GitHub Actions. Jenkins is highly flexible and supports a wide range of plug-ins, making it suitable for complex CI/CD pipelines, but it demands significant maintenance. GitHub Actions is user-friendly and integrates well with GitHub, making it perfect for teams using GitHub for version control. It is easier to set up than CodeBuild and Jenkins but may not offer the same level of customization as Jenkins.

Use Cases of AWS CodeBuild

AWS CodeBuild excels in various scenarios within the software development lifecycle. It's particularly well suited for automating continuous integration and delivery (CI/CD) pipelines, enabling teams to create fully automated release processes that promote code changes through multiple deployment environments. It can replace the complexity of managing traditional build servers, allowing organizations to run existing jobs without the hassle of configuring and maintaining build nodes. Additionally, it can integrate with source code repositories, automatically initiating builds from source code and posting results back, making it an ideal choice for open source projects and collaborative development efforts.

Key Components of AWS CodeBuild

Here are the essential components:

1. **Build Projects:** Define the build environment, source code location, and build commands for each project

2. **Build Environments:** Preconfigured or custom Docker images that provide the necessary tools and runtime for building and testing code

3. **Buildspec:** A YAML file that specifies the sequence of commands to be executed during the build process

4. **Artifacts:** The output generated by the build process, which can be stored in a designated location or used in subsequent stages of a CI/CD pipeline

Features of AWS CodeBuild

AWS CodeBuild offers a range of powerful features:

1. **Automated Build Process:** The service fully automates the build workflow, including compiling code, running unit tests, performing static code analysis, and packaging deployable artifacts. This comprehensive automation ensures consistency and reliability in the software build process.

2. **Integration and Customization:** The service seamlessly integrates with various tools for end-to-end CI/CD workflows. It also supports custom build environments through Docker images, allowing teams to tailor the build process to their specific needs.

3. **Parallel and Distributed Builds:** It can execute multiple builds concurrently, significantly reducing overall build times. This feature is particularly beneficial for large projects with complex dependencies or extensive test suites.

CHAPTER 5   CLOUD DEVOPS

4. **Build Reports:** The service generates detailed reports for unit, functional, and integration tests, providing a visual representation of test results. This feature helps teams quickly identify and address issues in their codebase.

Advantages of AWS CodeBuild

AWS CodeBuild offers several benefits:

1. **Fully Managed:** As a serverless service, it eliminates the need for provisioning and managing build servers, reducing operational overhead and costs.

2. **Scalability:** The service automatically scales to handle multiple concurrent builds, ensuring that your development pipeline remains efficient even as your project grows.

3. **Cost-Effective:** With a pay-per-use model, you only incur charges for the compute resources used during builds, optimizing costs for teams of all sizes.

4. **Flexibility:** It supports a wide range of programming languages, build tools, and environments, accommodating diverse project requirements and tech stacks.

Disadvantages of AWS CodeBuild

Despite its many strengths, AWS CodeBuild has some limitations:

1. **Learning Curve:** New users may find it challenging to configure and optimize CodeBuild, especially when dealing with complex build processes or custom environments.

CHAPTER 5 CLOUD DEVOPS

2. **Limited Local Testing:** While it offers a local build simulation feature, it may not perfectly replicate the cloud environment, potentially leading to discrepancies between local and cloud builds.

3. **Vendor Lock-In:** Heavy reliance on this service and its integrations can make it difficult to migrate to alternative CI/CD solutions in the future.

Practical Guide to AWS CodeBuild

1. Log in to the AWS Console if you haven't already.

2. In the search bar, type "AWS CodeBuild." Click the "CodeBuild" result to access the CodeBuild Console as shown in Figure 5-2.

Figure 5-2. *CodeBuild Console*

3. To start a new CodeBuild project, select "Create Build Project." This will take you to the page shown in Figure 5-3.

245

CHAPTER 5   CLOUD DEVOPS

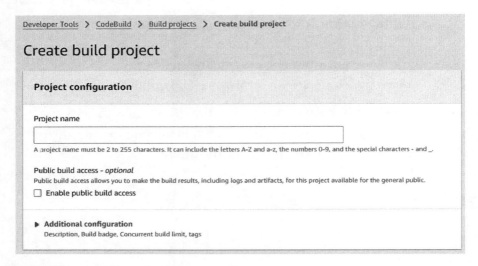

Figure 5-3.   *CodeBuild project creation*

4. Enter a name for your CodeBuild project.

5. The next step is to select the source as shown in Figure 5-4.

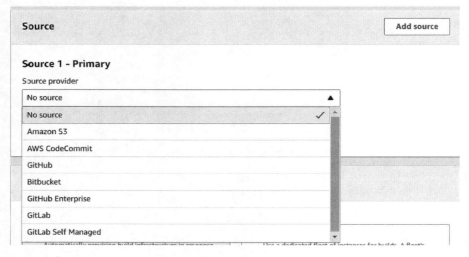

Figure 5-4.   *Source selection for build project*

246

6. You can select any source from the drop-down.

7. You can also add multiple sources for one project by clicking "Add Source."

8. The next step is to choose the environment settings for your CodeBuild project, including the compute type, operating system, runtime environment, and whether to use a new or existing role.

9. Then provide the build specifications.

10. You have the option to select S3 for storing your project artifacts and logs. This is not required, but it can be helpful. Once you've made your selections, you can create the build project.

AWS CodePipeline

AWS CodePipeline is a fully managed continuous delivery service that streamlines the software release process. It enables developers to model, visualize, and automate the steps required to release their applications and infrastructure updates. By integrating seamlessly with other AWS services and third-party tools, CodePipeline offers a flexible and scalable solution for implementing efficient DevOps practices, allowing teams to rapidly iterate on feedback and deliver new features to users faster.

With CodePipeline, teams can ensure consistent quality checks for all code changes by automating the build, test, and deployment phases. Its user-friendly interface and declarative pipeline definitions simplify the creation and management of release workflows, empowering teams to focus on innovation rather than manual processes.

CHAPTER 5   CLOUD DEVOPS

Use Cases of AWS CodePipeline

AWS CodePipeline excels in various DevOps scenarios, particularly in automating release processes for web applications, mobile apps, and microservices architectures. It's ideal for teams developing serverless applications using AWS Lambda and API Gateway, enabling continuous delivery workflows. Organizations practicing infrastructure as code benefit from CodePipeline's ability to automate testing and deployment of CloudFormation templates. It's also valuable in multi-environment setups, facilitating smooth progressions from development to staging and production environments.

Key Components of AWS CodePipeline

AWS CodePipeline comprises several essential elements:

1. **Pipeline:** Orchestrates the entire release process workflow, guiding code changes through various stages

2. **Stages:** Logical divisions within the pipeline, such as build, test, and deploy, each containing a sequence of actions

3. **Actions:** Specific tasks performed on code revisions, including building, testing, and deploying

4. **Artifacts:** Files or sets of files that actions work upon and pass between stages in the pipeline

5. **Transitions:** Connections between stages that can be enabled or disabled to control the flow of revisions.

CHAPTER 5   CLOUD DEVOPS

Features of AWS CodePipeline

CodePipeline offers a range of powerful features:

1. **Workflow Modeling:** Provides a graphical interface and CLI for creating, configuring, and managing pipelines. Users can easily visualize and model their release process workflow, defining stages and actions with flexibility.

2. **AWS Integrations:** Seamlessly integrates with various AWS services, including CodeCommit, CodeBuild, and CodeDeploy. This enables end-to-end automation of the software delivery process within the AWS ecosystem.

3. **Third-Party Integrations:** Supports integration with popular tools like GitHub and Jenkins through prebuilt plug-ins. Custom plug-ins can also be created to incorporate specialized tools into the pipeline.

4. **Parallel Execution:** Allows modeling of build, test, and deployment actions to run in parallel, significantly increasing workflow speeds and reducing overall release time.

Advantages of AWS CodePipeline

CodePipeline offers several benefits:

1. **Rapid Delivery:** Automates the software release process, enabling quick iteration on feedback and faster feature delivery to users

249

2. **Improved Quality:** Enforces consistent quality checks by automating build, test, and release processes for all code changes

3. **Flexibility:** Easily extendable to adapt to specific needs, supporting both prebuilt and custom plug-ins for various stages of the release process

4. **Visibility:** Provides detailed pipeline execution history and integrates with Amazon CloudWatch for comprehensive monitoring and troubleshooting

Disadvantages of AWS CodePipeline

Despite its strengths, CodePipeline has some limitations:

1. **AWS-Centric:** While it integrates well with AWS services, it may require additional effort to incorporate non-AWS tools and environments.

2. **Learning Curve:** Users new to AWS may face challenges in understanding the service's concepts and configuration options.

3. **Cost Considerations:** Pricing is based on active pipelines, which may impact costs for organizations with numerous pipelines or frequent executions.

Practical Guide to AWS CodePipeline

1. Log in to the AWS Console if you haven't already.

2. In the search bar, type "CodePipeline." Click the "CodePipeline" result to access the CodePipeline Console as shown in Figure 5-5.

CHAPTER 5   CLOUD DEVOPS

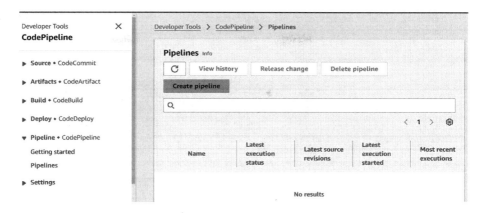

Figure 5-5.   CodePipeline Console

3. Click Create Pipeline; it will redirect to the page as shown in Figure 5-6.

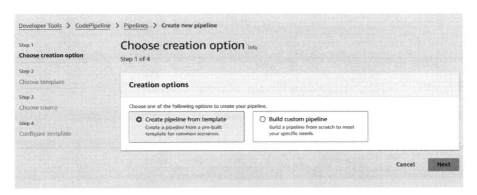

Figure 5-6.   Creation of CodePipeline

4. Either you can create a custom pipeline or you can create from an existing template.

5. To create a custom pipeline, you'll need to specify the pipeline name, execution mode, and role.

251

CHAPTER 5 CLOUD DEVOPS

6. Then you need to select the source stage, build stage, and then deploy stage; it will deploy as shown in Figure 5-7.

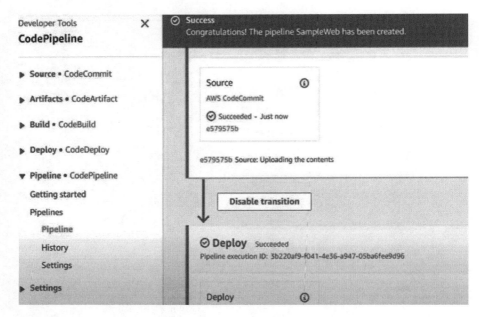

Figure 5-7. *Sample pipeline*

AWS CloudWatch Monitoring

Amazon CloudWatch is a powerful monitoring and observability service that plays a crucial role in managing serverless applications on AWS. It provides real-time insights into your application's performance, resource utilization, and operational health. By collecting and analyzing metrics, logs, and events from various AWS services, CloudWatch enables developers and operations teams to gain a comprehensive view of their serverless infrastructure.

CHAPTER 5   CLOUD DEVOPS

With CloudWatch, you can set up alarms, create custom dashboards, and automate responses to specific events or threshold breaches. This level of monitoring is essential for maintaining the reliability, scalability, and cost-effectiveness of serverless applications, allowing you to proactively identify and address potential issues before they impact your users.

Use Cases of AWS CloudWatch Monitoring

CloudWatch excels in several scenarios within the serverless ecosystem. It's particularly effective for monitoring Lambda function performance, tracking API Gateway requests, and analyzing DynamoDB table throughput. CloudWatch can help you identify cold starts in Lambda, detect abnormal API latencies, and optimize database read/write capacity. It's also invaluable for cost optimization, allowing you to track resource usage and set up alerts for unexpected spikes. Additionally, CloudWatch's ability to correlate logs and metrics makes it an excellent tool for troubleshooting complex serverless architectures, helping you quickly pinpoint the root cause of issues across multiple services.

Key Components of AWS CloudWatch Monitoring

CloudWatch consists of several essential components:

1. **Metrics:** Numerical data points representing the performance of your resources and applications over time

2. **Logs:** Text-based records of events and activities from your AWS resources and applications

3. **Alarms:** Notifications triggered when specific metrics exceed predefined thresholds

253

CHAPTER 5   CLOUD DEVOPS

4. **Dashboards:** Customizable visual representations of your metrics and logs for at-a-glance monitoring

5. **Events:** Near real-time streams of system events that describe changes in AWS resources

Features of AWS CloudWatch Monitoring

CloudWatch offers a range of powerful features:

1. **Custom Metrics:** Allows you to publish your own metrics, giving you the flexibility to monitor application-specific data points crucial for your serverless architecture

2. **Log Insights:** Enables you to perform interactive queries on your log data, helping you quickly analyze and troubleshoot issues across your serverless stack

3. **Anomaly Detection:** Utilizes machine learning algorithms to automatically identify unusual patterns in your metrics, alerting you to potential problems before they escalate

4. **Composite Alarms:** Lets you create alarms based on multiple metrics or conditions, providing a more comprehensive approach to monitoring complex serverless systems

You will see CloudWatch Alarms and Dashboards in more details in the upcoming sections.

Advantages of AWS CloudWatch Monitoring

CloudWatch offers numerous benefits for serverless application monitoring. It provides a centralized platform for observing multiple AWS services, eliminating the need for separate monitoring tools. The service's ability to automate responses to specific events or metric thresholds can significantly reduce manual intervention and improve overall system reliability. CloudWatch's integration with other AWS services, such as Lambda for custom metric publishing or SNS for alarm notifications, creates a robust ecosystem for managing serverless applications. Moreover, its pay-as-you-go pricing model aligns well with the cost-effective nature of serverless architectures.

Disadvantages of AWS CloudWatch Monitoring

While CloudWatch is a powerful tool, it does have some limitations. The service can become costly for high-volume logging or when storing metrics at fine granularity over extended periods. There's also a learning curve associated with effectively using CloudWatch, particularly when setting up complex alarms or custom metrics. Additionally, while CloudWatch provides extensive monitoring capabilities within the AWS ecosystem, it may not be as effective for monitoring external or on-premises components of hybrid architectures without additional configuration.

Practical Guide to AWS CloudWatch Monitoring

1. Log in to the AWS Console if you haven't already.
2. In the search bar, type "CloudWatch." Click the "CloudWatch" result to access the CloudWatch Console as shown in Figure 5-8.

CHAPTER 5   CLOUD DEVOPS

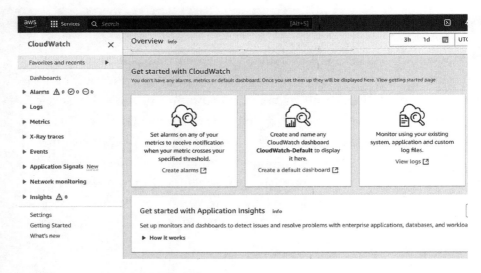

Figure 5-8. *CloudWatch Console*

3. To view the logs, click "View logs" as shown in Figure 5-8. This will take you to the Log Group screen where you can see detailed information about your services and activities.

4. You can create a log group as well for the logs.

5. You can also export the logs to our S3 bucket from the Actions tab.

6. By clicking the settings option, you can customize the view as shown in Figure 5-9.

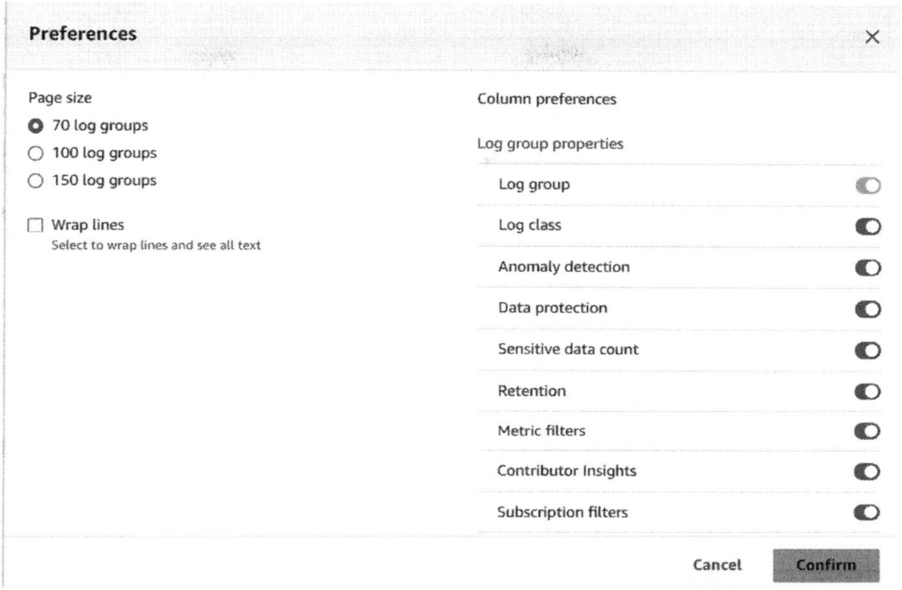

CHAPTER 5   CLOUD DEVOPS

Figure 5-9. Log screen settings

7. In Log Monitoring, you also have other options like Log Anomalies for detection using machine learning to automatically monitor your logs and surface an anomaly whenever unusual behavior such as a new ERROR message or a large increase in logs occurs as shown in Figure 5-10.

CHAPTER 5   CLOUD DEVOPS

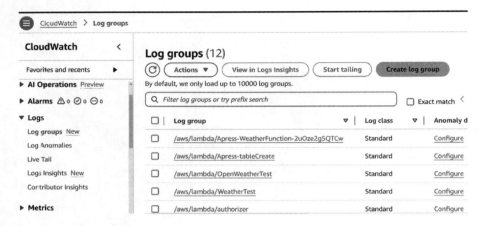

Figure 5-10. *Log groups page*

AWS CloudWatch Alarms

In the realm of serverless applications, maintaining optimal performance and reliability is crucial. AWS CloudWatch Alarms serve as a vigilant guardian, continuously monitoring your serverless resources and alerting you when predefined thresholds are breached. This powerful feature enables developers and operations teams to proactively manage their serverless infrastructure, ensuring smooth operation and minimizing downtime.

CloudWatch Alarms integrate seamlessly with various AWS services, allowing you to set up customized alerts for metrics such as Lambda function errors, API Gateway latency, or DynamoDB read/write capacity units. By leveraging these alarms, you can quickly identify and address potential issues before they impact your users, maintaining the efficiency and reliability of your serverless applications.

Use Cases of CloudWatch Alarms

CloudWatch Alarms are versatile tools that can be applied to numerous scenarios in serverless architectures. They excel in monitoring Lambda function performance, tracking API Gateway request rates, and observing DynamoDB table throughput. Alarms can be set to detect anomalies in serverless application behavior, such as unexpected spikes in error rates or unusual traffic patterns. They're particularly useful for cost optimization, alerting teams when resource usage approaches predefined limits. Additionally, CloudWatch Alarms can trigger automated responses, like scaling resources or invoking remediation Lambda functions, making them indispensable for maintaining high availability and responsiveness in serverless environments.

Key Components of CloudWatch Alarms

CloudWatch Alarms consist of several essential components:

1. **Metrics:** The foundation of alarms, representing specific data points collected from AWS resources over time

2. **Thresholds:** Predefined values that, when crossed, trigger the alarm state

3. **Evaluation Periods:** The number of consecutive time periods the metric must breach the threshold to activate the alarm

4. **Actions:** Responses triggered when an alarm changes state, such as sending notifications or executing AWS resources

CHAPTER 5   CLOUD DEVOPS

Features of CloudWatch Alarms

CloudWatch Alarms offer a range of powerful features:

1. **Metric Math Alarms:** These allow you to create alarms based on mathematical expressions involving multiple metrics, enabling more complex monitoring scenarios and providing deeper insights into your serverless application's behavior.

2. **Composite Alarms:** By combining multiple alarms using logical operators, you can create sophisticated alerting conditions that consider various aspects of your serverless infrastructure simultaneously, reducing noise and providing more meaningful alerts.

3. **Anomaly Detection:** This feature uses machine learning algorithms to analyze historical data and automatically detect unusual patterns in your metrics, helping you identify potential issues before they become critical problems.

4. **High-Resolution Alarms:** With the ability to evaluate metrics at 10-second or 30-second intervals, these alarms provide near real-time monitoring capabilities, allowing for rapid detection and response to critical changes in your serverless environment.

Advantages of CloudWatch Alarms

CloudWatch Alarms offer numerous benefits for managing serverless applications. They provide real-time monitoring and alerting, enabling quick responses to potential issues. The flexibility to set custom thresholds and actions allows for tailored monitoring solutions that align with specific application requirements. Integration with other AWS services facilitates automated remediation and scaling, enhancing overall system reliability. CloudWatch Alarms also support proactive management by identifying trends and potential problems before they escalate. Their ability to aggregate data across multiple resources provides a comprehensive view of serverless application health, simplifying complex monitoring tasks and improving operational efficiency.

Disadvantages of CloudWatch Alarms

While CloudWatch Alarms are powerful tools, they do have some limitations. The configuration process can be complex, especially for intricate monitoring scenarios, potentially leading to missed alerts or false positives if not set up correctly. There's a learning curve associated with effectively using advanced features like metric math and anomaly detection. CloudWatch Alarms may also generate additional costs, particularly for high-resolution monitoring or when dealing with large-scale applications generating numerous metrics. The default retention period for metric data is limited, which may restrict long-term trend analysis. Additionally, while CloudWatch Alarms excel at monitoring AWS resources, they may not provide comprehensive insights for all aspects of complex, distributed serverless applications without additional tooling or custom metrics.

Practical Guide to CloudWatch Alarms

1. Click Create alarms from the AWS CloudWatch Console as shown in Figure 5-8; it will redirect to the Alarms console as shown in Figure 5-11.

CHAPTER 5   CLOUD DEVOPS

Figure 5-11. *CloudWatch Alarms console*

2. Click Create alarm to create an alarm.

3. To set up an alarm, you'll need to define the metric, conditions, actions, name, and description. Once you've configured these settings, you can preview and create the alarm. The newly created alarm will be visible on the CloudWatch Alarms console page.

4. You can customize the view of Alarms by clicking the settings icon and then selecting the options as shown in Figure 5-12.

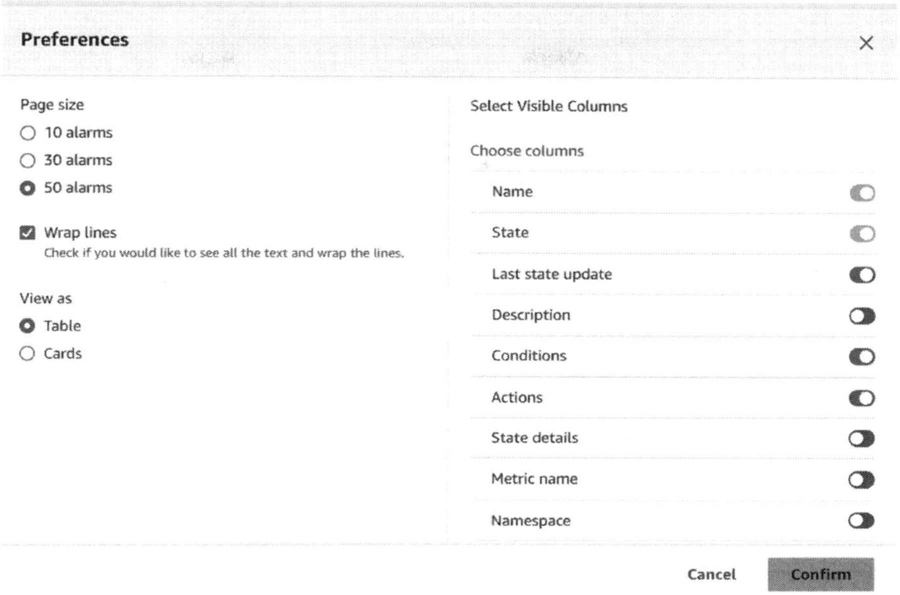

CHAPTER 5　CLOUD DEVOPS

Figure 5-12.　CloudWatch Alarms view settings

AWS CloudWatch Dashboards

Amazon CloudWatch Dashboard is a powerful tool within the AWS ecosystem that provides a centralized view of your cloud resources and applications. It allows you to create customizable, visual displays of metrics and alarms for your AWS resources, enabling real-time monitoring and troubleshooting. With CloudWatch Dashboard, you can gain valuable insights into the performance, health, and operational status of your serverless applications and infrastructure.

The dashboard provides a user-friendly and adaptable interface, enabling you to integrate various metrics, logs, and alerts into one cohesive view. This unified perspective assists DevOps teams in swiftly spotting problems, monitoring trends, and making data-driven decisions to enhance their serverless applications and maintain seamless operations within the AWS cloud environment.

CHAPTER 5   CLOUD DEVOPS

Use Cases of CloudWatch Dashboards

CloudWatch Dashboard is particularly well suited for various scenarios in serverless application monitoring and management. DevOps teams can leverage CloudWatch Dashboard to monitor the performance of Lambda functions, API Gateway endpoints, and DynamoDB tables in real time. It's ideal for tracking resource utilization, identifying bottlenecks, and optimizing costs across serverless architectures. The dashboard is also valuable for creating custom views for different stakeholders, such as executives who need high-level overviews or developers who require detailed performance metrics. Additionally, it's excellent for setting up proactive alerts and visualizing long-term trends in application behavior, enabling teams to make informed decisions about scaling and resource allocation.

Key Components of CloudWatch Dashboards

CloudWatch Dashboard comprises several essential components that work together to provide a comprehensive monitoring solution:

1. **Widgets:** These are the building blocks of a dashboard, representing various types of visualizations such as line graphs, bar charts, and number displays. Widgets can be resized and arranged to create custom layouts.

2. **Metrics:** The core data points collected from AWS services and custom applications. Metrics provide quantitative information about the performance and health of resources over time.

3. **Alarms:** Configurable thresholds that trigger notifications or automated actions when metrics exceed specified limits. Alarms help in proactive monitoring and issue resolution.

4. **Logs:** Aggregated log data from various AWS services and applications, which can be visualized and analyzed directly within the dashboard for troubleshooting and insights.

Features of CloudWatch Dashboards

CloudWatch Dashboard offers a range of powerful features to enhance monitoring and analysis:

1. **Cross-Region and Cross-Account Monitoring:** This feature allows you to create dashboards that display metrics and alarms from multiple AWS regions and accounts in a single view, providing a holistic perspective of your entire infrastructure.

2. **Auto Refresh and Time Range Selection:** Dashboards can be set to automatically refresh at specified intervals, ensuring you always have the most up-to-date information. You can also easily adjust the time range for all widgets simultaneously.

3. **Sharing and Permissions:** Dashboards can be shared with team members or external stakeholders, with granular control over permissions. This facilitates collaboration and ensures that relevant information reaches the right people.

4. **Custom Widgets:** In addition to prebuilt widgets, you can create custom widgets using math expressions, text, or even Lambda functions to display complex metrics or business-specific KPIs tailored to your needs.

CHAPTER 5   CLOUD DEVOPS

Advantages of CloudWatch Dashboards

CloudWatch Dashboard offers numerous benefits for monitoring and managing serverless applications. It provides a centralized, customizable view of your entire AWS infrastructure, enabling quick identification of issues and trends. The real-time data visualization helps in making informed decisions and reduces mean time to resolution for incidents. Its integration with other AWS services allows for seamless automation and scaling based on performance metrics. The dashboard's flexibility in creating custom views caters to different roles within an organization, from developers to executives. Additionally, the ability to correlate metrics, logs, and traces in a single interface significantly enhances troubleshooting capabilities and overall operational efficiency.

Disadvantages of CloudWatch Dashboards

Despite its many advantages, CloudWatch Dashboard has some limitations. The learning curve can be steep for users unfamiliar with AWS services or metrics. Creating complex dashboards may require significant time and expertise. While powerful, the dashboard's customization options can sometimes lead to information overload if not carefully designed. There are also constraints on the number of metrics that can be displayed simultaneously, which may be limiting for large-scale applications. Additionally, costs can accumulate quickly when monitoring numerous resources or using advanced features, potentially impacting budgets for smaller organizations.

CHAPTER 5 CLOUD DEVOPS

Practical Guide and Examples of CloudWatch Dashboards

1. Click Create a default dashboard from the CloudWatch Console as shown in Figure 5-8.

2. It will redirect to the CloudWatch Dashboard page as shown in Figure 5-13.

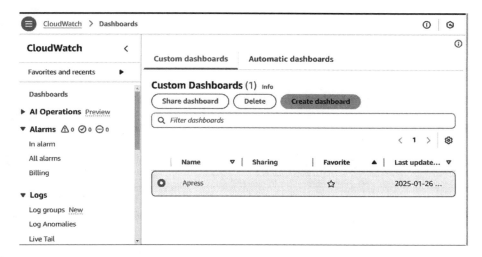

Figure 5-13. *CloudWatch Dashboard Console*

3. Click Create dashboard and then give a name to your dashboard.

4. As shown in Figure 5-14, you need to add the widgets to your dashboard.

267

CHAPTER 5   CLOUD DEVOPS

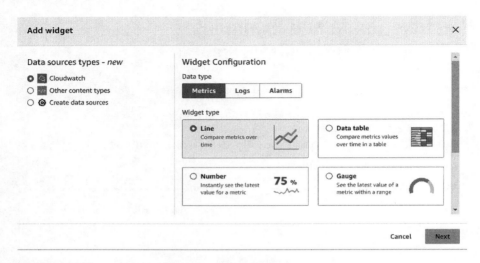

Figure 5-14. *Adding widget to dashboard*

5. If your widget's data source is CloudWatch, you'll need to specify whether the data type is metrics, as shown in Figure 5-15, logs, or alarms.

CHAPTER 5 CLOUD DEVOPS

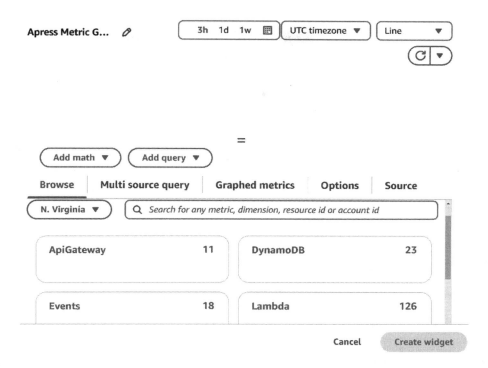

Figure 5-15. *Sample metric graph widget selection page*

6. You can also create your own data source as shown in Figure 5-16.

269

CHAPTER 5   CLOUD DEVOPS

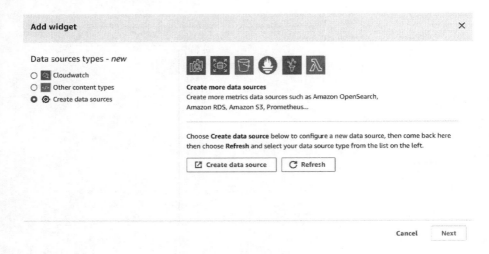

Figure 5-16. *Creating a data source for conclusion*

Conclusion

As you conclude our exploration of AWS Cloud DevOps for serverless applications, let's summarize the essential insights:

1. AWS CodeCommit enhances collaboration and version control, providing a secure and scalable repository for serverless application code. It integrates seamlessly with other AWS services, enabling teams to maintain code integrity and track changes effectively throughout the development lifecycle.

2. AWS CodeBuild automates the build and testing processes, significantly reducing manual errors and improving overall code quality. By leveraging AWS CodeBuild, teams can ensure consistent builds across different environments and catch potential issues early in the development cycle.

CHAPTER 5   CLOUD DEVOPS

3. AWS CodePipeline orchestrates the entire CI/CD workflow, automating the software release process from source control to production deployment. This service enables rapid and reliable delivery of new features, allowing teams to respond quickly to user feedback and market demands.

4. AWS CloudWatch Alarms provide proactive monitoring and alerting capabilities, enabling teams to respond swiftly to critical events in their serverless applications. By setting up appropriate alarms, developers can ensure high availability and performance of their applications.

5. AWS CloudWatch Monitoring offers comprehensive insights into application performance, resource utilization, and user behavior. This feature allows teams to identify bottlenecks, optimize resource allocation, and make data-driven decisions to improve application efficiency and user experience.

6. AWS CloudWatch Dashboards provide a centralized view of key metrics and logs, enabling teams to visualize and analyze application performance at a glance. These customizable dashboards help in identifying trends, troubleshooting issues, and making informed decisions about application scaling and optimization.

In essence, the synergy of these AWS services creates a formidable Cloud DevOps ecosystem, empowering teams to construct, deploy, and monitor serverless applications with unparalleled efficiency and dependability.

CHAPTER 6

Getting Hands-On: Creating First Serverless Application

Introduction

Welcome to the final chapter of *Practical Serverless Applications with AWS*!

In this chapter, we'll embark on a practical journey to create your first serverless application from scratch. By the end of this chapter, you'll have a fully functional, scalable, and cost-effective solution deployed in the AWS cloud.

The goal is to guide you through the entire lifecycle of a serverless application, from understanding the problem statement to monitoring the deployed solution. We'll leverage various AWS services, including Lambda, API Gateway, DynamoDB, CloudWatch, and more, to build a robust and efficient application. We'll focus on using the services which we have already gone through in the previous chapters of this book.

We'll start by clearly defining the problem statement, ensuring we have a solid foundation for the solution. Then, we'll dive into the design phase, where we'll architect our serverless application using best practices and AWS-recommended patterns. With our design in place, we'll meticulously plan our implementation, breaking down the project into manageable tasks. The heart of this chapter lies in the implementation phase, where we'll write code, configure AWS services, and bring our serverless application to life.

By the end of this hands-on chapter, you'll have gained practical experience in building, deploying, and monitoring a serverless application on AWS, setting you up for success in your serverless journey.

Understanding the Problem Statement

You are going to design a serverless weather information system that provides weather data based on postal codes (PIN/ZIP codes). This system will serve as a practical demonstration of AWS serverless architecture.

The system consists of several key components that work together:

1. An OpenWeatherAPI integration for fetching current weather data
2. A Lambda function to process and transform the weather information
3. A database for persistent storage
4. An S3 bucket for file storage
5. A secure API Gateway for client access
6. CloudWatch for monitoring and logging

CHAPTER 6   GETTING HANDS-ON: CREATING FIRST SERVERLESS APPLICATION

The system will

1. Fetch corresponding weather data from the OpenWeatherAPI based on the list of available uploaded in the S3 bucket

2. Process and store the weather information in a database

3. Accept city name inputs through an API endpoint

4. Fetch corresponding weather data from the database

5. Return formatted weather data to end users

6. Maintain logs and configurations for system management

Designing the Solution

In designing our serverless weather application on AWS, we'll follow a structured approach that emphasizes scalability and efficiency. The solution architecture centers around a Lambda function that serves as the core processor, interacting with the OpenWeatherAPI to fetch weather data based on county name. As shown in Figure 6-1, this design incorporates various essential AWS services. By leveraging these serverless components, we create a robust system that automatically scales with demand while maintaining cost efficiency and performance. Let's have a look in detail.

CHAPTER 6   GETTING HANDS-ON: CREATING FIRST SERVERLESS APPLICATION

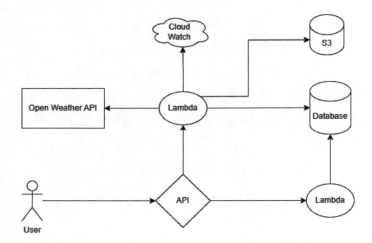

Figure 6-1. Solution diagram

System Architecture Components

1. The system begins with an OpenWeatherAPI integration that serves as the external data source for retrieving near real-time weather information.

2. A Lambda function processes incoming requests and handles the data transformation, acting as the central processing unit of the system.

3. The processed data is stored in an RDS MySQL database, which provides persistent storage and efficient data retrieval capabilities.

4. CloudWatch is implemented for comprehensive monitoring and logging of the entire system's operations.

5. An S3 bucket is used to maintain the City list csv file.

6. DynamoDB is used to store the city list from which lambda will list the city and request for weather report from the OpenWeatherAPI.

CHAPTER 6   GETTING HANDS-ON: CREATING FIRST SERVERLESS APPLICATION

7. The system exposes its functionality through an API Gateway that provides secure endpoints for client access.

8. Security is enforced through security groups, IAM roles, policies, subnet configurations, and VPC settings to ensure proper access control and network isolation.

Data Flow

1. The "csvprocessing" Lambda function retrieves CSV data from Amazon S3 and subsequently stores the "City Code" and "City Name" attributes within an Amazon DynamoDB table.

2. The "fetchweatherdata" Lambda function retrieves the city name from the DynamoDB table. Subsequently, it utilizes the "OpenWeatherAPI" to acquire the corresponding weather data, which is then persisted within the MySQL database table.

3. CloudWatch initiates the data retrieval from the OpenWeatherAPI periodically.

4. Users initiate requests by providing a city name and the authorization key through the API Gateway endpoint.

5. The Lambda function retrieves corresponding weather data from the MySQL database for the specified location.

6. After successful data retrieval, the Lambda function processes and transforms the weather information into a structured API response format.

CHAPTER 6   GETTING HANDS-ON: CREATING FIRST SERVERLESS APPLICATION

7. The system returns formatted weather information to end users through the API Gateway while maintaining proper security protocols

Planning the Implementation

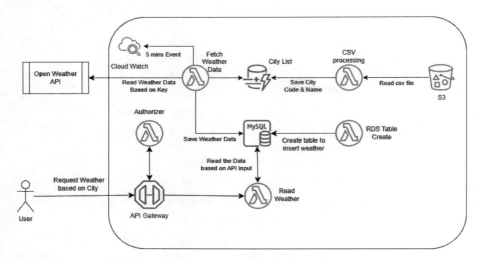

***Figure 6-2.** Overall infrastructure architecture*

Figure 6-2 shows the overall infrastructure architecture of the implementation. To begin implementing this solution, start by logging in to the AWS Console using your credentials. Once logged in, you'll need to provision all the required AWS resources as outlined in the infrastructure architecture for this implementation. You have two options for creating these resources: using CloudFormation templates or directly through the AWS Console user interface. In this particular use case, we'll employ a combination of both methods to set up the necessary resources efficiently. This approach allows for flexibility in resource creation while leveraging the benefits of both automated and manual provisioning techniques. Let's see it step by step:

CHAPTER 6   GETTING HANDS-ON: CREATING FIRST SERVERLESS APPLICATION

Essentials

1. Kindly Install and configure the most recent Python version on your local machine.

2. Prior basic knowledge of Python is essential, as your Lambda functions will be implemented in the Python language.

3. MySQL Workbench is utilized as the client for connecting to the AWS RDS MySQL instance; you can use any other tool based on your comfort.

API Gateway Creation

An API Gateway will be implemented to facilitate the retrieval of weather report data through an API:

1. Access your AWS Management Console account. Proceed to the API Gateway console and commence the API creation process by selecting the "REST API" option, as illustrated in Figure 6-3.

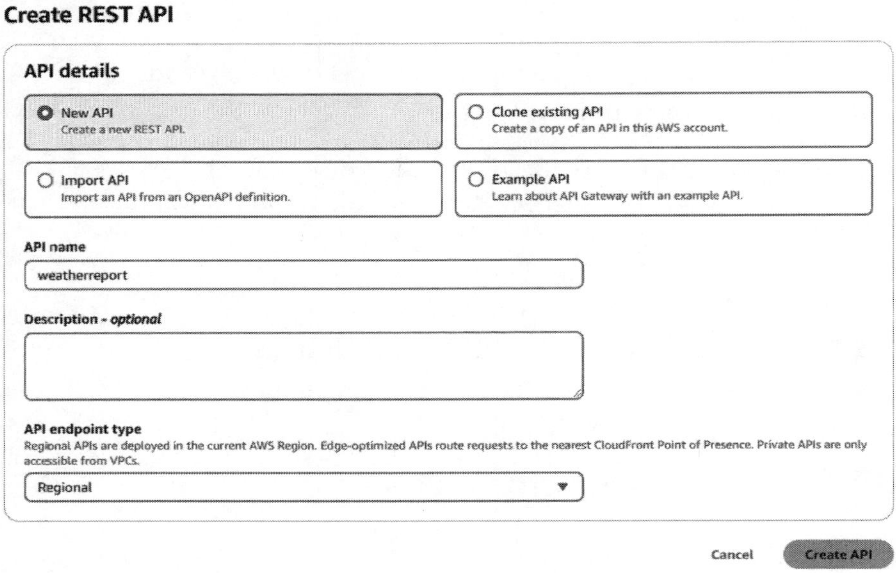

CHAPTER 6   GETTING HANDS-ON: CREATING FIRST SERVERLESS APPLICATION

Create REST API

API details

- ● New API
  Create a new REST API.
- ○ Clone existing API
  Create a copy of an API in this AWS account.
- ○ Import API
  Import an API from an OpenAPI definition.
- ○ Example API
  Learn about API Gateway with an example API.

API name

weatherreport

Description - *optional*

API endpoint type
Regional APIs are deployed in the current AWS Region. Edge-optimized APIs route requests to the nearest CloudFront Point of Presence. Private APIs are only accessible from VPCs.

Regional ▼

Cancel   **Create API**

***Figure 6-3.** Creation of API Gateway using AWS Console*

2. Specify the API name as "weatherreport," choose "Regional" for the API endpoint type, and then click the "Create API" option.

3. Upon successful creation of the REST API, proceed to create a resource within the API Gateway console by clicking the "Create Resource" button. Assign the resource name as "countryweather" and subsequently click "Create Resource." This action will result in the successful creation of the resource, as depicted in Figure 6-4.

CHAPTER 6   GETTING HANDS-ON: CREATING FIRST SERVERLESS APPLICATION

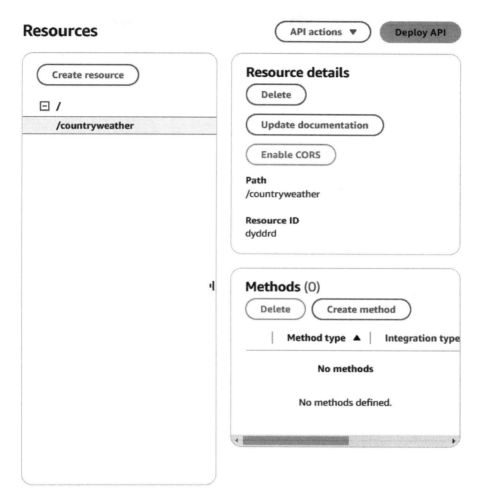

Figure 6-4. *API resource creation*

    4. Prior to defining the GET method for the resource, it is necessary to create the "readweather" Lambda function, which will be responsible for executing the GET method logic.

CHAPTER 6   GETTING HANDS-ON: CREATING FIRST SERVERLESS APPLICATION

5. Navigate to the Lambda Console and initiate the creation of a new function. Assign the function name as "readweather" and select "Python 3.13" as the runtime environment.

   Note: Always try to select the latest version, and it should be the same as the version which is running your local machine.

6. Click the "Create function" button. This will generate a Lambda function with basic Python code as illustrated in Figure 6-5. Subsequently, make the necessary modifications to the default code within the function body.

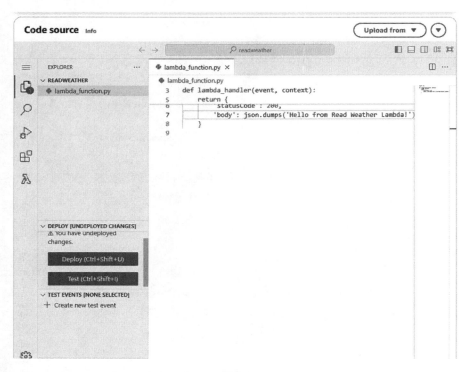

Figure 6-5. *Creation of readweather Lambda function*

CHAPTER 6   GETTING HANDS-ON: CREATING FIRST SERVERLESS APPLICATION

7. Proceed to deploy the Lambda function with the incorporated changes by clicking the "Deploy" button. Upon successful deployment, create a test event to validate the functionality of the Lambda function and observe the output.

8. To integrate the "readweather" Lambda function with the API, return to the API Gateway console. Select the "weatherreport" API, navigate to the resource, and then click the "Create method" option.

9. Select "GET" as the method type and configure the integration type as "Lambda." Choose the ARN of the "readweather" Lambda function and then click "Create method" to complete the process. The resulting method will be as shown in Figure 6-6.

CHAPTER 6   GETTING HANDS-ON: CREATING FIRST SERVERLESS APPLICATION

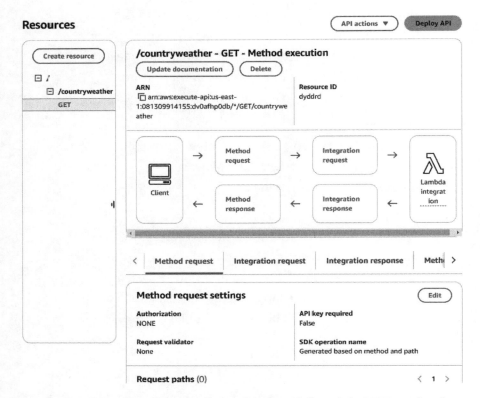

Figure 6-6. *Configuring readweather lambda with GET method*

10. From the Resource page, click the "Deploy API" button. Choose "New Stage" as the deployment stage and specify the stage name as "Dev." Click "Deploy API" to deploy the API. Upon successful deployment, the system will automatically redirect you to the Stages page.

11. We can now invoke the URL associated with the method that was previously created, as illustrated in Figure 6-7.

284

CHAPTER 6   GETTING HANDS-ON: CREATING FIRST SERVERLESS APPLICATION

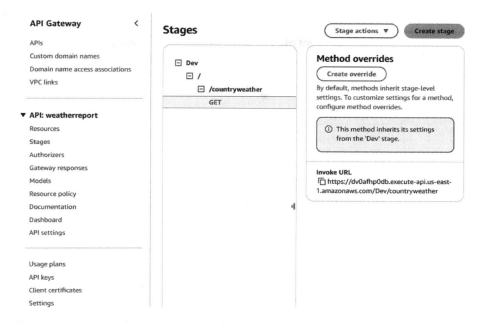

Figure 6-7. Deployment stage for weatherreport API

12. To test the Invoke URL, you can either open a new browser tab or utilize tools like Postman or any other API testing tool.

Authorizer Lambda Creation

To enhance security, we will now create an Authorizer Lambda function to interact with the Weather API instead of directly utilizing the Open API:

1. Create Authorizer lambda for API Gateway by using the AWS Console page by giving the name "authorizer" and select the Runtime as Python.

2. Please replace the default code with the code in Figure 6-8.

285

CHAPTER 6   GETTING HANDS-ON: CREATING FIRST SERVERLESS APPLICATION

```
import json
def generate_policy(principal_id, effect, resource):
    auth_response = {
        'principalId': principal_id
    }
    if effect and resource:
        policy_document = {
            'Version': '2012-10-17',
            'Statement': [
                {
                    'Action': 'execute-api:Invoke',
                    'Effect': effect,
                    'Resource': resource
                }
            ]
        }
        auth_response['policyDocument'] = policy_document
    return auth_response

def lambda_handler(event, context):
    token = event['authorizationToken']

    valid_token = "apressweatherapi"

    if token == valid_token:
        return generate_policy('countryweather', 'Allow', event['methodArn'])
    else:
        return generate_policy('countryweather', 'Deny', event['methodArn'])
```

Figure 6-8. *Authorization Lambda*

CHAPTER 6　GETTING HANDS-ON: CREATING FIRST SERVERLESS APPLICATION

3. *generate_policy*: This function generates a policy document for API Gateway based on the provided principal_id (ID of the principal making the request), effect (request should be allow or deny), and resource (resource for which policy is being generated).

4. *lambda_handler*: It retrieves the authorizationToken from the event and compares the authorizationToken with a valid_token. If the token is valid, it calls generate_policy to generate an "Allow" policy for the resource specified in event['methodArn']. If the token is invalid, it generates a "Deny" policy for the resource.

5. Deploy the Lambda.

6. To configure the Authorizer Lambda, access the API Gateway console and navigate to the "Authorizers" section. Click "Create Authorizer" and provide the name "weatherauthorizer."

7. Select the ARN of Authorizer Lambda in the lambda function and then select "Lambda event payload" as "Token."

8. Then provide the token source as "auth-token."

    Note: You need to pass this field while you are invoking the Weather API.

9. Disable the "Authorization caching" and then click "Create authorizer." It will create the Authorizer successfully as shown in Figure 6-9.

CHAPTER 6   GETTING HANDS-ON: CREATING FIRST SERVERLESS APPLICATION

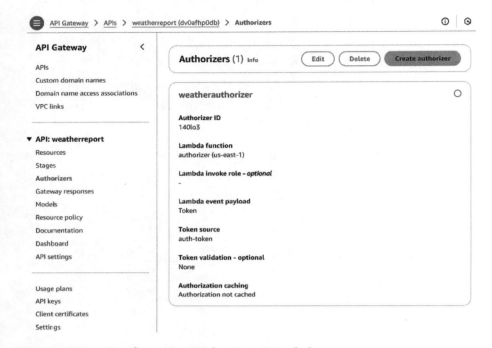

Figure 6-9. *Configuring Authorizer Lambda*

Configuring the Authorizer for GET Method Invocation

To integrate the Authorizer, we need to add it to the "GET" method that was defined for the "countryweather" resource":

 1. Go to the GET method from the API Gateway console page and then click the "Method request" and then "Edit."

 2. By default, Authorization is "None." Select "weatherauthorizer" which you created in Figure 6-9 and click Save as shown in Figure 6-10.

288

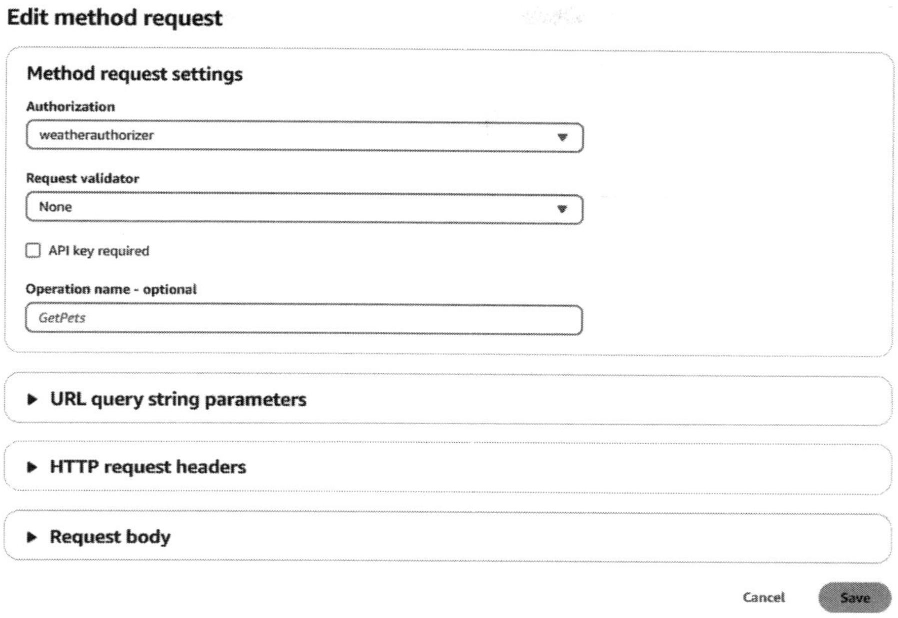

CHAPTER 6   GETTING HANDS-ON: CREATING FIRST SERVERLESS APPLICATION

Edit method request

Method request settings

Authorization

| weatherauthorizer ▼ |

Request validator

| None ▼ |

☐ API key required

Operation name - optional

| GetPets |

▶ URL query string parameters

▶ HTTP request headers

▶ Request body

Cancel Save

Figure 6-10. *Adding Authorizer to GET method*

3. Once you have Authorizer added successfully, then you need to deploy the API to reflect the latest changes.

4. To test your API, utilize the API Invoke tool as shown in Figure 6-11. Ensure that the following header is included: "auth-token: apressweatherapi." Navigate to the "Stages" page and click the "GET" method to obtain the Invoke URL.

CHAPTER 6   GETTING HANDS-ON: CREATING FIRST SERVERLESS APPLICATION

Figure 6-11. Testing API Authorization

Creating S3 Bucket and DynamoDB

1. *S3 Bucket*: Next, you will create an S3 bucket using the AWS Console as you followed the steps in Chapter 2 – Simple Storage Service.

2. Give the bucket name as "apressbucket" and upload "citylist.csv," which contains city codes and city names as shown in Figure 6-12.

```
"CityCode","CityName"
"TK","Tokyo"
"SY","Sydney"
"PA","Paris"
"DX","Dubai"
```

Figure 6-12. Sample city list

3. *DynamoDB*: You will then create a DynamoDB table to store the city name list.

4. Go to AWS DynamoDB console page, then click the Create table.

290

CHAPTER 6 GETTING HANDS-ON: CREATING FIRST SERVERLESS APPLICATION

5. Fill the details as shown in Figure 6-13.

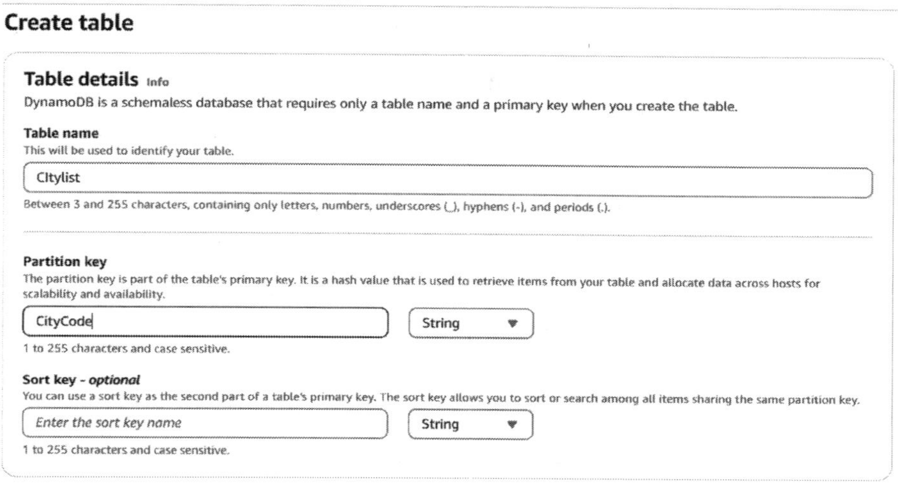

Figure 6-13. DynamoDB table creation

6. Keep the other values as default and then click Create table. It will create the DynamoDB table as shown in Figure 6-14.

Figure 6-14. DynamoDB table list

291

CHAPTER 6   GETTING HANDS-ON: CREATING FIRST SERVERLESS APPLICATION

7. Click the table; it will redirect to the landing page, then click "Action," "Create item," and then "Add new attribute" as "String" and give the values as shown in Figure 6-15.

Create item

You can add, remove, or edit the attributes of an item. You can nest attributes inside other attributes up to 32 levels deep. Learn more

Attribute name	Value	Type
CityCode - *Partition key*	LN	String
CityName	London	String

Figure 6-15. Adding new attribute with values to DynamoDB table

8. Now you will insert the remaining data into the DynamoDB table by reading the file from S3 bucket file "citylist.csv" using the "csvprocessing" Lambda function.

Process S3 CSV with Lambda, Stored in DynamoDB

1. Create lambda "csvprocessing" with Python runtime and assign DynamoDB full permission and S3 bucket full access to the "*csvprocessing-role-xxxx*" role.

292

CHAPTER 6   GETTING HANDS-ON: CREATING FIRST SERVERLESS APPLICATION

Note: The "-xxxx" suffix within the role name will be dynamically generated by AWS, resulting in a unique value for each instance.

2. Go to IAM Roles in the AWS Console and select the role "*csvprocessing-role-xxxx*." Click "Add Permission" and then Attach Policies.

3. Search for DynamoDB and select "AmazonDynamoDBFullAccess" and search for S3 and select "AmazonS3FullAccess" and then click Add permission.

4. Now you will read the file from S3 and insert data into DynamoDB with lambda code as shown in Figure 6-16.

CHAPTER 6   GETTING HANDS-ON: CREATING FIRST SERVERLESS APPLICATION

```
import boto3
import csv
def lambda_handler(event, context):
    s3_client = boto3.client('s3')
    dynamo_client = boto3.resource('dynamodb')
    table_name = dynamo_client.Table('Citylist')
    S3_BUCKET_NAME = 'apressbucket'
    file_name = 'Citylist.csv'
    response = s3_client.get_object(Bucket=S3_BUCKET_NAME,
    Key=file_name)
    filebytes = response['Body'].read().decode('utf-8')
    csv_reader=csv.reader(filebytes.splitlines())
    header = next(csv_reader)
    for row in csv_reader:
        result = dict(zip(header, row))
        print(result)
        try:
            table_name.put_item(Item = result)
            print("Item added successfully!")
        except Exception as e: print(e)
```

Figure 6-16. *Sample code to read from S3 and upload into DynamoDB*

9. Deploy and test the Lambda; this setup will enable your Lambda function to read the citylist.csv file from S3 and insert its content into the "Citylist" DynamoDB table.

CHAPTER 6   GETTING HANDS-ON: CREATING FIRST SERVERLESS APPLICATION

Note: You need to increase the Lambda function's timeout in case you get a timeout error for this lambda. Navigate to the "Configuration" tab, click "Edit," and adjust the timeout value to five minutes.

RDS Database Creation

The next step is to create an RDS instance using the AWS Console to store city weather information:

1. Navigate to the AWS RDS Console page.

2. Click the Database link from the left navigation and then click the "Create database" button.

3. While creating the database, please select the "Standard create" option and engine type as "MySQL" and select templates as "Free Tier."

4. Give the database name as "weatherreport." In the Credentials settings, set the master username to "apress." Opt for self-managed credential management and enter a master password and confirm the master password of your choosing.

5. Keep the default instance configuration, storage values, VPC, and subnet group.

6. Select Option "Yes" for external access to the database outside the VPC is required. However, this is not recommended for real-time applications due to security concerns.

7. Keep other options as default.

8. Select the Database authentication option as "Password authentication." Keep other values as default, then click "Create database." It will create the database as shown in Figure 6-17.

Figure 6-17. *Successful creation of MySQL database*

Key Consideration: Security is crucial. Make sure to configure appropriate security group rules and use strong passwords. Consider enabling Multi-AZ deployment for production workloads to ensure high availability. Choose the appropriate instance size and storage type based on your performance and storage requirements. Monitor your RDS instance regularly to ensure optimal performance and identify any potential issues.

9. By default, it will create a few databases in RDS like "information_schema," "mysql," "performance_schema," and "sys."

10. If you want to create your own database in AWS RDS, then you can create it with the help of MySQL Workbench.

CHAPTER 6   GETTING HANDS-ON: CREATING FIRST SERVERLESS APPLICATION

11. To connect a database from a local machine using MySQL Workbench, you should allow 0.0.0.0/0 in your security group inbound rule.

12. To modify the DB security group, click the "weatherreport" DB identifier, then click "VPC Security Groups" in the "Security" column; it will redirect to the Security Groups Console page, then click security group which is attached to your "weatherreport" DB identifier.

13. Then click "Edit Inbound Rules" and then Add Rule. While adding a rule, select type "All traffic" and source "Anywhere-IPV4" and save.

14. To configure with MySQL Workbench, you have to use the endpoint, port, user, and password of the "weatherreport" DB identifier.

15. You will create a database with the name "weatherreport" by using MySQL Workbench.

16. Now you will create a Lambda function to perform CRUD operations on this RDS instance, and this can be done directly from the AWS Lambda Console.

17. Name the function "rdstablecreate" and use Python as the runtime. Once it is successfully created, connect the Lambda function to the RDS database by using the "Configuration" tab and RDS database link as shown in Figure 6-18.

297

CHAPTER 6   GETTING HANDS-ON: CREATING FIRST SERVERLESS APPLICATION

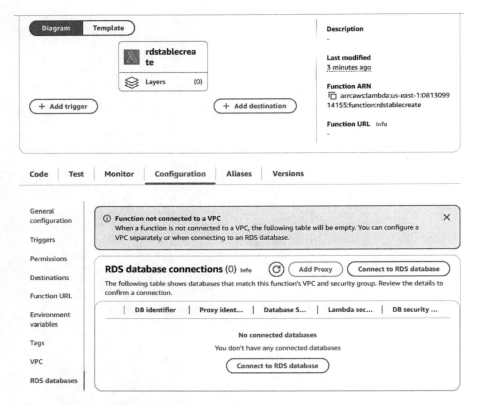

Figure 6-18. *Lambda connection with RDS*

18. Click "Connect to RDS database." It will redirect you to the page where you need to select the RDS which you created with the name "weatherreport."

19. Once you click the "Create" button, it will take care of updating permissions which are required for lambda to connect to RDS.

20. It will take some time to update the Lambda function.

21. Next, you will create a table in the "weatherreport" database to store weather information.

298

CHAPTER 6   GETTING HANDS-ON: CREATING FIRST SERVERLESS APPLICATION

22. *pymysql* is utilized to establish a connection to the MySQL database.

23. To utilize the *pymysql* library within your "rdstablecreate" function, you must include it as a dependency. Install *pymysql* locally by using "`pip install pymysql --target .`", package it as a ZIP file, and upload this ZIP file to your Lambda function as shown in Figure 6-19.

Figure 6-19. *Adding pymysql package to Apress-tableCreateLambda*

24. Update Python file code, as shown in Figure 6-20, in the new "rdstablecreate" function.

299

Chapter 6 Getting Hands-On: Creating First Serverless Application

```
import pymysql
def lambda_handler(event, context):
    connection = pymysql.connect(
host='weatherreport.c3sew2om25ii.us-east-1.rds.amazonaws.com',
        user='apress',
        password='yourpassword',
        database='weatherreport' )
    cursor = connection.cursor()
    create_table_query = """ CREATE TABLE weatherdata
     ( id INT AUTO_INCREMENT PRIMARY KEY,
     city VARCHAR(50) NOT NULL,
     temperature FLOAT,
     humidity INT,
     description VARCHAR(100),
     created_at TIMESTAMP DEFAULT CURRENT_TIMESTAMP ) """
    cursor.execute(create_table_query)
    connection.commit()
    connection.close()
    return { 'statusCode': 200, 'body': 'Table created successfully'
}
```

***Figure 6-20.** Lambda code to create table in database*

25. The RDS configuration should be your own database configuration.

    Key Consideration: AWS Secrets Manager helps you manage, retrieve, and rotate secrets throughout their lifecycle. Secrets can be database credentials, passwords, API keys, OAuth tokens, TLS certificates, and other sensitive information. Instead of hardcoding secrets in your applications

CHAPTER 6   GETTING HANDS-ON: CREATING FIRST SERVERLESS APPLICATION

or storing them in plain text, you can use Secrets Manager to securely store and retrieve them. AWS Secrets Manager is a valuable service for enhancing the security and management of your sensitive information in the AWS cloud.

26. Test the Lambda function, and it will create a table successfully.

Creating Account in OpenWeatherAPI

1. Please make sure that you create an account in https://home.openweathermap.org/.

2. Once you create the account, you can generate your own API key as shown in Figure 6-21.

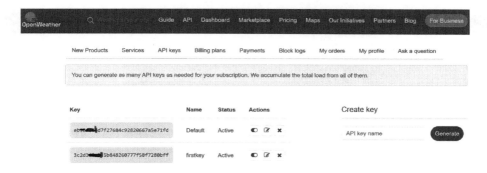

Figure 6-21. *OpenWeatherAPI custom keys*

CHAPTER 6   GETTING HANDS-ON: CREATING FIRST SERVERLESS APPLICATION

Lambda to Fetch OpenWeatherAPI

We will now proceed to create the "fetchweatherdata" Lambda function within the AWS Console. This function will retrieve a list of countries from the DynamoDB table, subsequently fetching weather information for each city from the "OpenWeatherAPI." Finally, the retrieved weather data will be stored in the MySQL database.

1. To accommodate the anticipated longer execution time, you need to increase the Lambda function's timeout. Navigate to the "Configuration" tab, click "Edit," and adjust the timeout value to five minutes.

2. To connect "fetchweatherdata" lambda to DynamoDB and RDS, do the required configuration by clicking "Permissions" in the Configuration tab.

3. Click the role name "*fetchweatherdata-role-qgswt2t7*"; it will redirect to the Roles page.

4. Then click Add permission and attach the policies as shown in Figure 6-22.

CHAPTER 6   GETTING HANDS-ON: CREATING FIRST SERVERLESS APPLICATION

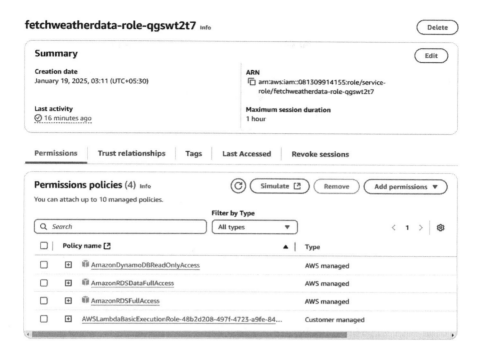

Figure 6-22. *DB permissions to Lambda*

    5.   Then add code shown in Figure 6-23 in "fetchweatherdata"; to execute the code, you need to add the "requests" and "pymysql" Python libraries. Install "*requests*" locally by using "`pip install requests --target .`", and "pymysql" package is already in your local machine make a ZIP file of both the packages, and upload this ZIP file to your Lambda function as shown in Figure 6-19.

CHAPTER 6   GETTING HANDS-ON: CREATING FIRST SERVERLESS APPLICATION

```python
import json
import boto3
import requests
import pymysql

def lambda_handler(event, context):
    dynamodb = boto3.resource('dynamodb')
    table = dynamodb.Table('Citylist')
    base_url = "http://api.openweathermap.org/data/2.5/weather"
    headers = {
        "Content-Type": "application/json"
    }
    connection = pymysql.connect(
        host='weatherreport.c3sew2om25ii.us-east-1.rds.amazonaws.com',
        user='apress',
        password='apress#weather',
        database='weatherreport' )
    cursor = connection.cursor()
    insert_data_query = """ INSERT INTO weatherdata (city, temperature, humidity, description) VALUES (%s, %s, %s, %s) """

    response = table.scan()
    items = response['Items']

    city_names = [item['CityName'] for item in items]
    while 'LastEvaluatedKey' in response:
        response = table.scan(ExclusiveStartKey=response['LastEvaluatedKey'])
        items.extend(response['Items'])
        city_names.extend([item['CityName'] for item in response['Items']])

    for city_name in city_names:
        params = {"q":{city_name},"appid":"1196cd362b174690705a898ce384e396"}
        urlresponse = requests.get(base_url, headers=headers, params=params)
        responsedata = urlresponse.json()
        city = json.dumps(responsedata['name'])
        temperature = json.dumps(responsedata['main']['temp'])
        humidity = json.dumps(responsedata['main']['humidity'])
        description = json.dumps(responsedata['wind'])
        cursor.execute(insert_data_query, (city, temperature, humidity, description))
        connection.commit()
      connection.close()
    return {
        'statusCode': 200,
        'body': json.dumps('Hello from Fetch Weather Data Lambda!')
    }
```

Figure 6-23. *Fetch weather report to county list from OpenWeatherAPI*

CHAPTER 6   GETTING HANDS-ON: CREATING FIRST SERVERLESS APPLICATION

6. Deploy and test the lambda; it will insert the data into the MySQL table "weatherdata."

   Note: Figure 6-23 is a sample code. You have to use your database and OpenWeatherAPI configurations.

Automating the Lambda Function

To create a CloudWatch Events Rule, do the following:

1. Go to Amazon CloudWatch in the AWS Console.

2. Click the Rules under Events.

3. Click Create Rule and define the rule in detail as shown in Figure 6-24.

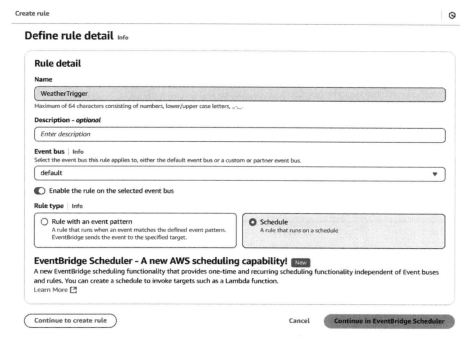

Figure 6-24. *Rule creation for scheduler*

305

CHAPTER 6   GETTING HANDS-ON: CREATING FIRST SERVERLESS APPLICATION

4. Then click Continue to create rule and select the option "Schedule," then define the Schedule pattern as shown in Figure 6-25.

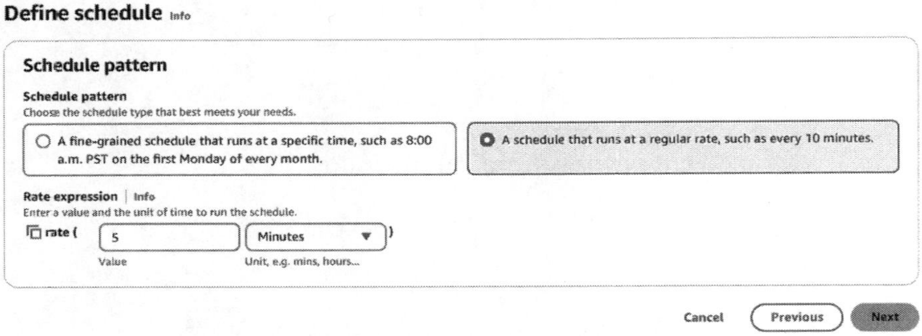

Figure 6-25. Schedule pattern

5. Set the Schedule expression to rate (5 minutes) to trigger the Lambda function every 5 minutes.

6. Click Next and then select the Target as Lambda function and then select function "fetchweatherdata."

7. You can also add multiple targets at a time; for now, you will add a single target.

8. Click "Next" twice to skip tag configuration, and then click "Create Rule."

Reading Weather Information from MySQL DB

We will use "readweather" lambda which we created in Figure 6-5 to fetch the data from the MySQL database:

1. As a first step, you need to add necessary permissions to the lambda.

CHAPTER 6   GETTING HANDS-ON: CREATING FIRST SERVERLESS APPLICATION

2. Go to "readweather" lambda configuration, then click "Permissions," and then click "Role name."

3. It will redirect to the IAM console page. Click "Add permission" and then select "AmazonRDSReadOnlyAccess," as shown in Figure 6-26.

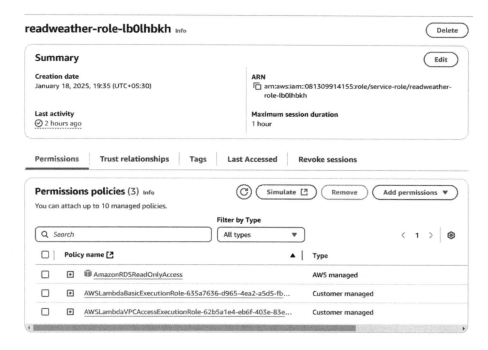

Figure 6-26. *Adding DB readonly access to readweather lambda*

4. Update lambda code as shown in Figure 6-27. Please add the "pymysql" package manually by zipping it locally and upload to the "readweather" lambda.

CHAPTER 6   GETTING HANDS-ON: CREATING FIRST SERVERLESS APPLICATION

```
import json
import pymysql

def lambda_handler(event, context):
    Location = event['headers']['location']
    LikeLocation ="%"+Location+"%"
    connection = pymysql.connect(
    host='weatherreport.c3sew2om25ii.us-east-1.rds.amazonaws.com',
    user='apress',
    password='apress#weather',
    database='weatherreport' )
    cursor = connection.cursor()
    select_data_query = "SELECT city,temperature,humidity,description FROM weatherdata WHERE city LIKE %s"
    dbresult = cursor.execute(select_data_query,LikeLocation)
    rows = cursor.fetchall()
    connection.commit()
    connection.close()
    return {
        'statusCode': 200,
        'body': json.dumps({
            'message': "Values received successfully",
            'Location': rows[0] })
    }
```

Figure 6-27. *Lambda code to fetch weather report from database*

CHAPTER 6   GETTING HANDS-ON: CREATING FIRST SERVERLESS APPLICATION

5. Deploy the Lambda code; before doing a test, you need to add the mapping template in API Gateway. Go to the "weatherreport" API and click the "GET" method and then click "Integration Request." Edit the settings of "Integration Request," keep the integration type as lambda function, scroll down, then go to Mapping templates to configure as shown in Figure 6-28.

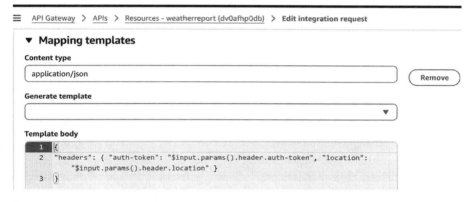

Figure 6-28. *Mapping template configurations*

6. Save and deploy the API to reflect the changes.

7. Test the API by passing a location value using a tool as shown in Figure 6-29.

309

CHAPTER 6   GETTING HANDS-ON: CREATING FIRST SERVERLESS APPLICATION

Figure 6-29. API testing

CloudWatch Monitoring

We can monitor the logs based on the groups which we created:

1. Log in to the AWS Console, if not logged in already.

2. In the AWS Management Console, go to "Services" and then select "CloudWatch" under "Management & Governance.

3. In the left-hand navigation pane, under "Logs," click "Log groups" as shown in Figure 6-30.

310

CHAPTER 6   GETTING HANDS-ON: CREATING FIRST SERVERLESS APPLICATION

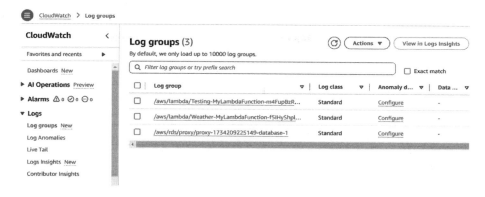

Figure 6-30. *CloudWatch log groups*

4. You'll see a list of all your log groups. You can search for a specific log group using the search bar.

5. Click the name of a log group to view its log streams. A log stream represents a sequence of log events originating from a specific source.

6. You can also navigate to CloudWatch Logs Insights, which provides a powerful query language that allows you to search and analyze your log data.

CloudWatch Dashboards

You can create CloudWatch dashboards to visualize key metrics derived from your logs:

1. In the CloudWatch Console, click "Dashboards" in the left-hand navigation pane as shown in Figure 6-31.

311

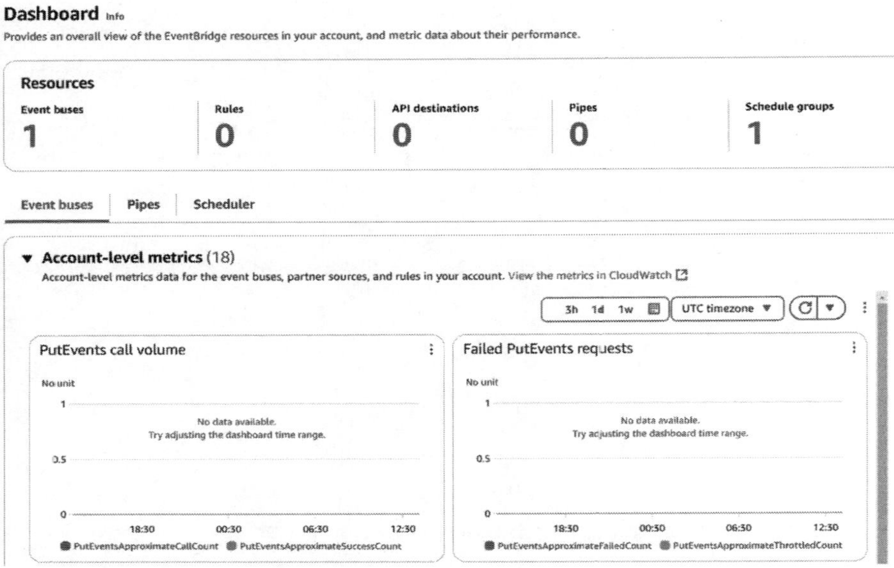

CHAPTER 6   GETTING HANDS-ON: CREATING FIRST SERVERLESS APPLICATION

Figure 6-31.   CloudWatch dashboard

2. Create a new dashboard or edit an existing one.

3. Add widgets to the dashboard to display metrics and graphs. You can create widgets that visualize data from your logs using Logs Insights queries. For example, you could create a widget that displays the number of error messages per hour.

Key Considerations

- **Log Retention:** CloudWatch Logs has a retention policy that determines how long log data is stored. You can configure the retention policy for each log group.

- **Log Stream Naming:** Using a consistent and informative naming convention for your log streams makes it easier to find and analyze your log data.

CHAPTER 6   GETTING HANDS-ON: CREATING FIRST SERVERLESS APPLICATION

- **Logs Insights Query Syntax:** Familiarize yourself with the Logs Insights query syntax to effectively search and analyze your logs.

- **Cost Management:** CloudWatch Logs charges for data ingestion, storage, and analysis. Be mindful of your log volume and retention settings to manage costs.

Conclusion

In this chapter, you explored the practical implementation of a serverless weather information system using AWS services. Through hands-on development, we created a robust solution that integrates the OpenWeatherAPI with AWS Lambda, API Gateway, and RDS MySQL. The system efficiently processes postal code-based weather queries while maintaining security through IAM roles and VPC configurations. You've implemented comprehensive monitoring using CloudWatch and established proper logging mechanisms. This project demonstrated the power of serverless architecture in creating scalable, cost-effective solutions while providing valuable experience in working with multiple AWS services in a real-world application context.

Index

A

Access control, 17, 22, 72, 81–83, 101, 102
Access Control Lists (ACLs), 23, 69, 72, 82, 220
ACLs, *see* Access Control Lists (ACLs)
AcmCertificateArn, 105
ACM, *see* AWS Certificate Manager (ACM)
ALB, *see* Application Load Balancer (ALB)
Aliases, 105
Amazon CloudFront
    applications area, 91
    architecture, 93, 94
    CDN, 91
    description, 91
    distribution types, 95, 96
    Edge locations, 95
    integrating with frontend development, 102–105
    key features and advantages, 92, 93
    performance optimization, 105–107
    Regional edge caches, 95
    security features, 100–102
    setting up, 96–99
Amazon Cognito, 53, 61, 62
Amazon ElastiCache
    advantages, 230
    Cache type selection, 232
    create Redis cache, 233
    ElastiCache Console, 232
    features, 229
    in-memory caching service, 227
    key components, 228
    limitations, 231
    Memcached creation page, 234
    serverless environments, 227
    use cases, 227
Amazon S3, 11, 22, 45, 68, 88, 111, 112, 137, 141, 144, 146, 156, 157
Amazon Simple Queue Service (AWS SQS)
    benefits, 216, 217
    features, 215, 216
    key components, 214, 215
    limitations, 217
    practical guide, 217, 218
    types, message queues, 214
    use cases, 214
    vs. SNS, 219

INDEX

Amazon Web Services (AWS), 43
    categories, 8
    definition, 8
    ECS, 235, 236
    EKS, 235–237
    importance, 9
    tools and products, 8
Amplify
    advantages, 47, 48
    comprehensive platform, 43
    description, 44
    features, 44–46
    functions, 48
    practical guidelines, 49–51
    unified interface, 44
Anomaly detection, 254, 260
API caching, 67
API Gateway
    API development and management, 52
    core components, 55, 56
    description, 51
    functions, 54
    handling tasks, 51
    integration, frontend development, 63–65
    integrating AWS Lambda and other services, 57
    key features, 52, 53
    key use cases, 53, 54
    pay-as-you-go pricing model, 52
    performance optimization, 65–68
    RESTful APIs *vs.* WebSocket APIs, 56, 57
    security features, 61–63
    setting up, 58–60
API-specific throttling, 62
Application Load Balancer (ALB), 183, 184, 188, 190
Array Jobs, 129
Automated schema discovery, 116
Availability Zones, 1, 14, 16, 41, 42, 185, 188, 216
AWS, *see* Amazon Web Services (AWS)
AWS Analytics services, 12
AWS API Gateway's integration, CloudWatch, 63
AWS architecture, 40
    architectural styles, 10
    best practices, 10
    cost optimization, 11
    definition, 9
    flexibility, 10
    reliability, 10
    scalability, 10
    security, 10
AWS Athena, 160
    advantages, 145, 146
    complex queries handling, 142
    description, 141
    disadvantages, 146, 147
    features, 144, 145
    key components, 143
    open source Presto engine, 142
    pay-per-query model, 142

INDEX

practical guide, 147–149
use cases, 142
AWS Batch, 160
   advantages, 131, 132
   definition, 127
   disadvantages, 132, 133
   features, 129–131
   key components, 128, 129
   practical guide, 133, 134
   process automation, 127
   use cases, 128
AWS Certificate Manager (ACM), 101, 105
   advantages, 195
   AWS services, 191
   components, 192, 193
   data privacy, 191
   disadvantages, 195, 196
   features, 193, 194
   practical guide, 196, 197
   public and private certificates, 191
   serverless applications, AWS ecosystem, 191
   use cases, 192
AWS CloudFront, 71
AWS CloudTrail, 13, 83–84, 158, 200
AWS CloudWatch Monitoring, 271
AWS CodeBuild, 270
   advantages, 244
   architecture, 241
   build servers, 241
   CodeBuild Console, 245

CodeBuild project creation, 245, 246
   components, 242
   continuous integration service, 240
   disadvantages, 244
   features, 243, 244
   GitHub Actions, 241, 242
   Jenkins, 242
   programming languages, 241
   source selection, build project, 246
   use cases, 242
AWS CodeCommit, 239, 240, 270
AWS CodePipeline, 271
   benefits, 249, 250
   CodePipeline Console, 250, 251
   continuous delivery service, 247
   creation, 251
   features, 249
   key components, 248
   limitations, 250
   sample pipeline, 252
   use cases, 248
AWS Global Infrastructure, 14
AWS Glue, 159
   advantages, 117, 118
   components, 113–115
   definition, 112
   disadvantages, 118, 119
   ETL jobs, 113
   features, 116, 117
   practical guide, 119–127
   supported-data sources, 112

INDEX

AWS Glue (*cont.*)
    tools, 112
    use cases, 113
AWS Glue Data Catalog, 112, 114, 116, 143
AWS Glue's serverless architecture, 118
AWS IAM policy, 82
AWS Lambda functions, 57, 62, 68, 161, 277
    advantages, 166, 167
    configuration settings, 165
    create new Lambda function, 168, 169
    disadvantages, 167
    event sources, 164
    execution environment, 164
    execution environment, code, 162
    features, 165, 166
    handler function, 164
    Lambda architecture, 163
    Lambda code output, 171
    Lambda code source console, 170, 171
    Lambda Console page, 168
    Lambda role selection, 169, 170
    multiple programming languages, 162
    serverless architecture, 162
    successful creation, 170
    use cases, 163
AWS managed policies, 22
AWS Management Console, 76

AWS Networking, 42
    cloud services, 32
    cloud services amalgamation, 32
    IGV, 36, 37
    NAT Gateway, 38, 39
    request-response model, 32
    route table, 37, 38
    Security Groups, 35, 36
    subnets, 34
    VPC, 33, 34
AWS offerings, 40
AWS Redshift, 160
    advantages, 138, 139
    analytical workloads, 135
    definition, 134
    disadvantages, 139, 140
    features, 136, 137
    flexibility, 135
    key components, 136
    practical guide, 140, 141
    use cases, 135
AWS Regions, 14–16, 41
AWS S3 lifecycle configuration, 75
AWS Secrets Manager, 300
    advantages, 201
    AWS Secrets Manager Console, 202, 203
    Choose secret type, 203
    cloud security, 197
    configure rotation, 206
    configure secret, 205
    disadvantages, 202
    features, 197, 199, 200

INDEX

hardcoding secrets, application code, 197
key components, 198, 199
other options to configure secret, 206
other type of secret, 204, 205
sample code, 207
use cases, 198
username and password screen, 204
AWS services, 117
    Analytics, 12
    Business Applications, 13
    compute services, 11
    database, 12
    Identity and Compliance services, 13
    IoT, 13
    machine learning, 12
    Management and Governance, 13
    networking and content delivery, 12
    security, 12
    storage, 11
AWS Step Functions
    advantages, 175, 176
    create Step Function, 178
    disadvantages, 176, 177
    event view, 182
    execution, 173
    Execution, 179, 180
    features, 174, 175
    graph view, 181, 182
    state machines, 172, 173
    state machines list, 183
    Step Function console page, 177
    Step Function Hello World, 178, 179
    successful execution, 180, 181
    tasks, 173
    transitions, 173
    use cases, 172
AWS SQS, *see* Amazon Simple Queue Service (AWS SQS)
AWS subnets, 34

B

BI, *see* Business intelligence (BI)
Big Data Analytics, 68, 71, 74
Bucket policies, 69, 72, 81–83, 98, 99, 103
Built-in transformations, 117
Business intelligence (BI), 12, 112, 134, 135, 138, 142, 159

C

CA, *see* Certificate Authority (CA)
Cache invalidation, 66, 105, 106
Cache policies, 105, 106
Caching, 66, 67, 106
Caching strategies, 106
CDK, *see* Cloud Development Kit (CDK)
CDNs, *see* Content delivery networks (CDNs)

319

INDEX

Centralized certificate management, 194
Certificate Authority (CA), 192, 193
Classic Load Balancer (CLB), 183, 185
CLB, *see* Classic Load Balancer (CLB)
Cloud-based data analysis, 145
Cloud computing, 4, 40
    advantages, 6, 7
    components and services, 5, 6
    definition, 2
    disadvantages, 7, 8
    growth, 2–4
    model types, 5
    service types, 4, 5
Cloud Development Kit (CDK), 1, 26–29, 40, 41
Cloud DevOps, 239, 270, 271
CloudFormation, 26–28, 41
CloudFront caches, 105
CloudWatch, 42, 276, 277
    access methods, 30
    advantages, 255
    aspects, 30
    AWS services metrics, 30
    CloudWatch Console, 255, 256
    components, 253, 254
    create custom dashboards, 253
    disadvantages, 255
    features, 254
    Log groups page, 257, 258
    Log screen settings, 256, 257
    metrics transfer, 30
    monitoring and observability service, 252
    real-time surveillance, 30
    use cases, 253
CloudWatch Alarms, 271
    advantages, 260
    AWS services, 258
    CloudWatch Alarms console, 261, 262
    components, 259
    disadvantages, 261
    features, 260
    practical guide, 261, 262
    use cases, 259
    view settings, 262, 263
    vigilant guardian, 258
CloudWatch Dashboard, 271
    add widgets, 267, 268
    benefits, 266
    CloudWatch Dashboard Console, 267
    components, 264
    create data source, 269, 270
    features, 265
    limitations, 266
    Sample metric graph widget selection page, 268, 269
    use cases, 264
CloudWatch dashboards, 311–313
CloudWatch log
    log event, 31
    log groups, 32
    log streams, 31
CloudWatch monitoring, 310, 311

INDEX

CloudWatch's monitoring and logging, 63
Cluster computing, 3
Composite alarms, 254, 260
Comprehensive job management, 130
Compute Environments, 129, 134
Consistency framework, 73
Constructs, 28, 52
Content delivery networks (CDNs), 73, 88, 91
CORS, *see* Cross-Origin Resource Sharing (CORS)
Crawlers, 113, 115, 118, 122, 157
Cross-Origin Resource Sharing (CORS), 63–65
Customer-Managed Policies, 22
Custom route table, 38

D

Database credential management, 198
Database Migration Service (DMS), 157
Databases
  NoSQL (*see* NoSQL databases)
  SQL, 220
Data governance, 114, 153, 155, 158, 159
Data lake, 68, 71, 111, 113, 135, 136
  advantages, 153, 154
  architecture design, 156–158
  data ingestion and organization practices, 158, 159
  data types, 149
  description, 149
  disadvantages, 155
  ETL process, 150
  features, 152, 153
  implementation, serverless architecture, 150
  key components, 151, 152
  use cases, 150, 151
Data visibility, 159
DDoS, *see* Distributed denial-of-service (DDoS)
Dead letter queue (DLQ), 210, 216
Default route table, 37
Distributed denial-of-service (DDoS), 12, 91, 93, 188
Distributed systems, 3
DLQ, *see* Dead letter queue (DLQ)
DMS, *see* Database Migration Service (DMS)
Domain name system (DNS), 12
Dynamic resource provisioning, 130
DynamoD, 224
DynamoDB, 12, 58, 164, 187, 224, 226, 264, 276
dynamodb.create_table() function, 226
dynamodb.delete_item() function, 227
dynamodb.get_item() function, 226
dynamodb.update_item() function, 226

321

INDEX

E, F

ECS, *see* Elastic Container Service (ECS)
Edge locations, 95
Edge locations/PoPs, 95
EKS, *see* Elastic Kubernetes Service (EKS)
Elastic Container Service (ECS)
　container orchestration service, 235
　deployment options, 235
　streamlined workflows, 235
　use cases, 236
　user-friendly interface, 235
Elastic Kubernetes Service (EKS)
　AWS services, 236
　Kubernetes service, 236
　use cases, 237
Elastic Load Balancers (ELB)
　advantages, 188
　ALB, 184
　architecture, 184
　CLB, 185
　disadvantages, 189
　essential components, 186
　features, 187, 188
　load balancing solutions, 183
　NLB, 185
　practice guide, 189–191
　sample dashboard, 190
　TCP/UDP load balancing, 183
　use cases, 185
　WebSocket, 183

ELB, *see* Elastic Load Balancers (ELB)
ETL, *see* Extract, transform, and load (ETL)
ETL Jobs, 113, 115, 118
ETL workflows, 117, 157
Event sources, 164
Execution environment, 162–164
Extract, transform, and load (ETL), 111–113, 115–118, 127, 150, 157, 159

G

GitHub Actions, 241, 242
Glue architecture, 114
Grid computing, 3

H

Handler function, 164
High-resolution alarms, 260
Hybrid cloud, 5, 236

I

IAM, *see* Identity and Access Management (IAM)
IAM authentication, 61
IAM capabilities
　accessibility and cost, 19
　global operation, 18
　identity federation, 19
　MFA, 18

INDEX

password policy management, 18
seamless integration, 18
IAM group, 20–21
IAM policies, 23
    ACLs, 23
    actions, 25, 26
    creation, JSON/YAML documents, 24
    identity-based, 22
    JSON document outlining permissions, 21
    organizations SCPs, 23
    permissions boundaries, 23
    resource-based, 22
    session policies, 24
IAM user credentials, 19–20
IAM users, 19, 20
Identity and Access Management (IAM), 40, 41, 158, 199, 200
    advantages, 17
    AWS account, 17
    capabilities (*see* IAM capabilities)
    entities view, 17
    granular permission assignment, 17
Implementation plan, serverless weather information system using AWS services
    add new attribute with values, DynamoDB table, 292
    API Gateway creation, 279–281
    API resource creation, 280, 281

deployment stage, weatherreport API, 284, 285
readweather Lambda function Creation, 282
readweather lambda, GET method, 283, 284
API test, 310
Authorization Lambda, 286
Authorizer, GET Method Invocation, 288, 289
Authorizer Lambda Creation, 285, 287, 288
Automating Lambda function rule creation, scheduler, 305
schedule pattern, 306
CloudFormation templates, 278
create account, OpenWeatherAPI, 301
create S3 bucket, 290
DB permissions to Lambda, 303
DynamoDB table creation, 290, 291
DynamoDB table list, 291
infrastructure architecture, 278
Lambda connection with RDS, 298
Lambda to Fetch OpenWeatherAPI, 302–305
OpenWeatherAPI custom keys, 301
process S3 CSV with Lambda, Stored in DynamoDB, 292, 295

323

INDEX

Implementation plan, serverless weather information system using AWS services (*cont.*)
  RDS database creation, 295–301
  read weather information, MySQL DB, 306–309
  testing API Authorization, 290
Infrastructure as a Service (IaaS), 4, 8
Integration services, 58, 116, 240
Internet Gateway (IGV), 1, 34, 36–37, 42

J

Job Definitions, 128
Job Queues, 129, 134, 214
Jobs, 111, 113, 115, 118, 128–132, 160, 163

K

Key Management Service (KMS), 81, 196, 198, 200
Key Management System (KMS), 199
Kubernetes, 162, 235, 236

L

Lambda architecture, 163
Lambda Authorizers, 53, 61–62
Lambda@Edge, 91–94, 105, 107

Legacy system integration, 54
Lifecycle policies, 68, 69, 71, 75–76, 89, 157
Load Balancers, 32, 34, 161, 163, 183–190, 238
Log event, 31, 32, 311
Log groups, 32, 256, 258, 311, 312
Log streams, 31, 32, 311, 312

M

Mainframe computing, 3
Massively parallel processing (MPP) model, 134, 137, 138
Methods, 56
Metric math alarms, 260
MFA, *see* Multifactor Authentication (MFA)
Microservices architecture, 53
Mobile and web applications, 54
MPP model, *see* Massively parallel processing (MPP) model
Multifactor Authentication (MFA), 18
Multi-node Parallel Jobs, 129
MySQL database, 296, 302

N

NAT Gateway, 38, 39
Network Load Balancer (NLB), 185
NLB, *see* Network Load Balancer (NLB)
NoSQL databases

INDEX

Amazon DynamoDB, 224
   benefits, 225
   features, 224
   lexible schemas and horizontal scalability, 223
   limitations, 225
   practical guide, 226
   use cases, 224

O

OpenWeatherAPI, 276, 277, 304

P

PaaS, *see* Platform as a Service (PaaS)
Pay-as-you-go pricing model, 118
Pay-per-query pricing model, 146, 147
Pay-per-use model, 165, 166
Performance optimization, 65
Performance optimization, best practices, 67, 68
Platform as a Service (PaaS), 4
Private-bucket, 103
Private cloud, 5
Private NAT gateways, 39
Public and private certificates, 194
Public cloud, 5
Public NAT gateways, 39
Publisher-subscriber model, 208
pymysql, 299

Q

Query engine, 143

R

Real-time communication, 54
Real-Time Messaging Protocol (RTMP), 96
Redshift Spectrum, 137
Regional edge caches, 95
Relational databases, 220
Representational State Transfer (REST), 57
Request-response model, 32
Resources, 55
REST, *see* Representational State Transfer (REST)
RESTful APIs, 57
RTMP distribution, 96
RTMP, *see* Real-Time Messaging Protocol (RTMP)

S

S3, *see* Simple Storage Service (S3)
S3 Access Logs, 84
S3 bucket, 276
S3 functionalities
   buckets and objects, 72, 73
   data consistency model, 73
   lifecycle policies, 75, 76
   storage classes, 74
   storage needs, 71
S3 Glacier, 74

INDEX

S3 Glacier Deep Archive, 74
S3 intelligent-tiering, 74
S3 One Zone-IA, 74
S3 performance optimization
    best practices
        data compression, 90
        data retrieval, 90
        monitoring and analytics, 91
        multipart uploads, 90
    caching strategies, CloudFront integration, 88, 89
    and cost management, 89
    strategies and tools, 88
S3's data consistency model, 73
S3's disaster recovery, 71
S3 security features
    ACLs, 82
    AWS IAM, 81
    bucket policies, 82
    bucket policy, 83
    comprehensive suite, security controls, 81
    encryption techniques, 81
    logging and monitoring capabilities, 83, 84
S3's global infrastructure, 70
S3's lifecycle policies, 69
S3 standard, 74
S3 Standard-IA, 74
S3's versioning, 69
SaaS, *see* Software as a Service (SaaS)
Schedulers, 129
SCPs, *see* Service Control Policies (SCPs)
Security, 161, 277, 296
Security Groups function, 35, 36
Serverless architecture, 116, 143
Serverless weather information system
    CloudWatch dashboards, 311–313
    CloudWatch log group, 311
    CloudWatch monitoring, 310, 311
    implementation plan (*see* Implementation plan, serverless weather information system using AWS services)
    key components, 274
    solution design
        AWS services, 275
        data flow, 277, 278
        system architecture components, 276, 277
    solution diagram, 276
Server-side encryption (SSE), 81
Service Control Policies (SCPs), 23
Service orientation, 4
Session policies, 24
Signed cookies, 102
Signed URLs, 101
Simple Notification Service (SNS)
    AWS serverless ecosystem, 207
    benefits, 211
    broadcast communication, 219
    features, 209, 210

INDEX

key components, 208, 209
limitations, 212
practical guide, 212, 213
publisher-subscriber model, 208
publish-subscribe model, 219
seamless dissemination, messages to multiple subscribers, 207
use cases, 208
Simple Storage Service (S3)
   architecture, 68
   definition, 68
   functionalities (*see* S3 functionalities)
   integrating with frontend development, 84–88
   key features and benefits, 69, 70
   performance optimazation (*see* S3)
   security features (*see* S3 security features)
   setting up, 76–79
   storage classes, 69
   structure, 68
   use cases, 70, 71
SNS, *see* Simple Notification Service (SNS)
Software as a Service (SaaS), 5
SQL databases
   advantages, 221
   disadvantages, 222
   features, 220, 221
   practical guide, 222, 223

relational databases, 220
use cases, 220
SQL interface, 143
SSE, *see* Server-side encryption (SSE)
SSL/TLS encryption, 100, 101
Stages, 56
Standard SQL, 145
Strategic planning, 158
Structured query language (SQL), *see* SQL databases

T, U

Throttling and rate limiting, 62
Time to live (TTL), 105
TTL, *see* Time to live (TTL)
Triggers, 115
TTL settings, 106

V

Virtualization, 3
Virtual Private Cloud (VPC), 33, 34
VPC, *see* Virtual Private Cloud (VPC)
VPC route table, 37, 38

W, X, Y, Z

WAF, *see* Web Application Firewall (WAF)
Web 2.0, 3
Web Application Firewall (WAF), 93
Web distribution, 95
WebSocket APIs, 57

327

Printed in the United States
by Baker & Taylor Publisher Services